BRODART   Cat. No. 23-221

Message in a Bottle

Message in a Bottle

THE MAKING OF
FETAL ALCOHOL SYNDROME

◆ ◆

Janet Golden

HARVARD UNIVERSITY PRESS

Cambridge, Massachusetts

London, England · 2005

Library of Congress Cataloging-in-Publication Data

Golden, Janet Lynne, 1951–
Message in a bottle : the making of fetal alcohol syndrome / Janet Golden.
p. cm.
Includes bibliographical references and index.
ISBN 0-674-01485-5 (alk. paper)
1. Fetal alcohol syndrome.
2. Alcoholism in pregnancy—Complications.
I. Title.

RG629.F45G655 2004
618.3′26861—dc22   2004052251

For Alex, Ben, and Eric,
and in memory of Joani Unger

♦ ♦

Contents

1

◆◆

"We Realized We Were onto Something": Naming FAS

The call came to David Smith, professor of pediatrics at the University of Washington School of Medicine in Seattle in 1973. Shirley Anderson, a physician who ran the pediatric outpatient department at Harborview Medical Center, the county hospital, asked him to come see eight children, all of whom had been born to alcoholic mothers. Smith went over to the hospital, bringing along his research fellow Kenneth Lyons Jones. Jones recalled the experience clearly: "We walked into this room and there were eight kids, all born to chronic alcoholic women, sitting there. We looked at those eight kids and they were all developmentally delayed, but four of the eight, on examination, looked alike." They were small in size with flat faces, and they had the small eye slits and drooping eyelids that would eventually be recognized as characteristics of alcohol exposure in the uterus.[1]

Jones had completed his pediatric residency and was training under Smith in dysmorphology, defined as "the area of clinical genetics that is concerned with the diagnosis and interpretation of patterns of structural defects." His training taught him that appearances mean a lot, and also that, while they can be the key to diagnosis, they can be easily overlooked. Malformations such as a cleft lip are easy to recognize. Internal defects such as congenital heart problems are also relatively simple for physicians to diagnose from a medical examination. But infants and children with subtle differences in their features need to be seen by a dysmorphologist, a physician trained to see and interpret the significance of minor abnormalities—those that appear in less than 4 percent of the general population. Clusters of minor malformations occurring in association with one another often signal the existence of an underlying condition: a syndrome.[2]

1

To date, hundreds of syndromes have been described and the causes of many of them identified. Some stem from chromosomal abnormalities. Others are inherited disorders. And then there are those caused by environmental agents that damage an embryo or fetus. In the majority of cases—about 60 percent—the etiology of a particular syndrome cannot be determined, and it is possible that these are caused by a combination of factors. While prenatal genetic testing, elective abortion of fetuses with detectable abnormalities, and the avoidance of substances known to cause birth defects may decrease the incidence of particular syndromes within a population, it is not possible to eliminate all risk.[3]

Pregnancies are events with uncertain endings, and when they end in disappointment parents and physicians invariably ask what went wrong. Sometimes the question arises later, when children appear to be developing abnormally. Smith and Jones asked themselves what was "wrong" with the children they had seen. Four of the eight shared a number of common abnormalities, including growth deficiencies, a small head circumference, and mental deficiencies. Their condition had no name. Smith wrote down the information and then returned with Jones to his office to examine his "unknown" files. For each of the individuals in the files, Smith had listed the three most prominent malformations, along with other information about their personal histories.

Such careful record keeping displayed Smith's interest in organizing, classifying, and exploring data about birth defects in order to find underlying patterns and causes. A leader in the field of dysmorphology (a term he had coined) before his early death in 1981, Smith trained many eminent clinicians, published numerous articles, and wrote several important books. His reputation for cataloging information very carefully, and for ordering his data with graphs and pictures so that he could refer to them in later investigations, is apparent in his seminal work *Recognizable Patterns of Human Malformations,* the essential textbook of dysmorphology diagnosis, which he published in 1976. Kenneth Lyons Jones compiled the more recent editions of this work, which now bears the name *Smith's Recognizable Patterns of Human Malformations.*[4]

While medical research is often thought of as a laboratory-based enterprise involving experimentation and studies of microscopic bits of material, much of it in fact remains rooted in clinical practice, with the slow accumulation of data and the imaginative leaps that allow physicians finally to connect their observations to a judgment about diagnosis, or treatment.

Jones and Smith soon made such a leap. After the examinations at Harborview, they combed Smith's files for children with the same pattern of abnormalities. They found two. Next, they looked at the mothers' charts; in both cases the women were described as alcoholics. "We realized we were onto something," Jones recalled.

Smith left town the next day for a stint as a visiting professor in Akron, Ohio. While there, he asked to see any children born to alcoholic women. The chief resident recalled a recent case and asked the mother to bring in her child. When Smith examined the child, he found the same features that appeared in the other six cases. Now there was a seventh. Back in Seattle, Jones found the eighth: called to examine a baby at Children's Orthopedic Hospital who had been born to an alcoholic mother, Jones observed the same features he had seen earlier. So within the span of a few days, Smith and Jones had examined eight children, male and female, ranging in age from eleven weeks to four years, representing three different ethnic groups. All of them had the same distinctive facial features, were extremely small, and were developmentally delayed. Most significantly, they had one other common feature: mothers who had abused alcohol during their pregnancies. Smith and Jones concluded that in utero alcohol exposure had somehow caused the physical and developmental problems of these children, or, as a dysmorphologist would put it, they came to believe that alcohol was a teratogen.

The linguistic root of the word *teratogen* lies in the Greek *terata*, meaning monstrous formations or births. A number of teratogens were known to physicians by the late twentieth century. These included infections such as syphilis and rubella (German measles), environmental hazards such as ionizing radiation, and certain substances, the most notorious of which was thalidomide. Marketed in the late 1950s as a safe sleeping pill, thalidomide caused children to be born with missing or truncated limbs. Approximately 10,000 children worldwide were born with these birth defects before physicians recognized thalidomide as the agent responsible; the drug was removed from the market in 1961. Thalidomide, a new substance, was quickly identified as a problem because it was, as one physician termed it, "flamboyantly" teratogenic, causing severe deformities in the majority of fetuses exposed at a critical stage of development.[5]

The idea that alcohol could be a teratogen came as a surprise. It had a long history of use and of observations about its possible effects on gestation. Still, researchers knew that tobacco use by pregnant women posed risks to fetuses, and so it was not entirely unbelievable that another agent in common use could prove to be dangerous.

Jones and Smith wrote up their findings, working with two coauthors: Ann Streissguth, a psychologist who did the performance testing of the children and who subsequently became a prizewinning fetal alcohol syndrome researcher, and Christy Ulleland, who, as a pediatric resident at Harborview in 1968, recognized and described the small size, low birth weight, and failure to thrive that characterized the children of alcoholic mothers. While on call one evening, Ulleland had been asked by an obstetrics resident whether she knew anything about the effects of alcohol on an unborn baby, because an alcoholic woman was about to deliver her infant. Ulleland checked the medical literature and found nothing. Her interest was apparently piqued, however, and she continued to study children born to alcoholic women in 1968 and 1969. Ten of the twelve cases she observed during that time were what she called "undergrown," five had retarded development, and three others were borderline retarded. Their mothers, she noted, were of relatively advanced age, had had a number of pregnancies, and only four of the twelve had received prenatal care. In a 1972 article, she concluded: "Chronic alcoholism" had to be "added to the list of maternal factors that create an unhealthy intrauterine environment for the developing fetus; the consequences of which may be lifelong." Her patients were the children Jones and Smith would later examine at Harborview.[6]

Jones and Smith mailed their article to the British journal *Lancet,* one of the most prestigious medical journals in the world. The vast majority of articles submitted to academic journals are rejected. Those that are accepted typically have to be revised in response to peer reviewers' comments, and the revised version, in turn, may be sent back to the reviewers for approval before an article is finally accepted for publication. After that, it may be many months before the article appears in print. The article from Seattle, which the authors titled "Pattern of Malformation in Offspring of Chronic Alcoholic Mothers," apparently did not undergo this process. News of its acceptance came within a week, presumably because *Lancet's* editors recognized its importance. It appeared on 9 June 1973.[7]

Five months later Jones and Smith published a second article in *Lancet* in which they described three more children, also born to alcoholic women, who displayed the cluster of abnormalities described earlier. They also discussed earlier descriptions of alcohol-related birth defects, including an 1834 report to the British House of Commons in which the children of women inebriates were said to have "a starved, shriveled and imperfect look"—a description more evocative but less clinically precise than their own. In this article, Jones and Smith named the particular pattern of abnormalities seen in the eleven youngsters the "fetal alcohol syndrome." They had created a diagnosis.[8]

The term *fetal alcohol syndrome* is now in common use, and its abbreviation, FAS, is employed by the public as well as the medical community. FAS is defined and described in medical textbooks and in educational materials for secondary school classrooms. It is discussed in the pages of popular magazines, referred to in newspaper articles, and mentioned on television news and entertainment shows. Pregnant women who obtain prenatal care are now routinely asked about their drinking habits, and information about FAS is distributed in the waiting rooms of obstetricians. Since 1989, all alcoholic beverages sold in the United States have carried a federally mandated warning label that includes the statement: "Women should not drink alcoholic beverages during pregnancy because of the risks of birth defects."

Syndromes are sometimes named for their discoverers or for those who offered the first major clinical description. The commonly recognized Down's syndrome, for example, is named for the English physician J. Langdon H. Down, who in 1866 described the condition that now bears his name. Syndromes caused by teratogens, however, are more typically named for their causal agent. Yet even if this naming tradition for teratogens had been ignored, FAS would not have been termed Ulleland syndrome or Jones-Smith syndrome. It would have been called Lemoine syndrome, for the lead author of a 1968 article in a French medical journal that described 127 children born to 69 alcoholic families. Those children, whose mothers were alcoholics, had the same appearance and deformities as the children Jones and Smith would describe in their articles five years later. Paul Lemoine, the pediatrician who first observed the abnormalities in infants with alcoholic mothers, presented his work at a professional meeting, published his findings, and made a point of teaching his students about alcohol-affected infants and children. He acknowledged that other French researchers had also suspected the damaging effects of maternal alcoholism.[9]

Jones learned about Lemoine's findings while attending the Fourth International Conference on Birth Defects, just a few months after his own coauthored publication appeared. He recalled that it was Widukind Lenz, one of the discoverers of thalidomide teratogenesis, who informed him of Lemoine's article. After returning to Seattle, Jones wrote to Lemoine and received a long letter in reply. Lemoine told him that when he presented his data to his French colleagues in 1968, none of them believed him, and according to Jones, Lemoine added "They don't believe me to this day." Jones and Smith did believe him, and they cited his work in their subsequent publications. When FAS gained credibility, Lemoine recalled being able to finally indulge, as he put it, "in a certain amount of satisfaction and amusement."[10]

Like Lemoine's claims, those made by Jones and Smith met with skepticism. Several physicians wrote to offer alternative explanations, suggesting that Jones and Smith had either made a faulty diagnosis or were wrong to impute the children's abnormalities to alcohol. A letter from two physicians suggested that the children described by Jones and Smith had a form of Noonan's syndrome, a condition of unknown etiology also characterized by short stature, mental retardation, and distinct facial features. Another doctor wondered whether the Seattle team had completed the work necessary to reach such a bold conclusion, noting the variety of abnormalities in the children they described and the fact that chromosomal studies had been done on only two of them. A Tennessee physician familiar with moonshine culture suggested that the problem may have been lead—a suspected teratogen—which was sometimes found in large amounts in "untaxed" (homemade) alcohol.[11]

For every skeptic, however, there were several others who saw the article as a breakthrough. To these grateful doctors and their patients, Jones and Smith were master detectives who had succeeded in deciphering symptoms that had long eluded them. A group of Swiss pediatricians sent a letter and photograph to *Lancet* describing a child with FAS, and soon other journals began receiving case reports as well. Boston pediatricians found three children in one family who showed the features of FAS; a report from Ireland discussed a child who had been misdiagnosed until the work of Smith and Jones suggested the proper explanation for the youngster's failure to grow.[12]

The literature on FAS grew quickly in the years following the first report by Jones and Smith. Clinical case reports detailed particular patients' anomalies, expanding the list of physical features associated with the syndrome. Further confirmation of the developmental effects of alcohol came from professionals who worked with the mentally retarded and found, in reviewing their cases, that a significant number had mothers who were chronic alcoholics. At the same time, experts who worked with alcohol-abusing women began to see more clearly the effects of drinking during pregnancy, including higher rates of stillbirths, miscarriages, and low-birth-weight babies (a condition linked to higher mortality rates).

Jones, Smith, and their Seattle colleagues turned from individual case reports to an epidemiological study of a large population, comparing the offspring of women who abused alcohol in pregnancy with the offspring of women not known to have been alcoholic. The data came from the records of the Collaborative Perinatal Project (CPP). Under the sponsorship of the National Institute of Neurological and Communicative Disorders and Stroke, the CPP had gathered information about more than 55,000 mother-child pairs seen at fourteen different university-affiliated hospitals around the country between 1958 and 1965. The research was initially undertaken to determine factors related to the risks of cerebral palsy and other neurological disorders, and the study data were mined once again after the thalidomide disaster to see what other drugs might be associated with birth defects. During their pregnancies, the women were interviewed in detail about their drug use and their reproductive, medical, and social histories. No one thought to ask about their use or abuse of alcohol in pregnancy—important testimony about medical beliefs at that time, when social drinking was the norm and abusive drinking was thought to be largely a problem among men. Information about the children was collected during the first week after birth, at regular intervals during the first twenty-four months of life, and annually thereafter.[13]

Despite the omission of alcohol from the research protocol, the charts of 23 of the women identified them as alcoholics. The expected number of alcoholics in a population this size would be far greater; even a conservative estimate of 1 percent would yield 550. Clearly, physicians had not been looking to make the diagnosis or even to acknowledge it; they had written it down in these cases only because the women's alcoholism appeared so unmistakable and so serious that it could not be overlooked. The Seattle group matched each of the women identified as alcoholic with two others of the same age, race, socioeconomic status, and education, and according to other relevant characteristics. They then compared the offspring of the two groups. Perinatal mortality (death before one week of age) among the children of the women identified as alcoholic was 17 percent; among the others it was 2 percent. Thirty-two percent of the children whose mothers were alcoholic were retrospectively diagnosed with FAS; none of the children born to women in the second group received this diagnosis. Additionally, 44 percent of the children born to alcoholic mothers had an IQ of 79 or lower; the figure for the comparison group was 9 percent. The conclusion seemed clear: children could be damaged for life by their prenatal exposure to high levels of alcohol.[14]

Further evidence of the lifelong effects of heavy alcohol exposure in the womb came when researchers explored the histories of children diagnosed with FAS. A decade after their original report, two of the original Seattle team members, Streissguth and Jones, along with Sterling Clarren, a physician in the pediatrics department at the University of Washington, reported on the status of the eleven children originally identified as having FAS. Two were dead, four had borderline intelligence and required remedial teaching, and the remaining four were severely handicapped and needed supervision outside the home; one had been lost to follow-up. Of eight survivors, four lived in adoptive homes, two in foster homes, and only two with a biological parent. Three of the biological mothers had died of alcohol-related causes, an indication of the severity of their drinking. Further details of one case came out in 1996, when a Seattle newspaper profiled the first child diagnosed with FAS: Wesley Perkins. He was by then twenty-three years old, mentally retarded, and still living with the legal guardian who had taken him home from the hospital. Perkins had been abandoned by his mother, who had given birth to seven other children and was later found dead in a flophouse.[15]

In France, Lemoine also followed up his original cases, with the aid of his physician son. After winning an international award for his work, he used the prize money to see how his early patients were faring in adulthood, some thirty years after his first investigation. The findings proved discouraging. Of the 127 individuals, 105 were living in institutions. A number were profoundly mentally retarded, and others suffered from a variety of emotional disorders. Lemoine also examined fourteen siblings of the individuals he had earlier identified and found that they had similar difficulties.[16]

Like all scientific discoveries, the observations of Jones, Smith, and Lemoine raised many questions. Could their observations be replicated? If chronic abuse of alcohol during pregnancy caused birth defects, was it really alcohol that was to blame? Was there perhaps some other chemical in the drinks or an alcohol by-product that was responsible for the problem?

By what means did alcohol—if it was shown to be the cause—act on the fetus? Was the damage dose related? Was time of exposure during pregnancy a critical variable? Did damage depend on the genetic susceptibility of the fetus? Did factors such as the mother's age, race, income, health habits, access to prenatal care, or number of previous pregnancies play a role in the expression of the syndrome? Were there cofactors, such as smoking, poor maternal nutrition, mineral or vitamin deficiencies, that determined the expression of the syndrome or its severity? Many questions would begin to be answered in the following years through a variety of human and animal studies undertaken by researchers around the world.

The journey that began one day with a visit to a Seattle pediatric outpatient clinic would take Kenneth Lyons Jones into courtrooms and onto the evening television news. He would find himself on the witness stand offering testimony in a lawsuit brought against an alcoholic beverage manufacturer for "failure to warn," and he would participate in a clemency appeal for a notorious death-row inmate who suffered from FAS. It all began with some simple observations and the awareness that "we were onto something."

This book follows the evolution of FAS in the United States from its naming in 1973 through its appearance in death-penalty appeals in the 1990s. It is, in essence, the biography of a diagnosis. While I argue throughout that it is pivotal to focus on the process by which diagnoses evolve, I do not claim that diagnoses are entirely socially constructed—that they describe conditions that have no existence outside of the one created for them and merely reflect cultural norms and social values. Nor do I take the stance that FAS must be regarded as a demonstrated "fact" with a fixed meaning. Neither intellectual posture can capture the fullness of the syndrome's history in the late twentieth century. A social constructionist viewpoint denies the historical continuities involved in the search to name and understand the subjective human experience of disease, difference, frailty, and death. A positivist model of medicine rejects the myriad ways in which subjective and culturally rooted experiences shape the interpretation and meaning of a disease or syndrome. FAS is real because, to paraphrase historian Charles Rosenberg, in certain ways we have agreed that it is real. Federal, state, and local government and private organizations are involved in its study and prevention because it has been identified as an important medical diagnosis. FAS is also a disputed diagnosis. In some instances, individuals who claim FAS as a mitigating factor in criminal cases, and particularly in death-penalty appeals, are said to be making excuses. FAS, according to legal scholar Alan Dershowitz, is one of many "abuse excuses"—a claim made by criminal defendants with "a goal of deflecting responsibility from the person who committed the criminal act onto some else who may have abused him or her."[17]

Message in a Bottle: The Making of Fetal Alcohol Syndrome looks at the emergence of multiple claims about the definition and meaning of FAS and analyzes what I term the mutually constituted medicalization and demedicalization of FAS. The chapters that follow acknowledge that FAS is a birth defect diagnosed by clinicians in the offspring of alcoholic women. They emphasize, however, how the meaning of that particular diagnosis is shaped by cultural concerns, legal debates, medical authorities, media analyses, and political decisions.

Medicalization and demedicalization are linked, distinct, and highly contentious historical processes. Medicalization refers to the acquisition by physicians of the power to define as sickness certain behaviors and afflictions that were once interpreted in religious, legal, or moral terms. A perfect example is alcoholism, which shifted from being understood as a moral weakness in the early nineteenth century, to a sign of hereditary degeneration in the late nineteenth century, to a disease in the late twentieth century. To some, the medicalizing of alcoholism was a means of removing stigma and shifting control from the criminal justice system to the medical arena, where those who were "diagnosed" with the disorder might receive more compassionate care than they could in the drunk tank of a local jail. Defining alcoholism as a disease also meant that scientists undertook a search for its cause and cure. To others, the medicalizing of alcoholism was the beginning of what soon became a surging stream of diagnoses that threatened to engulf existing social structures and weaken the foundation of society by offering individuals an opportunity to elude responsibility for their actions by invoking a their particular disability.[18]

Scholars see the beginnings of medicalization in the scientific revolution of the seventeenth century and its advancement in the eighteenth and nineteenth centuries, when physicians took increasing responsibility for defining sickness and managing healing. The culmination of medicalization occurred in the twentieth century, as physicians gained professional autonomy and took control of vital health-care institutions, including hospitals, medical schools, and asylums, and accrued the power to label and treat disease and oversee the health of the public. Obviously medicalization is closely linked to other phenomena often placed under the rubric of modernization—industrialization, urbanization, secularization, and the transformation of social welfare by the rise of modern capitalism. The growing cultural authority of science and medicine helped to reorder daily life and to change the way people understood themselves and their society. While historians define medicalization as a process inextricably linked to the development of modern Western society, social theorists focus on its meaning and its links to definitions of deviance.

Medicalization was (and remains) a highly contested and uneven process, with equivocal results. The power that accrued to the medical profession was used to label the socially marginal as sick, to shroud in the mantle of science racial and gender hierarchies, and to force people to undergo "treatments," against their will. Yet medicalization was also used to attack social inequality, as health became an index of well-being and as the provision of health services served at times as a proxy for other, more dramatic social interventions. Medicalization did not follow a single path; conditions were medicalized or demedicalized or fell somewhere along that continuum according to particular circumstances. Medical authority was never absolute; the claims of medical professionals were always countered by the claims of other professionals and interest groups, and therefore medicalization always met with challenges.[19]

Demedicalization is also a historical process. It involves the diminishing cultural authority of medicine and the yielding of the power to diagnose social ills and individual disorders to other professions and authorities. The sources of demedicalization are numerous and entangled. In the late twentieth century, physicians' decision making at the bedside faced ethical challenges, government regulation, legal sanctions, and censure from patient activists, all of which disputed doctors' autonomy and authority. A classic example of demedicalization is the removal of the label "mental disorder" from the official definition of homosexuality, a change that resulted from interest-group pressure in contesting medical judgments. And like medicalization, demedicalization is never absolute. Some scientists continue to search for the genetics of homosexuality, and many in the public continue to regard homosexual behavior as "sick."[20]

The emergence of a new economics of health-care delivery and the creation of new government programs since the 1960s also limited the power of medicine, adding new parties to negotiations over what constituted a diagnosis. Third-party payers sometimes rejected claims for court-ordered addiction treatment and often imposed coverage limits on mental illness, setting boundaries on the medical domains of diagnosis and treatment. The intervention of government and privately funded health insurers in the sickroom coincided with an expanding quest for health and longevity among the middle and upper classes. As their individual "lifestyle" choices were granted social capital, those living in poorer circumstances and in need of medical services came to be seen as less deserving of medical care because they failed to manage their own health appropriately. The triumphs of scientific medicine in the twentieth century—increased life expectancy, the vanquishing of many infectious diseases, and the development of effective treatments and technologies for chronic conditions—resulted, ironically, in an increased personal accountability for health.[21]

Finally, demedicalization gained momentum in the closing decades of the twentieth century as critics dissected the theoretical underpinnings of medicalization. They viewed it as a way to ascribe personal failings to biopathology, accidents of birth, heredity, or the environment. Medicalization, in their eyes, conferred absolution not through divine forgiveness but through the banishing of agency via diagnosis. For the most part, attacks on medicalization were not conscious critiques of Western medicine and its secularizing effects but simple expressions of anger at individuals who attempted to shift the blame for their actions from their choices to their "conditions."

During its brief history, FAS has been medicalized and, at times, demedicalized. It is a diagnosis, a scientific subject, and a public health problem. It is also a symbol of maternal misbehavior, evidence of moral decay within particular communities, and a claim asserted by death-penalty opponents as well as condemned prisoners. These framings have occurred simultaneously or in close succession; I have separated them to make the point that FAS, like other diagnoses, has multiple, contingent meanings that emerge from scientific discoveries, popular beliefs, legal battles, and popular narratives. Discussions of FAS turn on critical issues in modern American society: the meaning of motherhood, the interpretation of alcohol abuse and addiction, the status of the fetus, the obligations of individuals to society and the duties of the government to its citizens. Undoubtedly other syndromes, diseases, and illnesses can offer equally compelling ways of examining these ideas. I chose FAS as a means of exploring these themes in part because it has a strong public presence in contemporary society and in part because alcohol-related birth defects and the contexts in which they are seen and interpreted have such a long and fascinating history.

The chapters that follow are loosely chronological and each focuses on a particular framing of FAS. Chapter 2 begins with a discussion of early sightings of alcohol-related birth defects (ARBDs). I argue that what was seen in the past was not FAS. The clinical features of ARBDs noted by eighteenth-, nineteenth-, and early twentieth-century observers unquestionably resemble those offered by late twentieth-century physicians because they were looking at the same physiological phenomenon. However, the meaning of these features was different because of the vantage point—historical, medical, and cultural—of those who described the particular infants and their parents. Early observations of ARBDs reflected contemporary beliefs about heredity and reproduction, about women's roles and responsibilities, and about the abuse of alcohol as an individual defect and a social problem. The discovery of FAS reflected other and more recent ideas about these same topics, but in ways that make FAS very different from ARBDs.

Chapter 3 takes up the question of why the assertion of alcohol teratogenesis met with relatively rapid acceptance in the 1970s. Prior encounters with thalidomide and other teratogens laid the foundation, as did the growing acknowledgment of alcohol abuse among women in the wake of feminist health activism and in the midst of a war on drugs. Finally, abortion, which had been recently legalized, made FAS appear to be a problem with a solution. This was the cultural soil in which the observations of Jones and Smith took root. Their further investigations and those of others were nourished by federal dollars flowing from the newly created National Institute on Alcohol Abuse and Alcoholism (NIAAA).

Scientific research about alcohol teratogenesis and the context in which that research took place, amid an expanding public discussion over the cultural status of the fetus, are the focus of Chapter 4, which also explores how physicians incorporated the new scientific findings into their professional literature and, more hesitantly, into their clinical practices. Early claims about FAS inspired a worldwide research enterprise that ultimately documented the effects of heavy drinking on the fetus but left open to interpretation the effects of light or moderate drinking. In the United States, the growing political, medical, and cultural position of what might be called "the fetal citizen" made it imperative that alcohol, rather than extremely heavy drinking during pregnancy, be seen as a threat.

Chapter 5 follows the public health crusade that resulted from the scientific findings. Warnings about alcohol and birth defects appeared in school health programs; in public service announcements on television, radio, and in print; and on signs placed in retail stores, bars, and restaurants. They also appeared on bottles of alcohol. Political debates over bottle labeling challenged the disease model of alcoholism, which argued that alcohol problems resided in the drinker, not the drink. The question then was whether the state should become involved in policing pregnancy and drinking.

The media response to FAS, primarily through an analysis of its portrayal on evening news broadcasts and also in Michael Dorris's prizewinning book *The Broken Cord*, an account of his son's struggle with FAS, is the focus of Chapter 6. Media accounts of FAS shifted dramatically in the 1980s as the moral panic over crack cocaine framed substance abuse in pregnancy as a national calamity. There were calls for pregnancy policing, and ultimately laws were enacted to permit the incarceration of pregnant substance abusers.

Were women or alcoholic beverage manufacturers responsible for FAS? This question came before a federal district court in Seattle in 1989, the same year that federally mandated warning labels began appearing on alcoholic beverages. The lawsuit against one distiller and the civil trial that resulted are examined in Chapter 7. The case, *Thorp v. James A. Beam*, tested the seeming immunity of alcoholic beverage manufacturers from claims that their products were unsafe, and it tested the willingness of the public to see pregnant alcoholic women as having no responsibility for the health of their fetuses.

The final chapter looks at the new faces of FAS—the convicted criminal and the problem adoptee—that came into view at the end of the twentieth century. While those investigating FAS soon recognized that alcohol was a behavioral teratogen, damaging the brain in ways that resulted in cognitive and behavioral impairments, in the courtroom and elsewhere such claims had a mixed reception. Parents of children with FAS, especially children who had been adopted, organized to promote awareness of the syndrome and to gain much-needed assistance in rearing and educating youngsters affected by prenatal alcohol exposure. In other settings the diagnosis met with doubt. When those charged with or found guilty of crimes claimed that their behavior had resulted in part from prenatal exposure to alcohol, FAS began to be demedicalized. It shifted, in certain situations, from being perceived as a diagnosis anchored to several decades of medical research to being judged as an excuse—a free-floating social construction cooked up by lawyers scheming to exonerate their clients.

The voices of those diagnosed with FAS and those who care for them and work with them are largely absent from this narrative. It is not my intention to examine the lives of individuals, families, and communities affected by alcohol exposure in utero. I use the diagnosis of FAS as a window through which to view and interpret American culture and institutions. Readers should know, however, that many individuals and families profoundly and directly affected by alcohol teratogenesis have told their stories in other places and have created informative Web sites.[22] I urge that their words be read.

2

♦♦

"Conceived in Gin": Historical Sightings of Alcohol and Pregnancy

When Sheila Blume heard the news reports about alcohol teratogenesis in the early 1970s she recalled thinking, "Uh-oh." During her first pregnancy she had been sailing to Japan and, she remembered, "There wasn't much to do but drink." Blume's son, an adult by the time of FAS's discovery, turned out just fine. Still, Blume wondered about the clinical implications of the report. A psychiatrist specializing in addiction and the director of a hospital-based alcoholism program, Blume turned to her own records. After a review of her files and the relevant literature, she concluded that many alcoholic women spontaneously cut down on their drinking during pregnancy.[1]

Blume presented her findings in a talk on alcohol and pregnancy and then submitted the paper to a medical journal. In her paper she included a description of FAS. The manuscript quickly came back with a pithy note from the editor: "You've got to be kidding." She returned it, along with some additional supporting information about FAS. The editor apologized and asked why, if alcohol caused birth defects, no one had noticed this before. In her conversations with colleagues, Blume found that they voiced similar doubts. She remembered someone saying that if FAS really existed, it would be common in France, where heavy drinking and alcohol abuse was a problem. She recalled that remark in particular because, shortly after hearing it, she happened to go to Paris, and the very first child she saw there—in the airport—exhibited the physical stigmata of FAS.

The question posed to Blume—Why hasn't anyone seen this before?— made sense. So did the answer. Alcohol-related birth defects had in fact been observed previously. Literature searches revealed numerous early descriptions. Rebecca Warner and Henry Rosett researched a number of suggestive reports and in 1975 published a survey of 250 years of English-language writing about the effects of alcohol on offspring. The recent "discovery" of FAS, they concluded, "completed a historical cycle. The forgetfulness of the Prohibition era and the skepticism of the 1940s were over; the effects of alcohol on offspring had again gained scientific attention." Over the next decade Ernest Abel, a leading FAS researcher, published several books in which he described and analyzed historical accounts of alcohol-related birth defects. Even a federal government report would proclaim that "evidence" of alcohol's harmful effects on unborn babies went back "a long way."[2]

Critics of Kenneth Lyons Jones, David W. Smith, and their colleagues first accused them of tilting at windmills; later the Seattle investigators faced charges of resurrecting an old diagnosis rather than constructing a new one. A 1978 article suggested that the 1530 painting *A Bacchanale* by Lucas Cranach the Elder showed FAS because it contained images of infants with "droopy lids" and "dull, retarded appearing faces." A recent article in *Addiction* asserted that in 1819 C. von Bruhl-Cramer, a German-Russian physician, had described the effects of alcohol exposure in utero in his book on dipsomania. Bruhl-Cramer had observed children who were "feeble, meager, suffering from various diseases, really atrophic, often very stupid" and whose physiognomy differed from their siblings, with growth "incomplete and inadequate with regard to their age." However, neither Bruhl-Cramer nor Cranach the Elder saw FAS when he looked at the faces of children born to alcoholic parents. FAS is a late twentieth-century diagnosis derived from a particular combination of scientific findings and social experiences. Medical conditions, as historian Owsei Temkin explained, are neither natural phenomena nor are they entirely created by those who observe and record them; they are both.[3]

Diagnoses, at their core, reflect contemporary beliefs that give them meaning. The history of two pandemics, six centuries apart, the Black Death and HIV/AIDS, makes this clear. When the Black Death ravaged Europe in the fourteenth century, learned physicians explained to Philip the VI that the plague resulted from the triple conjunction of Saturn, Jupiter, and Mars. Many in the public saw the terrible ravages of disease as the wrath of God; still others alleged it was spread by the Jews. Astronomy, religion, and anti-Semitism, animating forces in late medieval life, helped to shape the questions asked and answered in the face of a devastating epidemic. To say that communities and states simply suffered an epidemic of bubonic plague is to rob the past of its complexity and reduce historical experience to mere case studies. Those who experienced the Black Death understood their disease in a particular way; its meaning came not from physiological "facts" they had no way of knowing, but from how they struggled individually and collectively to make sense of what they observed and suffered and from the judgments of others. To study disease is to understand its corporeal and cultural definitions.[4]

HIV disease, named for a virus that attacks the human immune system, giving rise to numerous diseases and life-threatening opportunistic infections, once bore the name GRID: gay-related immunodeficiency disease. The shift in nomenclature suggests how explanation and blame can overlap, whether the focus is on fourteenth-century sinners and strangers or the stigmatized groups of the twentieth century who are seen as responsible for their own suffering and that of others. In a religious world, sinners are said to bring sickness upon themselves and their children; in a secular society, failure to obey scientific and social authorities, by smoking, drinking, overeating, taking drugs, or having "inappropriate" sexual congress, earns opprobrium. Yet even when blame is cast on individuals and groups, it is also understood that they are not entirely responsible; environmental conditions, individual circumstances—even bad luck—are known to influence health and disease. Seen from this perspective, FAS can be understood as a description of the spectrum of effects resulting from heavy alcohol exposure in utero and as a way of naming the behavior of pregnant women. It is a condition reflective of both biopathological events and of late twentieth-century ideas about fetuses and mothers. Historical accounts of the condition of infants and children affected by alcohol exposure in the womb need to be scrutinized not simply as early sightings of FAS but also as useful illustrations of how scientific theories and social beliefs together shaped interpretations of the effects of alcohol on reproduction.

The "Gin Epidemic"

From a scientific perspective, the "gin epidemic" in eighteenth-century England might be termed a natural experiment, although it resulted from efforts to solve an economic crisis. Seeking to aid grain producers and the

Figure 1. William Hogarth's *Gin Lane,* 1751.

distilling industry—both of which were experiencing financial difficulties—the government lowered taxes on gin. Beginning in 1720, cheap gin
flooded the marketplace, replacing beer as the beverage of choice among
the poor and working classes. Thanks to the growing consumption of gin,
the industry recovered. However, there appeared to be other, unintended
outcomes. Mortality rates seemed to be climbing and social disorder, some
sensed, was growing. Whether gin drinking caused either or both is debat-

able; infant mortality rates were high before and after the gin episode. Nevertheless, many blamed the gin.[5]

Accounts of the epidemic have come to be seen, in retrospect, as sightings of FAS. The engravings of William Hogarth and the writings of Henry Fielding are referred to as descriptions of maternal alcohol abuse and its aftermath. Hogarth's engraving *Gin Lane* vividly depicts the effects of unrestrained gin drinking. In the foreground a baby falls from its drunken mother's lap; in the background, degradation and debauchery abound in a narrow street set between a pawnshop and a distillery. Hogarth was disparaging gin, not alcohol. In *Beer Street* he trumpets the value of malt, which was the traditional beverage of the laboring classes. In that image he shows beer-bellied drinkers sipping from their tankards while reading political tracts, as robust workers toil away in the background.[6]

Henry Fielding, a magistrate and the author of *Tom Jones,* cursed the gin epidemic in words rather than pictures. In describing the social misery it left in its wake, he asked: "What must become of an infant who is conceived in gin?" Fielding's criticism of gin was part of a larger commentary on crime, law, and the situation of the poor. His fears about the effects of "poisonous distillations" were never realized, however; tax policies changed in 1751 and the gin epidemic began to subside.[7]

Neither Fielding nor Hogarth depicted FAS, because FAS had yet to be created. Each saw the unruly lives of the urban poor and their excessive drinking of gin as a blight on the nation; neither interpreted women's abuse of alcohol as causing a problem in fetal development. Explanations of physical and mental defects in children in the eighteenth century differed from those in the late twentieth century. Physicians and laymen believed that children could be damaged in utero by maternal impressions formed during pregnancy. Bad experiences, unhealthy indulgences—both dietary and sexual—and disturbing thoughts were all thought to be manifested as physical or mental problems in a child. Such interpretations helped to account for otherwise inexplicable defects and deformities in newborns. Parental drunkenness at the moment of conception was also thought to harm a child, explaining Fielding's concerns about infants "conceived in gin." Jones and Smith referred to this belief in their second article on FAS when they noted that "in Carthage, the bridal couple was forbidden to drink wine on their wedding night in order that defective children not be conceived." But no one in ancient Carthage or eighteenth-century London emphasized alcohol's ability to damage fetuses; they framed the problem of alcohol abuse and pregnancy in terms of social disorder and specifically as a matter of drunken conceptions.[8]

Degeneration

In the late nineteenth century, social commentators voiced new concerns about inebriety, public order, and reproduction. Eschewing theories of maternal impressions and drunken conceptions, observers embraced new ideas about heredity. Alcohol, they argued, destroyed the health of future generations. As a result, advanced societies ceased progressing and began to degenerate as the population grew physically, morally, and mentally weaker. A leading proponent of this theory, French psychiatrist Bénédict Auguste Morel, helped popularize the concept of alcoholic degeneration in his influential work *Analysis of the Physical, Intellectual and Moral Degeneration of the Human Species* (1857).[9]

Alcoholic degeneration, a subset of the larger problem of degeneration, neatly encapsulated the fears of social observers troubled by the inebriety of the urban poor and the sentiments of reformers disturbed by the condition of their children. Although ill-defined—seen sometimes as the cause of national decline and at other times as the result—degeneration as a concept appeared to be steeped in science, drawing on the disciplines of heredity and psychiatry.

A generation after Morel, theories of alcoholic degeneration rested on an understanding of alcohol as a chemical agent that damaged reproductive cells. Auguste-Henri Forel, an influential Swiss psychiatrist and entomologist, deemed it a "protoplasmic poison" that damaged germ cells and left the next generation "more or less crippled." Conflating the effects of maternal and paternal drinking, Forel claimed that "about one-half to three-quarters of the idiots and epileptics can be shown to spring from alcoholic parents or at least fathers." Other investigators similarly identified multiple developmental problems in the offspring of inebriates. Like Forel, they failed to distinguish between the effects of maternal and paternal alcoholism, expressing no particular concern about alcohol abuse in pregnancy. Their focus was on the causes of deviance.[10]

In many instances, nineteenth-century social theorists provided precise measurements of the effects of alcohol abuse on social decay. Their efforts illustrated the expanding role of numerical data in social epidemiology and its application in political debates. Findings typically came from studies of institutionalized individuals, something made possible by the erection of asylums, hospitals, prisons, workhouses, and other institutions designed to confine and thereby aid sick, criminal, and disorderly citizens.[11]

Nineteenth-century Americans also mined records of inmates and patients in order to explore the causes of disorder. Early studies of intemperance included research on military personnel, cholera victims, and physicians. Not surprisingly, all of the inquiries revealed that drinkers suffered higher rates of illness and death. The particular effects of parental intemperance were noted in two early studies of the mentally retarded. In 1848 the well-known reformer Samuel Gridley Howe reported to the governor of Massachusetts that "out of 359 idiots" housed by the Commonwealth and with a known parental history, "99 were the children of drunkards." Following the lead of Massachusetts, the Connecticut state legislature appointed its own Commission on Idiocy and in 1856 learned that nearly a third of the individuals studied suffered from "idiocy" because of parental intemperance.[12]

Studies of intemperance continued into the twentieth century on both sides of the Atlantic. The *Quarterly Journal of Inebriety* published findings from a Swiss study of the birth dates of imbeciles that determined that a disproportionate number had been conceived during periods of peak drinking: New Year's, Shrove Tuesday, Easter, spring nuptials, and the grape harvest. The findings were said to prove Forel's theory that alcohol poisoned the germ plasm. Seeming to validate the theories of Morel, a French physician presented his findings about the contribution of alcohol (and syphilis) to insanity, epilepsy, and other nervous diseases in a neurology journal in 1901. In the United States, Henry Smith Williams, a physician at the Craig Colony for Epileptics in New York, reported that more than 22 percent of the residents had alcoholic parents. While the studies often described the generational effects of alcohol use or abuse, they can be seen as hinting at fetal effects only when viewed retrospectively by scholars familiar with modern investigations of FAS.[13]

Nineteenth- and early twentieth-century physicians and social critics viewed alcohol problems through a wide lens. It was not the method by which alcohol did its damage but the damage it did that captivated their interest. Whether children suffered from poor "alcoholic" heredity, poor parenting, poor living conditions resulting from parental intemperance, or from their own alcohol habit mattered less than the fact that they were liable to become disorderly and dependent citizens. Physician T. Alexander MacNicholl, reporting on his study of 55,000 New York City schoolchildren at the turn of the century, concluded that the majority—53 percent—of those deemed "dullards" were the offspring of drinking parents, as compared with only 10 percent of the children of abstainers. Equally troubling to MacNicholl was the dullness caused by the drinking done by children themselves. He reported that when one teacher asked an intoxicated nine-year-old boy where he'd gotten his drink, the boy pulled a card from his pocket and explained that "a hole was punched in the card every time he got a drink of beer and that whoever got the most holes in his card in a month got a prize." Other children in the class also had such cards. Saloons, MacNicholl reported, sometimes had "small furniture, picture books, toys and hobby-horses" for patrons' children to play with, so that the "taste for liquor" could be "surreptitiously cultivated." The veracity of his statistical and anecdotal reports aside, MacNicholl's work demonstrates how investigators understood the effects of alcohol on offspring in broad terms: drinking parents created damaged children, either by heredity or by example.[14]

MacNicholl was one of many temperance-minded physicians who studied the effects of alcohol on individual health and assessed its contribution to social disorder. Temperance doctors publicized alcohol's dangers and erected institutions to care for its victims. In the United States in the decades after the Civil War, their numbers were small and their influence negligible. Nonetheless, as true believers they maintained their faith. Eventually their cause came back to life, sparked by urbanization, immigration, and class antagonism.[15]

Temperance

Drunken men were hard to overlook in the growing urban centers of nineteenth-century Europe and the United States. Stumbling through the streets, abusing their wives and children, drinking up their wages, losing their jobs, dispatching their families to the workhouse, and dying young of cirrhosis of the liver and other ailments and accidents linked to their excessive consumption of alcohol, they were visible testimony to the problem of inebriety. As statistics gathered by social observers and temperance advocates suggested, many ended their days in institutions for the sick, the insane, the destitute, or the criminal. With male inebriety growing ever more visible, female inebriety (with the exception of drinking among urban prostitutes) became less visible.

In the United States the Women's Christian Temperance Union (WCTU), a nationwide organization created in 1874, gave voice to mainly white, middle-class women who used the cause of "home protection" to push for a vast array of social and moral reforms, including the outlawing of the production and sale of alcohol. The WCTU campaign portrayed women and children as victims or potential victims of unchecked male drinking, highlighting women's economic and legal dependency. Activists did not deny that women sometimes succumbed to inebriety themselves, but they viewed those situations as pitiful cases rather than a collective threat to the social order. Far more politically compelling and rhetorically dominant than the asides about weak-willed women who developed an excessive fondness for drink were descriptions of male drunkenness and disorder that threatened the harmony of the home, workplace, city, and nation.[16]

Medical interest in female inebriety was equally limited, except among those who argued that it led to increased rates of infant mortality. Falling birth rates in industrialized countries in the nineteenth century high-lighted the problem of infant deaths and led worried authorities to ponder the causes and solutions. American temperance advocates in the field of medicine seized on the evidence that alcohol played a role and in a few in-stances noted the particular problems of maternal drinking. Alarmed by the increase in drinking among women, Nathan S. Davis, a leading Ameri-can doctor and one of the founders of the American Medical Association, reported that alcohol "tends to produce in the offspring of drinkers an un-stable nervous system, lowering them mentally, morally and physically." But while Davis and his allies criticized women's drinking, the subject failed to provoke the same level of alarm as men's drinking.[17]

William Sullivan, deputy medical officer of the Convict Prison in Park-hurst, England, observed, measured, and described the effects of women's abuse of alcohol on their offspring. His early findings about women's drinking in pregnancy, published in 1899, are often hailed as critical find-ings about alcohol teratogenicity. Inebriate women, he showed, bore chil-dren with severe problems, and many of them died young. The women's sober sisters bore healthier, longer-surviving children. Sullivan also found that when alcohol-abusing women entered prison early in their pregnan-cies and could not continue their drinking, their children were healthier than those born during periods when the women were able to imbibe freely. Finally, he observed what later twentieth-century studies would confirm: that maternal alcoholism had a progressive effect. Infant death and morbidity rates were higher among the later-born children of inebriate women. Sullivan's investigations led him to conclude that alcohol had "a direct toxic action on the embryo."[18]

Ultimately, Sullivan's concerns about male inebriety and his commitment to the temperance crusade clouded his investigations and muddied his arguments about alcohol. In *Alcoholism: A Chapter in Social Pathology* (1906), he turned away from his findings on maternal alcoholism and focused to a great extent on parental inebriety. Seeking to ground his data within the scientific literature, he turned for intellectual support to scholars whose work testified to the problems of parental or even paternal intemperance. He cited an analysis of 1,000 French "idiots" that found that 62 percent were the offspring of alcoholics, findings that 30 percent of criminals and 45 percent of juvenile offenders in Swiss prisons were the offspring of alcoholics, and a report that 82 percent of Russian prostitutes came from alcoholic parents. In each case, the specific role of maternal alcoholism received no attention. Sullivan submerged his findings in a sea of claims about parental intemperance, and the result demonstrates how political rhetoric combined with contemporary scientific ideas to create an understanding of alcohol's effects on offspring. Like those who castigated the gin drinking of the English poor in the eighteenth century or decried the alcoholic degeneration of the masses in the nineteenth century, Sullivan understood inebriety as an individual defect with grave social consequences. His interpretation of the specific action of alcohol on offspring was tempered by his belief that it was drinking, not drinkers, that mattered and that male drinking mattered most of all. Clearly discerning the debilitating if nonspecific effects on infants of in utero exposure to high levels of alcohol, Sullivan did not see FAS—a diagnosis that rested on late twentieth-century constructions of mothering, drinking, and fetuses as well as on the ways in which clinical evidence was amassed and interpreted.[19]

Drinking for Health

Despite denunciations of inebriety and calls for temperance or even abstinence, men and women continued to enjoy alcoholic beverages. And while a few physicians decried this habit, many more prescribed alcohol to their patients. Those searching for the early sightings of alcohol-related birth defects cannot overlook the numerous discussions of alcohol's use as a therapy and a tonic in pregnancy, childbirth, and nursing.

Ironically, as theories of degeneration developed in the nineteenth century, so too did theories about the medical value of alcohol. The emphasis in therapeutics shifted from an early nineteenth-century focus on depletive therapies such as bleeding and purging, designed to reduce "overexcitement," to therapies intended to stimulate the body and restore it to its natural state. By the second half of the nineteenth century, doctors were increasingly prescribing alcohol as a tonic. In the United States and Europe, physicians ordered pregnant women suffering morning sickness—termed "deranged stomach"—to consume sparkling wines. Some obstetrics specialists pointed to champagne as particularly beneficial—an indication that they practiced among an elite population. These specialists also recommended other alcoholic drinks, such as brandy with soda. One explained that alcohol in general exercised "a specific influence" on the digestive system; most prescribed it as a general remedy and an appetite stimulant.[20]

Just as many in the public believed that common workers gained energy from strong drinks, some doctors concluded that women about to meet the physical challenges of childbirth needed alcohol to fortify them for the rough road ahead. For the same reason, they prescribed alcoholic beverages as restorative tonics after delivery. Moreover, doctors viewed alcohol as a remedy as well as a tonic. A popular midwifery text that went through several editions recommended it for treatment of puerperal fever (an infection following childbirth). Nevertheless, practitioners recognized that excessive use could lead to problems and were leery of inducing an alcohol habit in their patients. A physician who suggested alcohol could be used as a sedative in cases of mastitis and mammary abscess, for example, also warned against letting patients overindulge.[21]

In addition to treating medical problems, alcohol was thought to aid in the production of milk for breastfeeding. An American doctor writing in the 1870s recommended a glass of mild ale twice a day, but ordered women not to take wine, brandy, or whiskey unless prescribed by a doctor. An English contemporary prescribed twice that amount: "two good meat meals a day with two glasses of beer or porter." Aware of the differing cultural practices on each side of the Atlantic, American practitioners sometimes chided their counterparts. As one commented, "Some physicians, particularly the English, as a routine practice, make their patients drink freely of malt liquors in spirituous fluids during the whole puerperal period." He claimed that such a practice could "engender an appetite for alcoholic stimuli that may lead to ruin of both body and soul," adding, perhaps disingenuously, "I am not writing a temperance lecture."[22]

Temperance-minded doctors freely criticized their peers whose prescriptions for alcohol set women on the road to ruin. Nineteenth-century Massachusetts physician Horatio Storer asserted women were made into "inebriates by doctors and nurses and relatives" who used alcohol for painful menstruation or after birth. William Sullivan also blamed female inebriety on prescribing habits. A "notable proportion of cases" [of female inebriety], he declared, "have their origin in the use of alcohol as a tonic after childbirth and prolonged nursing." There were other consequences of drinking and nursing, according to some medical writers, who complained that it led to an alcohol habit in the infant. As one explained, "Drunkards are made many times by the unconscious indulgence of mothers."[23]

Eventually, calls for temperance and the declining use of stimulant therapies led physicians to prescribe smaller amounts of alcohol. On the eve of World War I, an English textbook for midwives called the popular reliance on stout after birth a "superstition," although the author said a small amount could be taken with meals. An American book from 1920 similarly permitted tonics and light wines, but only at supper. But even as alcohol tonics and treatments fell in and out of favor, alcohol itself remained a popular beverage. And while some disparaged its use, others found new, hidden benefits—claiming it eliminated the unfit before birth.[24]

Eugenics

The apparent social decay that so troubled temperance advocates also spurred twentieth-century supporters of eugenics—the science of better breeding. Like temperance promoters, eugenicists worked to change laws in order to achieve what they viewed as a justifiable social good. And, like prohibitionists, they succeeded, in part by pointing to the consequences of inaction: unchecked reproduction by the unfit, including the degenerate offspring of the intemperate. However, eugenicists, much like their contemporaries in the temperance crusade, failed to identify maternal inebriety as a major source of degeneration.[25]

The writings of eugenicists, although steeped in scientific rhetoric and

anchored to studies of the unfit, never fully elucidated the precise hereditary mechanism of alcoholic degeneracy. Whether the child of an inebriate
suffered from a physical disability, a moral deficit, a mental deficiency, or
an inherited fondness for drink did not seem to matter as much as the fact
that "weakness" passed from generation to generation. As Victor Vaughn,
dean of the University of Michigan Medical School, explained in a 1914
publication, while there were uncertainties as to whether alcoholism "is
begotten of, or begets, feeble-mindedness" the alcoholic and the feeble-
minded "belong to the same breed."[26]

Eugenicists based many of their conclusions on evidence obtained from
family studies that traced genealogies of the fit and the unfit. Syphilis, sexual promiscuity, alcoholism, criminality, and pauperism were signs that
one belonged in the latter category. In 1912 Henry H. Goddard, director of
the Vineland, New Jersey, Training School for Feeble-minded Boys and
Girls and a leading scholar in the field published *The Kallikak Family: A
Study in the Heredity of Feeble-mindedness* which made a clear case for alcoholic heredity. His book described two branches of a single family—one
side descended from a soldier and a feebleminded woman he had met in a
tavern; the other from the soldier and a "respectable girl from a good family." Although a thoughtful reader could guess what would be revealed
about the two lines of descent, Goddard provided the data and analysis.
What was surprising were the conclusions he drew about the direction of
influence: "feeble-mindedness," he inferred from his findings "is not due to
alcoholism, alcoholism is to a very large extent due to feeble-mindedness."
In short, degenerates became alcoholics; it was not, as earlier studies concluded, that alcoholics produced degenerates.[27]

In a recent retrospective analysis of Goddard's Vineland records, physician Robert Karp and colleagues argue that several of the Kallikak children
from the "degenerate" branch who were deemed feebleminded actually
suffered from the effects of alcohol exposure in utero. The lesson to be
drawn here is not that Goddard was mistaken in his understanding of feeblemindedness but that his conclusions rested on contemporary concerns
about degeneracy and the promise of eugenics, just as Karp's finding re-
flects his understanding of fetal development.[28]

Not all of the early twentieth-century eugenicists claimed to see the effects of alcohol on offspring. The most critical dissenter, Karl Pearson, a
leading scientist who directed the prestigious Galton Eugenics Laboratory
at the University of London, argued that alcohol did not damage germ

cells. Along with colleague Ethel Elderton, he undertook investigations using animals and applied advanced statistical techniques to the data he collected. The pair concluded that parental alcohol use had no significant hereditary effects. Understandably, their findings outraged both medical temperance advocates and fellow eugenicists who often chose to ignore this aspect of Pearson and Elderton's work.[29]

In time, the null hypothesis became the favored one. As historian Philip Pauly explained, the laboratory findings about alcohol and offspring offered conflicting interpretive possibilities. If alcohol-exposed animals gave birth to smaller litters, then alcohol could be said to be poisoning future generations in the womb. Or, as some argued, alcohol could be seen as offering a eugenic advantage by weeding out the weak in utero so that only the healthiest survived. The supposition that alcohol could serve the cause of race betterment so alarmed temperance advocates that one of its supporters, Frank B. Hansen, undertook laboratory research to prove the null hypothesis. Alcohol, he determined, had no effect whatsoever on offspring. As Pauly wryly explained, Hansen achieved the "liquidation of a scientific problem area," making clear that the question of alcohol's effects had been answered and no further investigations needed to be undertaken.[30]

Yet the argument that alcohol provided a long-term eugenic benefit remained popular with some scholars and experts, perhaps because it seemed so logical. In *The Eugenic Predicament* (1933), Berkeley zoology professor and eugenicist Samuel Johnson Holmes referred to "Drs. Reid and Haycraft" who "contended that alcohol is a racial blessing in disguise because it eliminates a number of weak-willed and nervously unstable people who drink themselves into an early grave." Similarly, Paul Popenoe and Rosewell Hill Johnson explained in their college text *Applied Eugenics* (1933) that regular exposure to alcohol had, over time, killed off some of the weaker members of society, leaving the strongest to survive and reproduce. It was, they noted, "a powerful agent of natural selection," although they were quick to point out to their college readers that encouraging the less fit to drink themselves to death before reproducing was not the ideal path to social betterment. On the one hand, great social and economic losses resulted from alcoholism; on the other hand, superior eugenic practices existed, including controls on reproduction and the outlawing of alcohol—both of which had been enacted.[31]

Advocates of both prohibition and eugenics scored important legal triumphs. By 1941 thirty states permitted compulsory sterilization and more than 38,000 individuals had been deemed unfit to breed and subjected to surgery. The temperance victory proved even greater. Twenty-seven states and a number of communities and municipalities had enacted Prohibition laws prior to ratification of the Eighteenth Amendment to the Constitution in 1919. Under the Volstead Act, which provided for enforcement of the amendment, the production and sale of intoxicating liquor ceased, except for alcohol manufactured for home, industrial, medicinal, and religious use. In many places Americans violated Prohibition laws, just as individuals that might be deemed "unfit" continued to bear children. But Prohibition did succeed in closing the door on scientific research on the effects of alcohol. When it opened again after the repeal of Prohibition in 1933, few scientists pursued new investigations. Studies of alcohol's effects on reproduction in particular had become, in Pauly's terms, "scientifically uninteresting."[32]

Doctors, Alcohol, and Pregnancy

When Prohibition ended, returning alcohol policies to the states, public taverns replaced hidden speakeasies in many cases, and new medical arguments about alcoholism slowly supplanted older ones about inebriety. In many circles, opponents of alcohol, called the "drys," began to be viewed as old-fashioned malcontents whose cries of alarm had led the nation to undertake a damaging social experiment. Discussions of medical and social problems linked to alcohol abuse seemed to have an air of fusty moralism that a new generation found disquieting or simply refused to listen to. Even data suggesting that alcohol abuse caused problems such as cirrhosis and esophageal cancer became suspect. Scientific research supported the emerging consensus that alcohol was harmless except to a small, vulnerable group of drinkers. Old findings were buried and forgotten—only to be retrieved decades later.

Evidence about alcohol's effects on reproduction also landed in the dustbin. Leading social scientists declared that the roots of childhood disorders lay in the child's environment, not in heredity and certainly not in alcohol-damaged germ cells. Poverty in its many guises came to be seen as the cause of childhood behavioral and physical limitations. Eugenics, stained by the horrors of Nazi Germany, was discredited, and many arguments about heredity that its supporters favored were also tossed away.[33]

After World War II a new science of alcohol emerged, based on an emerging disease theory of alcoholism that argued that a few individuals were so physically dependent on alcohol and so damaged by the consequences that they could not control their drinking. The majority, however, could drink without harming themselves. What separated alcoholics from other drinkers was not how much they consumed, but whether they drank involuntarily. Just as diabetics had no ability to compel themselves to produce insulin, alcoholics had no ability to stop drinking. And, like diabetics, alcoholics needed treatment and understanding.

In attempting to excise the moral stigma of abusive drinking and set scientists on a quest to find the genetic, environmental, physiological, and psychological underpinnings of alcoholism, experts promoting the disease concept initiated a profound change in American life. They taught the public to view alcohol abusers with compassion rather than contempt and they worked to replace punishment of alcohol abuse with treatment. In doing so, they changed the perception of alcohol from a product that might be dangerous to one that could be used safely and pleasurably by the vast majority. What temperance advocates labeled a poison, a new generation of alcohol experts called harmless, except to a few susceptible individuals.[34]

A coalition of interest groups underwrote the research leading to the development of the disease concept of alcoholism and propelled the findings into the political mainstream. Work began when Prohibition ended and the Research Council on the Problems of Alcohol, an organization affiliated with the American Association for the Advancement of Science, undertook a scientific study of alcoholism. In the 1940s the Yale School of Alcohol Studies (with major funding from the Research Council) initiated an investigation of alcoholism, working to educate the public about the nature of this disease and trying to devise treatments for sufferers. The Yale group published the *Quarterly Journal of Studies on Alcohol,* which became the leading journal in the field, and created a Summer School of Alcohol Studies to train professionals to work with alcoholics. They also developed Yale Plan Clinics, which pioneered outpatient alcoholism services. Led by E. M. Jellinek, America's foremost alcohol scholar, experts at Yale declared alcoholism a treatable medical condition. Jellinek published and edited a number of influential books and articles on alcoholism as a disease, including *The Effect of Alcohol on the Individual* in 1942 and in 1960 *The Disease Concept of Alcoholism.*[35]

When confronting questions about alcohol and reproduction, Jellinek staunchly rebutted old ideas about alcoholic heredity—that it was passed along as a single trait—and argued that alcohol had little direct effect on offspring. Echoing Goddard, Jellinek proclaimed that "moronism in the offspring of alcoholics is not due to the alcoholism of the parents, but to the moronic heredity of the drinking parent." Higher rates of miscarriage, infant mortality, feeblemindedness, epilepsy, and mental disorders among the children of what he termed abnormal drinkers, were explained, he said, by their higher rates of pregnancy, the disruptive home environments in which their children lived, and their eugenic liabilities. Blame the drinker, he argued, not the drink.[36]

His colleagues did just that. Responding to questions sent in to the Yale Plan Clinics, two of them explained that, while heavy drinking on the part of a pregnant woman might impair the health of the embryo, this was not due to the direct action of the alcohol. Rather, they said, it was because heavy drinking resulted in "unhygienic personal habits, particularly with respect to diet," that damaged the embryo. Anne Roe, a member of the Yale group who studied the children of alcoholics living in foster homes, found they were less gifted intellectually than children of nonalcoholics also reared in foster care. Nevertheless, she concluded that the difficulties experienced by the first group were not caused by the alcoholism of the parent, a reflection perhaps of the opinions of the Yale group, but not supported by her evidence. Succeeding generations of physicians and scientists would accept as valid assertions of alcohol's inability to directly affect offspring, despite the fact that such claims rested on suspect evidence, poor reasoning, or no evidence at all.[37]

With alcohol use and even abuse in pregnancy declared safe by leading experts, doctors felt free to brush off nervous patients and peers who questioned them about possible negative consequences of drinking. When a worried physician wrote to *JAMA* (the *Journal of the American Medical Association*) about a patient who drank thirty-six ounces of beer shortly after conception, the reply noted that "in human beings it is difficult to prove that alcohol has a deleterious effect on babies in utero, even when large amounts are taken." Medical textbooks invariably stressed the safety and benefits of moderate consumption, stating that it helped women to relax and to sleep. The only problem it posed came from the calories in the drinks, as doctors perceived excess weight gain in pregnancy as dangerous.[38]

In the early 1950s, doctors discovered new applications for alcohol in their obstetrical practices, as an analgesic and as a tocolytic agent (capable of halting premature labor). Several physicians described the experimental use of intravenous alcohol for relief of pain in childbirth, reporting good results: patients became euphoric, pain was effectively relieved, and alcohol, because it was a food, provided nourishment. Most important, it caused none of the complications that resulted from the use of other drugs for pain relief. The major limitation appeared to be that if given too early in labor, contractions ceased. This serendipitous observation led to clinical trials of alcohol as a tocolytic in the mid-1960s. The need for an agent capable of halting premature labor and preventing preterm births was vital; infants not born at full term had elevated mortality rates, and those who survived often experienced serious medical problems.[39]

When research into alcohol tocolysis first began, physicians believed that the placenta seemed to act as a barrier to the passage of alcohol from the mother's bloodstream to that of the baby. They soon learned this was not the case; as the mother's blood alcohol level rose, so did that of the fetus. However, alcohol appeared to halt premature labor in a number of instances, its mechanism of action made scientific sense, and it was safer than the other substances used for tocolysis at the time. New York obstetrician and gynecologist Fritz Fuchs, who conducted many important studies of alcohol tocolysis, argued against drawing broad conclusions from his early investigations and urged that controlled studies be done comparing the efficacy to alcohol infusion to bed rest. But, he admitted, it was not easy to establish such a trial, even in his own department. Staff members, he reported, "have become convinced of the beneficial effects of alcohol." So taken were doctors with the purported ability of alcohol to halt premature labor that one mused in a discussion following publication of one of Fuchs's papers that many of his patients who experienced habitual miscarriage and premature labor were "teetotalers." Perhaps medical science would demonstrate that *not* drinking during pregnancy posed a risk.[40]

One of the advantages of alcohol tocolysis was that while it might have to be given as an infusion in serious cases, in instances when patients experienced mild early contractions, they could drink at home. But as information about the risks of drinking during pregnancy began to be publicized after findings about FAS, many women rejected the treatment. Moreover, safer and more effective agents were becoming available.

Follow-up studies on children exposed to alcohol tocolysis showed that it did not lead to cases of FAS. Seen in retrospect, alcohol tocolysis may have had a greater impact on obstetricians than on mothers and babies. A cohort of doctors learned during their training that alcohol use in pregnancy was not merely benign but potentially beneficial. This may have made them dubious when, following the discovery of FAS, they were told to have their patients abstain.[41]

Contexts

When Sheila Blume's editor asked, regarding FAS, "Why hasn't anyone seen this before?" he posed a valid question. Until the second half of the twentieth century, no one had seen FAS. There had been astute descriptions of the effects on infants of heavy alcohol exposure in utero and shrewd observations of the damage women did to their infants and children when they spent their pregnancies in a state of constant intoxication. There had also been medical literature and medical practitioners who touted the benefits of alcohol use during pregnancy and scientific explanations of why alcohol could not harm an embryo or fetus. As a result, when FAS was named in 1973 it was something new: a diagnosis that emerged from a particular scientific understanding of fetal development and fetal risk in the context of a growing awareness of alcohol abuse among women of childbearing age.

3

◆ ◆

"A Clinically Observable Abnormality": Framing FAS

While attending the Rutgers University Summer School of Alcohol Studies in 1973, Carrie Randall arrived one day with an article she had clipped from the newspaper. It described a recent medical journal article that suggested a possible connection between alcohol and birth defects. The experts she showed it to were dubious, declaring that if alcohol damaged the fetus, someone would have noticed before. Randall and her fellow scholars were equally troubled by the small sample of cases reported by the authors, Jones and Smith. They had drawn a breathtakingly large conclusion from a small number of cases. Randall, a scientist conducting research on animals, figured it would be easy to demolish what seemed to be an insupportable claim. She wrote a grant for postdoctoral study on alcohol's ability to damage the fetus. "I thought it would be a very simple question to answer," she admitted, adding that she started out as "a skeptic."[1]

Randall conducted her study using mice, and she recalled being "much surprised to see grossly critical birth defects" linked to alcohol exposure. Shortly after she finished her research she attended a scientific meeting, where she remembers "running with my little bottle of mouse fetuses" to show them to Kenneth Lyons Jones. He referred her to Gerald Chernoff, a scientist who had made similar findings from his own studies of mice. Instead of quickly discrediting what she had assumed was an erroneous finding by doctors who mistook the effects of poor nutrition and smoking for alcohol effects, Randall—along with Chernoff and others who conducted animal research—helped confirm that alcohol was a teratogen. It was fortunate, Randall later remarked, that she and Chernoff had both used "sus-

35

ceptible" mice in their studies; had they used rats or a less susceptible strain of mice, they might have gotten negative results. A few years after her research on alcohol teratogenesis began, Randall found herself testifying before Congress in support of alcoholic beverage warning labels. Her research continues to this day and she admits, "I just never believed that thirty years later I'd still be doing it."[2]

Within a few years, FAS attained the status of a legitimate diagnosis and spawned an international research program. Scientific unbelievers like Randall were persuaded by the results of their own inquiries; the public was persuaded because, after the experience with thalidomide, there was a cultural framework in place for understanding alcohol teratogenesis. Most Americans had no interest in peering into tiny bottles of mouse fetuses or reading scientific reports in specialized journals. They did, however, find it easy to watch on television and to read stories about deformed babies born to severely alcoholic women and to accept the claim. The public understood that fetuses could be damaged in utero and knew that many women suffered from alcoholism, just like men. Equally critical to public acceptance of FAS was the fact that, although it was initially perceived to be a serious problem, it was understood as a medical problem with a medical solution. Thanks to the Supreme Court's *Roe v. Wade* decision, aborting the potentially damaged fetuses of pregnant alcoholic women was a viable medical option.

Teratogens

For decades, scientists and the public had shared a perception of the womb as a protective barrier not easily breached. Even those who understood that a fetus could be damaged by particular environmental agents believed the list of such dangerous agents was small. Alcohol was certainly not among them. A popular book by anthropologist Ashley Montagu, *Life before Birth* (1964), illustrates the thinking at the time. The book purported to teach prospective mothers how to influence the physical and emotional development of their children before birth, acknowledging the significance of prenatal experiences. In addition to providing commonsense and commonplace advice—urging women to eat well, eschew drugs, and quit working after the fourth or fifth month of pregnancy—Montagu offered readers the latest scientific findings about risks to fetal development from smoking and X-rays. And he staunchly defended the moderate use of alcohol, repri-

manding those who claimed it was dangerous: "It can be stated categorically that no matter how great the amounts of alcohol imbibed by the
mother or the father, alcohol as such affects neither the germ cells nor the
development of the fetus." He dismissed contrary advice, including the
"many publications [that] claim to show that alcoholics give birth to more
idiots, more malformed children, and more retarded children than do
sober individuals." Such assertions, he stated without hesitation, do not
"stand up to scientific examination." A little more than a decade after
Montagu's book appeared, Americans knew that lots of things, including
alcohol, could harm a fetus. Montagu amended the 1977 edition of his
book, chiding himself for his earlier advice and for overlooking the historical literature on alcohol's effects on offspring. He now told readers that
while there was no evidence of harm from an occasional drink, the wisest
course was abstinence. His rapid journey from doubter to believer demonstrated the power of the new scientific findings.[3]

Over a twelve-year period that began with the thalidomide tragedy and
concluded with the discovery of FAS, Americans completed a short course
in teratology. By the time *Newsweek* published a brief article about the
findings of Jones and Smith in 1973, the magazine's editors could assume
that readers would understand the parallels drawn among alcohol, nico-
tine, and thalidomide. Having discarded the idea that the womb func-
tioned as a shield surrounding and protecting the fetus, Americans now
perceived it as a boundary line—a thin membrane that could be easily
penetrated by man-made (and natural) substances. This was what thalidomide had taught them.[4]

The horrible damage done by thalidomide, a supposedly safe sleeping
aid, shook public confidence in medical science and the pharmaceutical industry. Thanks to the vigilance of FDA scientist Dr. Frances Kelsey, thalidomide, which was in use in Europe, Canada, and elsewhere, never received
approval for licensing in the United States. Nevertheless, the would-be
American manufacturer succeeded in distributing more than 2.5 million
capsules to more than 1,200 physicians for testing. When news of thalidomide's dangers broke, President John F. Kennedy took a few moments of
his weekly news conference to tell women they should check their medicine cabinets for the pills. For some, the warning came too late; at least seventeen American children sustained severe prenatal damage caused by
their exposure to the drug.[5]

The news media lauded Kelsey as a valiant physician who had stood up to the pressures exerted by the pharmaceutical company and its allies, underscoring the fact that Americans had narrowly avoided a massive tragedy. In magazines and on television, images of European infants born with missing limbs and of toddlers with prostheses strapped to their chests horrified viewers. When a Belgian woman, aided by her family and physician, killed her severely damaged baby, who was born with no arms, severe facial deformities, and an anal canal that emptied through the vagina, her arrest and trial received daily coverage in the American press. The front page of the *New York Times* announced her acquittal.[6]

For Americans, the most riveting case of all involved Sheri Finkbine. A pregnant Arizona mother of four and the host of *Romper Room*, a local television show for young children, Finkbine took some thalidomide that her husband had brought home from England. When she discovered the danger, she sought an abortion. A local hospital committee gave its approval, but final legal permission could not be obtained. Finkbine's identity, kept secret until then, became public when she sued to overturn the ruling. Week after week the media followed her quest to end her pregnancy, painting her agonizing pursuit against a backdrop of horror stories as the numbers of deformed thalidomide babies born in Europe and elsewhere continued to climb. Eventually Finkbine traveled to Sweden and obtained an abortion there. Following the procedure, a physician reported that the fetus had been seriously damaged.[7]

The thalidomide episode resulted in higher standards for testing new drugs both in the United States and abroad and expanded interest in drug safety during pregnancy. The 1962 Kefauver-Harris amendments to the Federal Food, Drug and Cosmetic Act, which came to be called the thalidomide law, mandated new controls on drug manufacturing, safety, effectiveness, reporting, approval, and labeling. Later the FDA adopted further guidelines for testing new drugs on animals to determine if they cause reproductive or structural defects. Such testing and investigation did not extend to foods, drugs, or chemicals already in use; their teratogenic properties awaited discovery by other means.[8]

Finding teratogens proved to be no easy task. Experimental research in which substances were given to pregnant laboratory animals to test for fetal effects provided some important information. Clinical investigations, sometimes sparked by observations of malformed children, yielded other kinds of data, but the fit between the laboratory science and the examination room proved to be imperfect. Substances found to be teratogenic in common laboratory animals, such as caffeine and aspirin, did no damage to human embryos or fetuses. Conversely, human teratogens were sometimes inert in laboratory animals or could not be found using standard testing protocols. Thalidomide had no effect on rat or mice embryos, unless, as researchers detected at a late date, the drug was given intravenously rather than orally. Many teratogens therefore awaited discovery by astute clinicians, like the ones who had made the connection between children born with missing limbs and their mothers' use of thalidomide during pregnancy.[9]

Americans learned other horrifying lessons about teratogens during a rubella epidemic that followed closely on the heels of the thalidomide episode. Following an outbreak in Australia in 1941, experts had clarified the link between first-trimester maternal rubella infections and birth defects. But the full implications of this became apparent to Americans only in the 1960s—the peak baby boom years—when somewhere between one-third of 1 percent and 4 percent of all pregnancies were affected. An estimated 30,000 infants born in the United States suffered from severe mental retardation, blindness, and deafness as a result of their exposure to rubella in utero. Another 20,000 pregnancies ended in elective abortion or stillbirth.[10]

Other teratogens also made news in the years preceding the discovery of FAS. In 1971, a team of Boston physicians observed a rare cancer of the vagina (clear-cell adenocarcinoma) in eight young women and linked it to their mothers' ingestion of a synthetic estrogen, diethylstilbestrol (DES), during pregnancy. It was the mother of one of the young women who suggested to physicians that DES might be the cause. The drug, prescribed to prevent miscarriage, later proved to be ineffective for that purpose. Further research showed that it also caused damage to the genital tracts of men exposed in utero. Soon after the DES story broke, Americans learned about "Minamata disease," the result of exposure to methyl mercury, which was dumped into Japan's Minamata Bay by the Chisson Chemical Company. In a brilliant and searing photo essay published in *Life* magazine in 1972, W. Eugene Smith showed the terrible effects of the mercury poisoning. The mercury had contaminated fish and, in turn, the local population that caught and ate the fish. Victims suffered physical deformities and progressive neurological symptoms, including paralysis, convulsions, and death. Methyl mercury was also severely teratogenic, causing such terrible defects that outsiders rejected young women from the town as marriage partners because they would bear deformed children.[11]

As the public received the news about industrial chemical and pharmaceutical teratogens, it also read about environmental pollution and its threat to fetal health, beginning with Rachel Carson's pathbreaking book *Silent Spring* (1962). Carson's work illuminated the damage done to animal fetuses by man-made pesticides and made clear that such toxins threatened human life as well. The revelations in her book helped spur the creation of the Environmental Protection Agency and to focus attention on the problems of environmental pollution. Radiation posed another threat. While post–World War II studies of the effects of atomic radiation primarily focused on genetic damage, they were followed by studies of the effects of nuclear fallout in the wake of an expanded nuclear weapons testing program. Eventually those living downwind from atomic test sites demonstrated that their exposure, including exposure in utero, had damaging effects on their health. Ironically, medical X-rays taken of pregnant women exposed greater numbers of fetuses to radiation than even military weapons testing. That practice ceased when scientists uncovered a link between such X-ray exposure and elevated rates of childhood cancers.[12]

Dramatic discoveries of new and old teratogens, particularly thalidomide and rubella, overshadowed the far more common risk of fetal harm from cigarette smoking by pregnant women. Beginning in the late 1950s, scientific studies revealed that fetal exposure to tobacco resulted in lower birth weights and higher rates of fetal and neonatal mortality. A subsequent review of the literature would find a higher incidence of pregnancy complications among smokers but a less consistent relationship between smoking and birth weight.[13] Eclipsed by much more deadly risks, such as lung cancer, other neoplasms, and heart disease, that together made an enormous contribution to adult mortality rates, the findings about fetal harm generated relatively little notice. Moreover, public health campaigns to educate Americans about smoking risks, including the Federal Cigarette Labeling and Advertising Act of 1965, which required that cigarette packages carry the caution, "Cigarette Smoking May Be Hazardous to Your Health," gradually helped to reduce the number of smokers and, consequently, the number of fetuses affected. Smoking prevalence among women was 33.9 percent in 1965. After 1974 rates declined rapidly, and by 1998 only 22 percent of women reported smoking. However, among those who smoked, only about half knew of the possible effects on a fetus. As a result of this finding, in 1985 the government began requiring that cigarette packages carry a set of four rotating labels, one of which referred to pregnancy: "Surgeon General's Warning: Smoking Causes Lung Cancer, Heart Disease, Emphysema, and May Complicate Pregnancy," and another of which addressed fetal health: "Surgeon General's Warning: Smoking by Pregnant Women May Result in Fetal Injury, Premature Birth and Low Birth Weight." The new statements reflected an increased concern with fetal health and the faith that public education via warning labels would prove effective.[14]

More than a decade of news about teratogens set the stage for the public's acceptance of the assertion that alcohol abuse by pregnant women could result in birth defects. The finding generated relatively little concern, however; the early reports suggested that FAS was a problem only when a pregnant woman was severely alcoholic. In addition, FAS was a medical problem with a medical solution: abortion.

Abortion

The discovery of FAS followed closely on the heels of the United States Supreme Court's decision in *Roe V. Wade*, which struck down all state abortion laws and implemented a system of abortion regulation based on the trimester of pregnancy. In the brief period before the antiabortion movement hushed those who spoke of the procedure openly, the subject of FAS and abortion would often be raised in tandem. A 1976 article in *U.S. News & World Report* entitled "Alcoholic Babies" described infants born "stunted in mind and body" because of their mothers' abusive drinking, and concluded that alcoholic women needed to use effective birth control and, should that fail, to be "offered the alternative of terminating the pregnancy."[15]

Elective abortions became an option for pregnant alcoholic women in part because of the earlier encounters with teratogens. The highly profiled Finkbine case made it possible for many Americans to think of abortion as a medical preventative to a potential family tragedy. The rubella outbreak reinforced this perception, as large numbers of pregnant women managed to obtain therapeutic abortions either with the permission of hospital committees or with the illegal assistance of private physicians. An editors' note at the beginning of a *Life* magazine article profiling abortions provided to women exposed to rubella bore the title "Two Mothers and a Brave Doctor," reflecting how abortion was slowly being reframed from a back-alley procedure into a medical technology. Yet the vast majority of women exposed to the rubella virus had no means of procuring one, a situation that helped spur the moment for change.[16]

As early as 1959 the American Legal Institute (ALI), a group of leading judges, law professors, and attorneys, developed a model state abortion law that explicitly justified termination of pregnancy for reasons of maternal health or if the child would be born with grave physical or mental defects. Abortion, the ALI argued, permitted compassionate parents to prevent the births of severely handicapped infants, thereby preserving the physical and emotional health of women. In the wake of the thalidomide and rubella episodes, physicians, lawyers, and members of the public increasingly came to side with this argument, enlisting in the battle for legalization. A survey of physicians, published in *Modern Medicine* in 1967, reported that the vast majority—87 percent—favored liberalizing abortion policies. Between 1967 and 1970, twelve states liberalized their abortion codes, and the ALI's model frequently served as both a template and a justification for the new laws. Then, in 1973, the Supreme Court issued its ruling.[17]

Roe v. Wade not only eliminated barriers to abortion, it led many physicians to discuss the abortion option with patients when they believed a woman herself might be at grave risk if she carried a pregnancy to term or when her baby might be severely disabled. Chronic alcoholism in a pregnant woman became a reason for raising the subject. Shortly after *Lancet* published the first article by Jones and Smith, it printed a letter from an American physician asking if the authors recommended abortion to "'severe chronically alcoholic' pregnant women." They replied: "As we indicated, the risk of adverse outcome of pregnancy of severe chronic alcoholic pregnant women is of sufficient magnitude (43%) to merit serious consideration of early termination of pregnancy by such women. This is a consideration for these women, and we feel they should be given every opportunity to make a decision relative to abortion with as many facts as are now available." They repeated this conclusion in other publications.[18]

Other doctors shared their sentiments. *Time* magazine reported that doctors warned prospective mothers to stop drinking heavily if they planned to become pregnant and "to consider having abortions if they became pregnant while addicted to alcohol." On network television, news anchor Barbara Walters told viewers: "The more alcohol consumed, the greater the risk. One obstetrician warned that the dangers of drinking during pregnancy are so serious, therapeutic abortion for alcoholic women may be advised." In this instance, the report seemed to confuse drinking and alcoholism. The medical textbooks, however, were more precise. A new edition of a popular obstetrics text that appeared in 1976 described the findings of Jones and Smith and, apparently persuaded by the evidence, suggested "early pregnancy termination" for alcoholic women. Other women could continue to drink, they concluded, writing that "use of alcohol by the pregnant woman has not been shown to produce any pathologic changes in the mother or fetus." But if the alcohol did no damage, why were alcoholic women candidates for abortion?[19]

European physicians also discussed abortion. Some German physicians described it as a choice meriting consideration, while a group of French doctors proposed hospitalization and detoxification of pregnant alcoholic women as an alternative. A German case report on the fetuses of three alcoholic women who underwent recommended abortions explained that all three fetuses had abnormal muscle tone and two were severely deformed. The authors stated: "Eugenically speaking, there is an absolute indication of interruption of pregnancy in alcoholics in the chronic phase of addiction." One of the authors later wrote, "I have recommended termination of pregnancy in four instances," going on to report that he did so when the women were in the chronic stage of alcoholism. The tone of the articles suggests that the doctors viewed elective abortion as an effective means of preventing the births of alcohol-damaged infants, just as they viewed it as a recourse when infants were liable to be born with other devastating handicaps.[20]

In the United States, open contemplation of abortion as a medical solution to FAS lasted only a short time. The *Roe v. Wade* decision ignited a political firestorm, and to escape the heat physicians and the media ceased recommending or even discussing the procedure. In 1981 Seattle physician Sterling Clarren wrote in *JAMA* of advising clinic patients about the hazards of alcohol abuse in pregnancy and the need to stop drinking. "Therapeutic abortion," he continued, "is often discussed as an option, but it is not actively recommended." Perhaps because of the mounting political debate, the term *abortion* was replaced in much of the medical literature by the term *pregnancy termination*. One of the last published discussions of this as an option to prevent FAS was in a 1986 textbook on genetic counseling that stated: "Women known to have consumed large amounts of alcohol during the first trimester should, if still in the second trimester, be counseled about their high risks and offered prenatal genetic studies, but also warned about the limited value of these tests and offered the opportunity to terminate their pregnancies." By the time these statements appeared, abortion opponents had returned to the Supreme Court and won cases involving the restriction of federal and state funding for abortions and permitting increased state regulation of the procedure and of abortion providers. Congress also placed restrictions on federal funding of abortions and considered passage of a "human life amendment" to the Constitution, supported by abortion opponents, that if passed would have granted political status to the fetus. The executive branch, too, became embroiled in the subject as abortion concerns infused presidential politics and appointments.[21]

The louder abortion and fetal rights debates grew, the quieter the medical discussion of abortion as a means of preventing of FAS became. Finally, silence fell. The problem, however, remained. Some pregnant women continued to abuse alcohol and gave birth to affected infants as a result. The *Newsweek* article announcing the first reports of FAS under the title "Martinis and Motherhood" had sounded an ominous warning: "There are an estimated 2 million alcoholic women in the U.S., and at least half of them are of childbearing age."[22]

Discovering Female Alcoholism

Thanks to the feminist movement, women's substance abuse came out of the shadows, and their struggles with addiction received new attention and greater understanding. The newfound visibility of alcoholic women helped legitimate the problem of FAS, but it did so by turning the spotlight away from the harm pregnant alcoholic women did to themselves and placing it on the fetus. Eventually the political debate about fetuses would transform narratives about the suffering of pregnant alcoholic women into morality tales about maternal obligation. But first Americans had to learn that women, like men, could be alcoholics.

After Prohibition, rates of female drinking slowly began to rise, although they lagged behind those of men. In 1940, 38 percent of all adult women drank as compared with 64 percent of men. By 1965 the figures stood at 60 percent for women and 77 percent for men. The narrowing gap said something about rates of consumption but nothing at all about rates of problem drinking.[23]

The evidence suggested that men's abusive drinking continued to be far greater than women's. Despite this fact, there was a "cultural preoccupation" with women's drinking, alcohol expert Kaye Middleton Fillmore noted, based on an unproved convergence thesis suggesting that the percentage of women abusing alcohol was coming close to the percentage of men. A *Time* magazine cover story on alcoholism in 1974 reported that in the 1950s one out of every five or six alcoholics was female, but that since then the gap had narrowed to one in four. "In some places," it reported, "the numbers are equal." Two years later, *Newsweek* published an account of the growing numbers of women joining Alcoholics Anonymous (AA) and asserted that deaths among women from alcohol-related diseases were climbing. Actual data on problem drinking varied according the measure being used—hospitalization, self-reporting, deaths from cirrhosis, membership in AA—and measurements best suited to assessing men's alcohol abuse did not necessarily provide accurate data about women.[24]

Ominous statements in the media about alcoholic women rested on very little evidence. According to the National Clearinghouse for Drug Information of the National Institute on Drug Abuse, between 1929 and 1970 only 28 English-language articles on the subject of women and alcohol appeared in research publications, compared with more than 1,000 articles about men and alcohol. With pressure from women's groups and the discovery of FAS, more investigations got under way, but the information gap remained wide. Between 1970 and 1976, according to a report issued by the National Institute on Alcohol Abuse and Alcoholism, 122 articles about women and alcohol appeared in the research literature.[25]

Despite the paucity of information, the subject of women's alcoholism stimulated investigations, public hearings, and press coverage. In a strange twist, the lack of data about women's alcoholism became evidence of "closeted" drinking. Once portrayed as scantily dressed skid-row prostitutes, female alcoholics began to be imagined as middle-class "lady tipplers" ensconced in their suburban homes, wearing aprons, and hiding their bottles in laundry hampers. Despite the change in venue and clothes, the public image of the woman drinker still reeked of sin. An analysis of the cinematic representations found alcoholic women depicted as "morally decayed, sexually promiscuous, tragically inadequate mothers and wives . . ."—and far more flawed than their male counterparts. These images and the judgments they subsumed would be amplified within the public discourse about FAS.[26]

Feminism helped women escape from the moralistic explanations of their alcoholism, but they did not get very far. Instead of being depraved, they were said to have been trapped—either in the role of homemaker or the role of worker—both of which could precipitate excessive drinking. *The Feminine Mystique*, Betty Friedan's 1963 best seller about unfulfilled middle-class women trapped in a web of low expectations and cultural biases, described homemakers taking "tranquilizers like cough drops" and drinking copious amounts of liquor because of their thwarted search for self-fulfillment. Friedan claimed there were "approximately a million known alcoholic housewives in America," hinting with her careful choice of words that many others remained hidden from view.[27]

Popular media presented the same message. A *Newsweek* article described women drinking in secret, explaining that while men drank to feel more powerful and masculine, women drank to feel more feminine and expressive. Television news broadcasts also focused on troubled alcoholic housewives. *NBC News* anchor David Brinkley told viewers that many women alcoholics were "home alone all day, bored, restless." But women who rejected existing social norms proved as vulnerable to alcoholism as those chafing against domestic boredom. Reporting on new data about increasing alcohol abuse by women, CBS television news anchor Walter Cronkite said that "doctors indicate women's liberation may play a role." Clarifying this, he explained that physicians credited the increase [in female alcoholism] to, among other things, changing women's roles, and jobs in which women face more pressure. A close reading (and watching) of the reports led to the conclusion that staying home made women drink and going to work made women drink, pressure made women drink and boredom made women drink.[28]

Feminists rejected these classic double binds and sought greater understanding and help for women dealing with substance abuse problems. In the politically charged 1970s their demands provoked a response from both government agencies and private organizations. The 1970 legislation creating the NIAAA contained language requiring states to identify the prevention and treatment needs of women. The National Council on Alcoholism established an office to deal with women's issues in 1976, and that same year Congress passed legislation requiring states to provide prevention and treatment programs for women. Forty-five states eventually created task forces on women and alcoholism. Feminism also reshaped the recovery movement. In 1975 Jean Kirkpatrick founded Women for Sobriety, a self-help group that incorporated many of the twelve steps used by members of AA but emphasized women's empowerment, rather than their help-lessness.[29]

The women's movement brought previously unspeakable topics, such as rape, domestic violence, and addiction, into public view, making it possible to understand them as social rather than individual problems and also giving a voice to survivors. A number of women alcoholics began to stand up and tell their stories. Hearings before a Special Senate Subcommittee on Alcoholism and Narcotics in 1969 featured testimony from Bill Wilson, the cofounder of AA, and also from Marty Mann, a recovered alcoholic and founder of the National Committee for Education on Alcoholism. Academy Award–winning actress Mercedes McCambridge also spoke to the senators: "As I sit here, scores of women like me are being arranged on slabs in morgues throughout the country with tickets that read 'Acute Alcoholism' or, if they have been protected as I was, those tags may read 'Liver Ailment,' 'Chronic Bronchitis' or 'Massive Hemorrhage.'" Seven years later the Senate Subcommittee on Alcoholism and Narcotics held hearings under the title "Alcohol Abuse among Women: Special Problems and Unmet Needs," a sign that women's alcohol abuse had been officially recognized. This time, it was actress Jan Clayton, a recovered alcoholic who once starred as the mother on the popular television show *Lassie*, who lectured the senators about society's "refusal to see the plight of the alcoholic woman." Her testimony aired on the evening news. Subsequently, other well-known women came forward to speak about their struggles with alcohol, including former first lady Betty Ford, who announced that she was addicted to alcohol and was undergoing treatment. Later she worked to promote awareness of women's alcoholism, standing before audiences and telling them, in the phrase favored by AA, "My name is Betty and I am an alcoholic." After her admission, it became far more difficult to categorize women's alcohol abuse as simply an expression of poverty, mental illness, hypersexuality, housewife boredom, or workplace stress.[30]

Along with the women's health movement, the government's War on Drugs served as a catalyst to the discovery of women's alcohol abuse. When calculating the toll of illicit drugs, it became impossible to overlook the significant problems caused by legal substances, whether obtained by prescription or purchased from a bartender or retail outlet. In 1975 the National Institute on Drug Abuse held the first federally funded conference devoted to the subject of women, alcohol, and drugs. Among its findings was that there were few differences between the needs of the woman drug addict and the woman alcoholic, and yet they were understood very differently. Alcoholism was a "disease"; drug use was an addiction. Whether women abused alcohol or drugs, or both, few wanted to enter treatment. Doing so often meant placing their children in foster care and risking loss of custody because of their self-identified needs. Others lacked the financial means to access care or did not meet the admissions criteria of being "employable." Women who, in spite of the obstacles, did seek help found it was not easy to obtain. An NIAAA study of services for alcoholic women in 1979 found that four out of five halfway houses restricted admission to men. Acknowledging women's alcoholism made it possible to accept the findings about FAS; FAS, in turn, made it necessary to find ways to help alcoholic women if the problem was to be prevented. However, the resources women needed—inpatient treatment, mental health services, and social supports for themselves and their children—were not forthcoming.[31]

The National Institute on Alcohol Abuse and Alcoholism

Responsibility for investigating the problem of alcohol teratogenesis and of women's abusive drinking rested with the NIAAA, a federal agency established only a few years before the discovery of FAS. Its creation owed much to Iowa senator Harold E. Hughes, a recovered alcoholic who said he felt he had been "brought to Washington to represent the millions suffering from addiction to alcohol and other drugs." In the late 1960s Hughes proposed legislation to support alcoholism treatment, and his efforts were rewarded when, in 1970, President Richard Nixon signed into law the Comprehensive Alcohol Abuse and Alcoholism Prevention, Treatment and Rehabilitation Act, which created the NIAAA. Scholars credit the founding of the NIAAA with accomplishing three goals of alcoholism-treatment advocates: defining alcoholism as a primary disorder, not an expression of mental illness; putting alcoholism experts rather than the mental health establishment in charge of the new agency; and supporting grant programs in the area of alcoholism treatment. The inauguration of the NIAAA occurred during a golden age in the history of alcoholism awareness, when there was growing support for medical as opposed to punitive treatment and also formal recognition by the Social Security Administration of alcoholism as a partially disabling impairment. The NIAAA embarked on a program of research, training, services, and public education for the prevention and control of alcohol abuse and alcoholism, assuming many of the tasks previously undertaken within the National Institute of Mental Health. Periodically it issued (and continues to issue) a special report to Congress, *Alcohol and Health,* which includes a statistical portraits and epidemiological analyses of the role alcohol plays in society and serves as a sobering reminder of what alcohol abuse costs the nation.[32]

The NIAAA's *Second Special Report to the U.S. Congress on Alcohol and Health* appeared in 1974, shortly after the early publications by Jones and Smith. It mentioned the articles but dismissed the findings: "It is difficult to comprehend how the small concentrations of alcohol that reach the fetus—they are not more than those in the blood of the mother—even in the case of heavy drinking, as by alcoholic people, could cause the sort of injuries and malformations described in these reports." Not content simply to brush off the claim, the report offered an alternative explanation: maternal malnutrition in pregnancy. Nevertheless, the second *Alcohol and Health* report included in its statement of findings an acknowledgment that heavy alcohol use in pregnancy could have adverse effects on offspring. The reluctance of the agency to fully embrace the evidence of a few clinical case reports can be accounted for by the paucity of data, the novelty of the findings, and an established theory of alcohol's safety in pregnancy. The judgment in the report echoed earlier arguments made by members of the Yale Alcohol Studies group, perhaps because the report's editor, Mark Keller, who was the editor of the *Journal of Studies on Alcohol,* had been a protégé of leading alcohol scholar E. M. Jellinek. Another reason for hesitancy may have been the fact that other data pointed to environmental and, particularly, familial causes for the problems experienced by the children of alcoholics.[33]

The NIAAA, under the leadership of its first director, Morris Chafetz, paid close attention to the children of alcoholics. In the 1980s, an era of blossoming social movements and citizen activism, they had become an organized group and had begun lobbying for recognition of their problems. A psychiatrist with special expertise in addiction, Chafetz described them as victims and argued for resources on their behalf. The COAs, as they quickly came to call themselves, comprised a varied social group of sufficient size to command attention; a study in the 1990s determined there were more than "20 million children of alcoholics over the age of eighteen in the United States." However, long before children of alcoholics formed an organized movement, scholars had been investigating their lives.[34]

Just as eighteenth-, nineteenth-, and early twentieth-century social observers had noted that the children of inebriates often led blighted lives, based on their numbers in institutions and assessments of their difficulties, so did late twentieth-century investigators note that a disproportionate number of the children of alcoholics suffered numerous problems. Studies found that a significant proportion exhibited emotional and physical problems. The search for the means by which alcoholism was transmitted from generation to generation consumed many researchers, leading from eugenic family studies to genetic studies involving twins. Environmental causes also received attention. The homes of alcoholic and non-alcoholic families were compared, with variables such as patterns of violence, communication, and social learning given close attention. Researchers also studied the particular problems plaguing the offspring of alcoholics, including conduct disorders, substance abuse, psychopathology, attention deficits, anxiety, depression, and interpersonal difficulties.

With abundant data implicating the genetic, environmental, and physical limitations of the offspring of alcoholic men and women, the value in pinpointing the particular problems resulting from intrauterine exposure to alcohol seemed minimal. As study after study revealed numerous social pathologies in the homes of alcoholics, the question of whether the damage occurred before or after birth aroused little interest. In clinical settings, as well, there was often little interest in asking about prenatal exposure to alcohol. When alcoholic women entered the delivery room suffering from multiple physical, mental, and social problems related to their years of extraordinarily heavy drinking—including poverty, malnutrition, and lack of prenatal care—physicians were not surprised that their babies were small and had a number of medical problems. And, when these children continued to experience physical, mental, and developmental delays, there was little reason to suspect that their problems had begun in the womb.[35]

Despite making public its doubts about alcohol teratogenesis, the NIAAA responded to the reports in the medical literature and in 1974 funded three major prospective studies on maternal alcohol use and pregnancy outcome. When the jury of scientists rendered its verdict, the agency changed its tune. The third *Alcohol and Health* report, released in 1978, devoted an entire chapter to FAS. Directly rebutting the agency's earlier statements, the new report stated categorically that "fetal alcohol syndrome (FAS) is a clinically observable abnormality." Soon, the agency began devoting substantial funds to FAS research. It sponsored a conference on women and alcohol in 1978 and again in 1984, funded more research projects, and began regularly reviewing the findings about alcohol and birth defects.[36]

One reason for the new perspective was a change in leadership. The agency's second director, Ernest P. Noble, admitted past neglect of the problem of women's drinking and supported new research in this area. Further support came from the Department of Health, Education, and Welfare. Subsequently, officials in the administration of President Jimmy Carter launched an alcoholism prevention and treatment program that tripled the funds devoted to the problem of alcohol abuse among women and targeted FAS prevention. Together, feminism, the War on Drugs, and a stream of federal research dollars would propel the FAS diagnosis into the medical and popular mainstream.

Accepting FAS

Educated by the thalidomide tragedy and experiences with other teratogens, many Americans found it easy to believe that even substances in common use, like alcohol and tobacco, might be dangerous. They stood ready to embrace a new catechism of health that asked pregnant alcoholic women to refrain from drinking for the sake of their unborn children or to have abortions. But questions about moderate drinking and, more specifically, how much alcohol pregnant women could safely consume, remained unanswered.

As women reflected on their own experiences and those of friends, relatives, and neighbors, they recalled many who drank moderately during pregnancy with no visible effects on their children. As one woman noted in a 1989 interview, "I have three very bright, beautiful children and three gorgeous grandchildren. I drank wine all the time when I was pregnant." Physicians, too, remained unperturbed by the new findings. They refrained from issuing edicts about abstinence to their patients and chose (naively in some cases) to believe that none of the women they saw in their own practices was engaged in abusive drinking. But while their clinical experiences proved reassuring, the data that began emerging from the laboratory would test their complacency.[37]

4

◆ ◆

"Not Quite Like Other Children": FAS, Science, and Medicine

On May 31, 1977, Americans met Melissa, the first child with FAS to appear on an evening network news program. The story on NBC opened with anchor David Brinkley reporting on a new warning to women about drinking during pregnancy. A local reporter then introduced three-year-old Melissa, shown on camera playing with her toys, and her mother, whom he described as "a reformed alcoholic who devotes much of her life to giving Melissa loving care, dreading the day she will have to tell her daughter what happened." As the camera zoomed in on Melissa's tiny and somewhat misshapen face, Kenneth Lyons Jones, who was interviewed for the story, described her physical features to viewers: "She's very, very small . . . She has microcephaly, which means that her head is very small. She also has short palpebral fissures, or small eye slits, and she is mentally deficient." The segment then turned to the scientific side of the story. Scientist Gerald Chernoff displayed skeletons of alcohol-exposed and unexposed mouse fetuses; the former were far smaller, and those with the highest level of exposure were not only tiny but deformed. Next came images of two children who further illustrated the effects of alcohol: a twenty-one-month-old boy with FAS who could not feed himself with a spoon and a "normal little girl of the same age" who had mastered the task.

In a mere three minutes and fifty seconds, Melissa's story introduced viewers to a new medical diagnosis, examples of ongoing research into the problem, and a doctor who told them how they could avoid the same fate for their children. Those who observed Melissa, with her tiny body and funny-shaped face, probably thought seriously about the warning. If

Melissa's condition failed to alert them, the ominous words of the local correspondent was designed to bring the message home. He began the segment wrap-up by noting, "Doctors still don't know how much alcohol is too much, but they do know that once the damage is done to an unborn child, medical science can't help." Then, in the closing moments of the Melissa segment, Jones offered two different warnings about FAS. First he remarked that "chronic alcoholic women should not get pregnant," a conclusion supported by the scientific evidence available at the time. He then advised women "not to drink anything" when pregnant, a suggestion derived from the core principle of teratology—that individual fetuses vary in their vulnerability to particular agents and thus there can be no absolutely safe level of exposure. A commercial for Pabst Blue Ribbon Beer followed the story.[1]

Jones's statements reveal the place of FAS in America in the late 1970s through the early 1980s. Scientific studies had demonstrated a link between alcohol abuse by pregnant women and birth defects in their children, but they had reached no definite conclusions about how much alcohol caused how much damage. Alcoholic women, researchers learned, drank at different rates and consumed varying amounts. They engaged in other risky behaviors as well, suffered from numerous medical problems, and often failed to get prenatal care. Nevertheless, government officials felt compelled to issue a warning to all women against drinking during pregnancy. At first they suggested prudent limits. Later, erring on the side of caution, they told pregnant women to drink no alcohol at all. The public, as well as many clinicians, responded to the warnings with ambivalence. They accepted the findings about FAS, yet wondered whether abstaining was necessary. And while many women gave up or curtailed their drinking during pregnancy, others did not.

First Warning

The day after viewers watched Melissa, the NIAAA and the National Council on Alcoholism (NCA) together announced that pregnant women who consumed six or more drinks a day incurred a significant risk of producing a child with birth defects. Pregnant women and those likely to become pregnant, their statement continued, "should limit themselves to two drinks of beer, wine or liquor a day" and "should discuss their drinking habits and the potential dangers with their physicians." All three national television networks reported on the warning, as did several news magazines. However, none of them gave it much exposure. The health and medicine section of *U.S. News & World Report* printed the advisory and quoted NIAAA director Ernest Noble, who stated, "It's important for the pregnant woman to realize that when she drinks she is taking a drug, and this can cause a problem." *Newsweek* devoted a few paragraphs to the announcement, as did the *New York Times*. Despite the brevity of news coverage, the announcement was an important event, signaling that in a few short years FAS had advanced from a "discovery" based on the observation of a few children to a problem meriting federal intervention.[2]

To make certain that medical professionals knew about the warning and informed patients about prudent drinking, an official statement appeared in both *Morbidity and Mortality Weekly Report,* a publication of the Centers for Disease Control (CDC) that reached 200,000 health professionals, and in the Food and Drug Administration's *FDA Drug Bulletin,* which was sent to more than 700,000. In 1979 the Research Society on Alcoholism's Executive Committee approved the statement that heavy drinking can be damaging and acknowledged, "We cannot say whether there is a safe amount of drinking or whether there is a safe time during pregnancy." The scientific research inspired by the observations of Jones and Smith left experts little choice; after examining the data they concluded that alcohol was a teratogen. The findings similarly left policy makers with no other course of action. Because children seemed at risk of lifelong damage unless their mothers were warned against drinking excessively during pregnancy, the government needed to broadcast a warning to the public as well as to the medical community.[3]

Unlike other alcohol-related problems, such as deaths from cirrhosis of the liver, cancer, automobile accidents, and crime, FAS combined the excitement of the new—a "scientific discovery"—with the promise of a quick fix: women would be warned, fetuses would be protected, and the problem would go away. So many other alcohol-linked problems seemed intractable, with lives lost, families destroyed, and society damaged. Alcoholics and those deemed "frequent heavy drinkers" had a substantially higher mortality rate than light or moderate drinkers. Some deaths resulted from the direct effects of alcohol, such as overdose or liver disease, some were indirect, resulting from automobile accidents or suicide, for example. The first *Alcohol and Health* report said that alcohol was implicated in half of all traffic fatalities; that a third of all homicide victims had significant amounts of alcohol in their bloodstream; that 4.5 million workers suffered from alcohol-related problems; that 9 million Americans had alcohol-related problems; and that the expense of medical care, lost work time, impaired job efficiency, and accidents linked to alcohol drained $15 billion a year from the economy. FAS may have been far down the list of afflictions, but at least it seemed as if it might be prevented. Public health advocates believed they could translate science into policy and that innocent babies could be saved from the effects of heavy alcohol exposure in utero.[4]

The science of alcohol teratogenesis ultimately delivered more and less than it promised. Together, scientists and clinicians created a substantial body of evidence that brought about new public health measures. However, when it came to preventing FAS, politics played a role, as well as science. Warnings went out to all women, not just those who abused alcohol and were most likely to give birth to alcohol-affected children. The emphasis on broad-scale public health education, rather than programmatic efforts to help severely alcoholic women through specialized inpatient programs, social service support, and prenatal care, meant that those at greatest risk of bearing affected babies received the same attention and resources as those least likely to have such children. Rates of FAS did not decline and the syndrome ultimately became a marker of maternal misbehavior rather than an indication that new measures were needed to help alcoholic women.

The Culture of the Fetus

Public health efforts aimed at preventing FAS echoed earlier efforts to control women's drinking by invoking their maternal obligations. What had changed was the context for determining those obligations. The warnings about FAS came out in an era of growing interest in the fetus. On the scientific side, there were new reproductive technologies, the growing use of genetic tests to determine whether fetuses were defective, and the possibility, in some cases, of performing surgery on the fetus. In the political arena, debate continued over access to legal abortions, and a political movement arose to give fetuses legal and constitutional rights.

In the 1970s, reproductive medicine reached a new frontier with the birth of the first "test-tube baby," born after an egg and sperm were united outside the body and the resulting fertilized egg was implanted in the uterus. In vitro fertilization began in Britain and quickly became established in the United States by the early 1980s. Demand for this procedure and for other types of assisted reproduction grew quickly as infertile couples engaged in expensive and time-consuming quests to become biological parents, and as the adoption of healthy, white babies grew increasingly difficult.[5]

Not only were babies "in demand" but also, with new pregnancy screening tools, fetuses could now be assessed. The development of prenatal imaging and diagnostic technologies—particularly amniocentesis, which involved chromosomal analysis of amniotic fluid taken from the womb, and ultrasound diagnosis, based on actual images of the developing fetus—allowed physicians and prospective parents to distinguish healthy fetuses from those that appeared to be damaged. When problems appeared likely, parents could choose to end the pregnancy. Some fetuses with life-threatening but correctable conditions were even operated on before birth, and in these cases they became "patients" in their own right.[6]

With these new diagnostic tools in place, new demands began to be made by parents. Parents sued for wrongful birth, claiming that physicians or other providers negligently kept them from being able to make an informed decision about pregnancy termination. These cases (which were also brought as malpractice claims) involved such claims as a failure to provide or to correctly interpret prenatal tests. Other legal actions involved charges against manufacturers for failing to warn consumers when products could result in fetal damage. State as well as private interest in what might be called the "fetal citizen" also expanded in the wake of elective and judicial triumphs by those opposing women's reproductive rights—specifically, their right to choose abortion.[7]

The public's heightened interest in and visualization of the fetus meant that federal officials faced with evidence about alcohol teratogenesis had little choice but to issue a warning. They knew that many women drank during pregnancy and that excessive consumption of alcohol might cause harm to a fetus. Policy makers thus began with the belief that all fetuses needed protection and that all women had a right to know the possible effects of excessive alcohol consumption in pregnancy.

The decision by federal officials to issue a warning in 1977 followed a meeting of researchers and public officials who reviewed the existing data about alcohol and pregnancy and concluded that a public statement needed to be made. Recalling the discussions surrounding the drafting and issuing of the warning, Kenneth R. Warren, the director of the Office of

Scientific Affairs of the NIAAA, noted that "many, if not most, of the clinicians and the public regarded alcohol as being totally safe during pregnancy. That was what you found in obstetrics books; that was what you found in Dr. Spock." Officials determined that, rather than an alarmist message, they would offer advice about a prudent limit for drinking. Using the best evidence available at the time, the NIAAA officials concluded that the limit was no more than two drinks a day. After consulting with officials in the Department of Health, Education, and Welfare on the evidence, the NIAAA received permission to release the statement on May 1.[8]

Investigating FAS

Over a period of about four years, FAS developed swiftly from an observation to a verifiable phenomenon. Researchers constructed an intellectual infrastructure for investigating the effects of alcohol exposure in utero and began reporting their findings in the medical literature. Their inquiries followed a well-trod scientific pathway from individual case reports to retrospective studies of the records of alcoholic women and their children to prospective studies that followed women through their pregnancies and after, to assess the effects of differing levels of alcohol consumption on their infants. In addition, investigators looked at alcohol teratogenesis in animals. The scientific enterprise engaged researchers throughout the world, and the similarity of their findings gave strength to the collective conclusion that heavy alcohol exposure posed a risk to the human fetus.

Creation of a precise definition of FAS in 1980 by the Fetal Alcohol Study Group of the Research Society on Alcoholism helped make international collaboration possible. The Study Group recommended that a diagnosis of FAS be made only when an individual had signs in each of three categories: pre- or postnatal growth retardation, central nervous system involvement, and characteristic facial features. In 1988 the Study Group coined another term *alcohol-related birth defects,* to refer to anatomical and functional anomalies that could be attributed to prenatal alcohol exposure, and further elaborations followed.[9]

With a formal definition, FAS literally and figuratively had a face, a fact that was made clear at a 1980 international workshop on FAS, where researchers from six countries gathered to report their findings. Host Ann Streissguth, a leading FAS scholar and coauthor of the first *Lancet* article with Jones, Smith and Ulleland, described it vividly: "We all used different

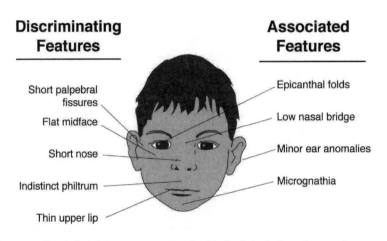

Discriminating Features

Short palpebral fissures

Flat midface

Short nose

Indistinct philtrum

Thin upper lip

Associated Features

Epicanthal folds

Low nasal bridge

Minor ear anomalies

Micrognathia

Figure 2. Craniofacial features associated with fetal alcohol syndrome, from *Alcohol Health and Research World* 18, 1994.

words and systems to describe the diagnostic process . . . But when we projected the pictures of our patients onto the big screen, the children all looked alike." The public got a glimpse of this when *National Geographic* ran a photographic essay in 1992 titled "The Preventable Tragedy: Fetal Alcohol Syndrome," with pictures of children from Sweden, France, Germany, Ireland, and the United States.[10]

Physicians who read the early reports of Jones, Smith, and their colleagues became aware of having seen in their own practices individuals damaged by in utero exposure to high levels of alcohol. Case reports were published quickly by doctors in Switzerland, the United States, and Ireland; other reports followed from Sweden, Spain, Italy, and Germany. Typically the articles detailed the histories of one or two children born to women who drank heavily during pregnancy. Often the authors pointed out previously unseen malformations and other medical problems that appeared to be linked to alcohol exposure.[11]

Three of the case reports offered particularly compelling evidence. In 1975, two pediatricians in the United States described the condition of fraternal twins, one of whom had full-blown FAS and one of whom had only minimal symptoms of alcohol exposure. The differences between the infants corresponded to a key principle of teratogenesis: the effects of a teratogen depend in part on the genotype of the individual fetus—or, in plain language, each individual has a unique level of susceptibility to a particular teratogen. Three years later, Sterling Clarren, a Seattle dysmorph-ologist who trained under David Smith, described autopsies conducted on four alcohol-exposed stillborn babies and deceased infants. They revealed a characteristic pattern of brain malformations, giving further weight to the argument that alcohol was a teratogen with a specific action and inti-mating that its major effects were on the developing brain. In 1981, Ger-man researcher Frank Majewski, who had published a number of detailed studies of what he called "alcohol embryopathy," presented an analysis of 108 cases. The sheer volume of subjects in his study underscored the valid-ity of the diagnosis.[12]

Early medical case reports of FAS discussed children with the character-istic physical features of the syndrome. Later, clinicians realized that indi-viduals outgrew the "FAS look" but not the behavioral effects of their ex-posure to alcohol before birth. A 1978 article by Streissguth and Sandra Randels described two young men diagnosed with FAS, neither of whom had the characteristic facial features. One was the son of a well-educated military wife who suffered from alcoholism; the other lived in a state insti-tution for the mentally retarded after having been abandoned by his alco-holic mother. Maternal histories, rather than the look of the individuals, made it possible to explain their condition. More commonly, adults and children received retrospective diagnoses of "suspected FAS" when there was no information available about their mothers' drinking. Many with FAS lived with relatives, foster families, or in adoptive homes and had no records of their birth or of their birth mothers' drinking.[13]

When evidence could be found, it typically revealed that the mothers of individuals diagnosed with FAS were long-term abusers of alcohol. A forty-one-year-old mother of a child with FAS reportedly imbibed a liter of beer and three to four liters of red wine each day. A report on seven cases of FAS included a discussion of one woman who had consumed six cans of beer and a quarter of a liter of scotch daily throughout her preg-nancy and another who had abused alcohol for at least ten years and as a result suffered from pancreatitis and liver problems. Other women de-scribed in the article suffered from equally serious health conditions, in-cluding gonorrhea, syphilis, liver diseases, anemia, gastritis, and kidney diseases. Jones and Smith offered the case history of a woman who had been an alcoholic for six years, consuming two quarts of red wine each day. Not surprisingly, she suffered from cirrhosis of the liver and during her pregnancy she experienced anemia, delirium tremens (delirium and acute physical symptoms resulting from alcohol withdrawal), and two episodes of intestinal bleeding related to alcohol gastritis, as well as a bout of diphtheria. A study of eight mothers noted that seven had alcohol "on their breath" at delivery, and many were in a similar condition when they visited their children in the nursery.[14]

Reports of binge drinking appeared frequently in the research. Clarren described a woman who consumed at least five drinks at a time during her weekly binges; she give birth to a stillborn fetus during her twenty-ninth week of pregnancy. Another patient described in the same article lost her infant at ten weeks of age. She reportedly drank several times a week, consuming up to a gallon of wine each time. Her level of consumption was not unique. A review of the literature by Ernest Abel found information about fifty-three mothers of children diagnosed with FAS; the women consumed an average of sixteen drinks a day. The findings underscored the perils of chronic alcohol abuse in pregnancy; they did little to determine whether a warning against light drinking was justified.[15]

Long-term abusive drinking took a heavy toll on women. The mothers of children with FAS died of alcoholism or were lost to follow-up at an extraordinarily high rate. Clarren estimated that 75 percent of the mothers of infants seen in his FAS clinic were missing or dead within five years of giving birth. A report on Native American children with FAS published in 2000 found a maternal mortality rate of 23.1 percent and referred to a German study in which eleven of sixty mothers of children with FAS (18.3 percent) had died by a ten-year follow-up.[16]

Alcoholic women differed from their nonalcoholic counterparts in myriad ways, making it difficult to find a control group to compare them with and difficult to pinpoint alcohol as the primary cause of their children's problems. The women were typically very poor, smoked heavily, ate poorly, received little or no prenatal care, suffered from numerous alcohol-related health problems, experienced high levels of stress in their daily lives, and, in many cases used dangerous and often illegal drugs. All of these factors appeared to influence the expression of the syndrome, and it proved impossible to disentangle their effects, although low socioeconomic status, according to Abel, was the critical variable.[17]

It also proved difficult to measure the effects of in utero alcohol exposure. When asked about their drinking, some women deliberately underestimated their consumption while others had trouble recalling the amount they consumed. A study comparing women's reports of their drinking during pregnancy and their recollections five years later of how much they had consumed found that many of them had initially understated their consumption. Studies demonstrating developmental problems in the children of self-declared moderate drinkers may well have been skewed by such underreporting. Researchers quickly learned that asking women how much they drank each week revealed very little—some might have two glasses of wine with dinner each evening while others might consume seven drinks each Friday and Saturday night, with both groups reporting the same total. As fetal blood alcohol levels came to be seen as a critical factor in FAS, researchers learned to ask about the amount consumed at each drinking episode. They also began to inquire about the size of the drinks, sometimes by letting women select a glass and pour water into it to show the amount they typically consumed. For some, a single drink consisted of seven ounces of hard liquor poured into an eight-ounce glass. Beyond the methodological hurdles in measuring alcohol use lay ethical barriers to research on alcoholic women. As one investigator pointed out, obtaining informed consent from subjects whose thinking was impaired by chronic alcoholism posed problems, as did the need to protect patient confidentiality in cases involving illegal drug use, which was not an uncommon practice among alcohol abusers.[18]

Despite their many limitations, studies of alcoholic women played a critical role in validating the claims of alcohol teratogenesis. Jones and Smith began the process by using the Collaborative Perinatal Project data. Other reports from research groups in Europe validated their findings. Soviet investigators found that the children born to women who were alcoholic during their pregnancies were far more impaired than the children whose mothers became alcoholics after pregnancy. In Göteborg, Sweden, an examination of the children of thirty chronically alcoholic women revealed that, compared with population norms, they had lower IQs, lower birth weights, and showed increased signs of brain damage. A report from a Belfast maternity hospital indicated that of twenty-three babies born to women who had been drinking heavily, only one was normal. While each of these studies involved a relatively small number of subjects, their findings pointed in the same ominous direction. However, a question remained: How many children and adults suffered from FAS? Studies of alcoholic women revealed that a sizable proportion gave birth to damaged children; studies of all women of childbearing age found few cases of FAS.[19]

Prospective investigations of pregnant women undoubtedly underestimated the incidence of FAS because severely alcoholic women often failed to obtain prenatal care and thus were underenrolled in the studies. The research nevertheless provided valuable information about the harm done by heavy drinking during pregnancy. By following large groups of women throughout their pregnancies, gathering data about health-related habits such as smoking and diet, collecting demographic information—such as age, parity (number of births), and social class—determining the status of their infants, and applying sophisticated statistical measures, researchers could tease out the effects of different levels of alcohol consumption and explore the interaction among the many variables. And there was another critical finding: interventions to help pregnant heavy drinkers reduce or halt their use of alcohol resulted in healthier babies than were born to similar groups of women who did not stop drinking heavily. Successful efforts were reported in Boston, Stockholm, and Helsinki.[20]

French researchers conducted one of the earliest prospective studies, tracking 9,236 births at thirteen maternity hospitals. They found that women whose average daily consumption of alcohol exceeded 1.6 ounces were more likely to have stillborn and small-for-dates children than those who drank less than that amount. However, they discovered no differences between the two groups in the rates of congenital malformations and neonatal mortality. Critics pointed out two methodological flaws that undercut the findings: the researchers had compared only two levels of drinking and in doing so had combined extremely heavy drinkers and those who consumed as little as 1.6 ounces daily in a single category, and the two groups of drinkers were not comparable in terms of age, marital status, parity, class, rates of smoking, and pregnancy complications. Nevertheless, statistical analysis implicated alcohol as a causal factor in infant size and showed that beer drinking posed a particular risk.[21]

The NIAAA provided funding for several prospective studies in the United States. Researchers followed women who gave birth at four southern California hospitals, recording, among other things, their use of alcohol and tobacco during pregnancy. They uncovered a link between heavy drinking and reduced infant birth weight and, like the French team, demonstrated an association between beer drinking and decreased intrauterine growth. In Boston, researchers administered a questionnaire about drug and alcohol use to 633 pregnant women. Later, physicians unaware of the mothers' histories examined their newborn children and discovered twice the rate of abnormalities among those whose mothers drank heavily. A prospective study in Cleveland of more than 12,000 pregnancies also revealed higher rates of FAS and neonatal problems among the children born to alcohol abusers, as well as higher rates of miscarriage.[22]

Seattle, where Jones and Smith had conducted their initial investigations, became a center of FAS research in the United States. Researchers at the University of Washington reached the controversial conclusion that moderate as well as heavy alcohol exposure led to problems in offspring—although their finding may have reflected the fact that women who drank heavily underreported their consumption, rather than an actual association between moderate drinking and effects on the fetus. While a study in Warwickshire, England, found that moderate drinking posed risks, investigations in Denver, London, and Dundee, Scotland, did not bear this out. The Seattle team's most vital contribution may have been its careful long-term follow-up of the children identified as alcohol-affected. The resulting publications provided a collective portrait and "natural history" of the syndrome that illuminated the many often-subtle effects of alcohol exposure.[23]

While studies of human populations offered conflicting or sometimes inconclusive findings, animal research demonstrated unequivocally that alcohol was a teratogen. By controlling variables that could not be controlled in human subjects—the amount of alcohol consumed, diet, genetic variability, and living conditions—scientists could distinguish the precise effects of alcohol on the embryo and investigate its mechanism of action. They noted that, in addition to causing malformations, alcohol was a behavioral teratogen. Among the effects they observed were hyperactivity, learning deficits, and sleep disturbances in newborns. Those engaged in human research began to observe and study similar phenomena.[24]

Epidemiology of FAS

Rather than asking whether alcohol is a teratogen and at what dose, epidemiologists inquired about the size and distribution of the FAS problem in the various populations. They investigated its prevalence (the number of cases within the population), incidence (the number of new cases each year), and rate (number of cases per 1,000 births) and studied variations among different population groups. Between 1977 and 1979, studies in France, the United States, and Sweden reported FAS rates of 1 in 1000, 1 in

700, and 1 in 600, respectively; later the French rate was given as 1 in 330, and a similar estimate appeared for Germany. Subsequent reports cited FAS rates of 1.9 per 1,000 births worldwide and 2.2 per 1,000 births in the United States, where the rates varied enormously among communities and among various kinds of drinkers. Some of the highest rates were found among Native Americans in New Mexico where the rate was 1 in 170, and among Native Americans in the Northern Plains, where it was an estimated 8.5 per 1,000. The highest rates of all appeared in the offspring of alcoholic women: an average of 59 per 1,000 births.[25]

Between 1981 and 1986 the CDC Birth Defects Monitoring Project collected data from 1,236 hospitals. From this sample of approximately 20 percent of births nationwide, the agency determined the rate of FAS was six times higher among African Americans than European Americans, and thirty-three times higher among Native Americans than among European Americans. Abel hypothesized that poverty, drinking practices, living conditions, and other factors—not simply race—accounted for the differences. Drinking patterns, he argued, reflect socioeconomic status, with high-income alcoholic women being more likely to consume alcohol throughout the day, thus maintaining a more constant blood-alcohol level than low-income women, who more typically drank in binges. Binge drinking he asserted, resulted in the highest fetal blood-alcohol levels, which in turn caused the greatest amount of damage.[26]

Just as nineteenth-century social observers counted the children of inebriates living in institutions and the costs to society, twentieth-century investigators calculated the contribution of FAS to the population living in congregate care facilities and came up with cost estimates. FAS was quickly recognized as the leading cause of mental retardation, a ranking that resulted, in part, from the fact that two other major causes—Down's syndrome and spina bifida—were being eliminated by prenatal testing and abortion. In 1978, the New York State Task Force on FAS estimated that 386 children with FAS would be born in the state that year, with another 1,563 having alcohol-related birth defects. The estimated lifetime cost of their medical services, remedial education, and custodial care was placed at $155 million, with the greatest expense coming from institutionalization. One estimate of national annual expenditures for FAS, made in 1991, was $249.7 million.[27]

The growing piles of data about the effects of alcohol exposure and the economic cost of FAS made many physicians and researchers into true believers, but a few remained outside the fold, skeptical of the claims made about FAS. They questioned the methods of investigators, the strength, validity, and reliability of their findings, and the sweeping declarations being made from what they viewed as relatively modest amounts of data. Prospective studies, they noted, found FAS occurring when many adverse factors were at work, including "lower maternal weight change, maternal illness, cigarette smoking and marijuana use." Other critics pointed to methodological problems rooted in the recall bias in women asked to report on their drinking. Additionally, they questioned whether researchers might be measuring the combined effects of alcohol and other agents. Finally, some were dubious of the attention being paid to FAS. They pointed out that it occurred infrequently and only among some of the children born to extraordinarily heavy drinkers. Despite their doubts, however, most agreed that heavy drinking, binge drinking, a lack of prenatal care, and multiple bad health habits risked harming fetuses; their quarrel was with the amount of attention FAS was receiving and the hyperbole about the risks of light and moderate drinking.[28]

Was the call for alcoholic abstinence during pregnancy based on solid scientific findings, or was it a political decision impelled by the moral status of the fetus? Did indulging in an occasional glass of wine with dinner truly put a fetus at risk? These questions troubled the doubters, particularly after the federal government issued a call for women to avoid drinking any alcohol at all during pregnancy. Reflecting on the attention paid to FAS, coauthors Armstrong and Abel, in an article exploring FAS as a "moral panic," pointed to two important developments affecting the issue: "expertise expansion," which drew physicians and researchers from many disciplines into the field, and "democratization," in which social problems largely affecting poor minority groups were nonetheless promoted as risks to all.[29]

The spreading interest in FAS, as well as the growing cultural interest in fetal protection, meant that the voices of those who questioned the amount of attention being paid to FAS went largely unheard. Instead FAS became a recognized public health problem, and data about the numbers of affected individuals and the cost of their care became part of the national discourse. As a result, the subject of how much alcohol might be too much was taken off the table.

Second Warning

In 1981 the acting surgeon general issued an official "Advisory on Alcohol and Pregnancy," telling pregnant women and those considering pregnancy "not to drink alcoholic beverages." With this message, the federal government indicated its concern for fetal health and the well-being of future citizens and demonstrated its continuing faith that health promotion via official warnings would serve the public interest by inspiring proper behavior. Like the first warning, the second one appeared in the *FDA Drug Bulletin* and was mailed to more than a million physicians and other health professionals. The new information included instructions for practitioners, asking them to "inquire routinely about alcohol consumption by patients who are pregnant or considering pregnancy" and to record information about alcohol consumption in medical records.[30]

Even as some questioned whether there was scientific justification for the new warning, others wondered about its potential effectiveness and possible unintended consequences. Would the warning lead women to choose abortion if they had had a drink or two before learning they were pregnant? *Time* magazine quoted NIAAA director John DeLuca, who defended the decision and asserted, "We don't know a safe level." A rebuttal came from Joe Simpson, a Northwestern University Medical School physician, who worried about inducing guilt in the occasional drinker: "Even if the studies are correct, it need not follow that every woman who had a drink and miscarried or had a baby with a problem did so because of alcohol." The last word in the *Time* article went to FAS researcher and physician Clarren, who offered a terse rejoinder: the risk might be small, he conceded, "but it is not zero." Teratology trumped epidemiology in 1981, and the victory proved to be long lasting. In 1990 and again in 1995 the Department of Health and Human Services would reiterate its advice that pregnant women and those planning to become pregnant should not drink any alcohol.[31]

In other nations, officials and experts reviewing the data came up with different guidelines. The Royal College of Psychiatrists in Great Britain issued a warning to women in 1979, advising them not to drink heavily in pregnancy, yet admitting there was no evidence about moderation. Three years later, after reviewing the latest scientific evidence, it began advising women to avoid alcohol altogether during pregnancy because an acceptable level of intake "remains uncertain." The Royal College of Obstetricians and Gynaecologists, however, recommended only that women "be careful about alcohol consumption in pregnancy and limit themselves to no more than one standard drink per day." Similarly, New Zealand authorities stated that there was "no conclusive evidence of adverse effects . . . below 15 units per week" and noted, "If one has in place a policy stating that no amount of alcohol is safe then there is a great potential for unnecessary anxiety, guilt and requests for therapeutic abortion." When the International Center for Alcohol Policies conducted a survey in 1999, it found that Australia, Austria, Denmark, Ireland, and Sweden recommended abstinence, while other nations, including Belgium, France, Germany, the Netherlands, Portugal, Spain, and Switzerland made no official recommendation. The continuum of advice illuminates how governmental bodies shape diagnoses into policies. National interests, including the value placed on individual and collective responsibility for health, beliefs about pregnancy and reproduction, public or private provision of medical services, experiences with alcohol abuse and harm-minimization policies and identified rates of FAS undoubtedly contributed to the variations.[32]

Textbook Medicine and Popular Advice

For decades, assertions about the safety of moderate drinking wore both the burnished glow of traditional wisdom and a patina of scientific logic. Both wore off, however, as the apostles of abstinence forced American physicians to rewrite medical textbooks to teach a new generation that any drinking during pregnancy was risky. In the years immediately following the discovery of FAS and the 1977 warning from the NIAAA, medical writers alluded to the new findings, warned against abusive drinking, and endorsed moderation. After the federal government's second warning, they toed the line and embraced abstinence.

Textbook authors had carefully followed the first reports on alcohol abuse and problems in infants. They openly discussed the possibility of abortion for alcoholic women but remained sanguine about light drinking. One stated authoritatively, "Alcohol ingestion during pregnancy in moderate amounts is not harmful to the fetus." Even as new data about the risks of moderate drinking began to sway the opinions of government policy makers, clinicians remained leery of the findings. The author of a chapter in one 1980 textbook on maternal and fetal medicine expressed some doubt as to whether a syndrome even existed, given the complex social and environmental factors at work. Women needed to be cautioned to limit their drinking, he wrote—because of the calories—but the demand that women drink nothing at all seemed to him both unnecessary and unlikely to be obeyed.[33]

Once the official word about abstinence went out from the surgeon general, medical authorities found it difficult to reject the new orthodoxy. Textbooks such as Benson's *Handbook of Obstetrics and Gynecology* called for "complete avoidance" of alcohol during pregnancy. In the journal *Patient Care,* a group of doctors advised their fellow practitioners to tell their patients to abstain from alcohol, tobacco, caffeine, and other drugs during pregnancy, and to obtain proof of their having done so. "If a patient refuses to adhere to one of your recommendations, consider having the patient sign a form documenting your entreatment and her noncompliance," the authors urged, explaining that "the form convinces patients of the issue's gravity and it also can help alleviate your liability."[34]

While few medical writers dared to challenge official government warnings, and many may have feared being held liable if they did so, an undercurrent of ambivalence remained palpable. The evidence that chronic heavy drinking posed a risk seemed solid; the data on light drinking less so. Moreover, common sense suggested that light drinking couldn't really be a problem. Millions of pregnant women had consumed alcohol in modest amounts without any harm to their offspring. Surprisingly, the American Medical Association also equivocated. A 1982 report, *Fetal Effects of Maternal Alcohol Use,* from the Council on Scientific Affairs, called for physicians to be aware of the dangers of moderate and heavy drinking and to "help their patients assess the risks and make informed decisions about drinking." While the AMA report stated that "with several aspects of the issue still in doubt, the safest course is abstinence," it also suggested future research would determine whether a safe level of drinking could be identified, an indication that findings the government considered conclusive were not regarded as such by clinicians.[35]

Popular health writing reflected the sentiments of clinicians, shifting slowly from careful statements about moderation to calls for abstinence in line with official government recommendations. Item eleven in a 1977 *Harper's Bazaar* article titled "How to Have a Health Baby" told readers: "Drink moderately or not at all." Not wanting readers to get too nervous about their before-dinner cocktails or after-dinner cordials, the piece quoted Dr. Frank A. Seixis, the medical director of the NCA, who stated that "full-blown FAS" appeared in babies whose mothers drank ten to fifteen ounces of alcohol a day. How much was safe? "I would venture a guess," he wrote, "that moderate amounts of drinking during pregnancy are insignificant in terms of the harm done to the baby. By moderate, I mean an ounce to an ounce and a half of alcohol or less a day." He did, however, warn against binge drinking. A similarly comforting statement appeared in an article in *Ladies' Home Journal* that same year: "Alcohol, despite recent scare stories, is probably not dangerous when limited to a drink or two at a party." The author presented a long list of "no-nos" during pregnancy, including the use of tranquilizers, DES, tetracycline, narcotics, tobacco, and laxatives, and conceded that "the equivalent of four or five shots of 100 proof alcohol may be hazardous." The warning seemed no scarier than the ones about "coffee nerves" in babies exposed to lots of caffeine. *Parents* magazine told readers that, while doctors "would not encourage their patients to get drunk during pregnancy, the occasional cocktail or glass of wine is unlikely to do any harm." Three years after the second government warning, the magazine's medical columnist still maintained that moderation—defined as a two drink limit—was fine.[36]

Eventually, however, women's magazines began instructing pregnant women to eliminate alcohol from their diet. Speaking directly to consumers (and indirectly to advertisers), the publications worked to allay fears women may have had about drinks consumed before they knew they were pregnant. A 1985 article in the fashion magazine *Vogue* stated: "If you usually drink a glass of wine with dinner and you find out that your are pregnant, the chances are small that you will have affected your unborn child. But, to give that child the best chance, you should eliminate alcohol from your diet or limit it to an occasional drink on a special occasion." In other cases, authors simply repeated the government warning without editorial comment. Only *Good Housekeeping* took a consistently conservative line on the subject of drinking, possibly reflecting of the overall tone of the magazine, its lack of alcoholic beverage advertisers, and the sentiments of its readers. From the beginning, *Good Housekeeping's* medical columnists confessed their ignorance and cautioned restraint: "Will an occasional 'social cocktail' affect the unborn child? We don't know. If you take a drink, you're betting it's harmless. Is it worth the risk?"[37]

Whatever their perspective on drinking and pregnancy, the magazines all assumed that pregnant women had a moral responsibility to their unborn children that required them to subordinate their own interests and desires. A typical statement appeared in *Essence*, a magazine for African American women, in 1979: "You should make a pact with your body—and your unborn child." Collectively the magazines told pregnant women to view their environment as being filled with many hazards besides the drinks offered at parties. A piece in *Parents* cautioned women to be "especially careful of things such as hair spray, paints, insecticides or anything else with an odor strong enough to cause [you] to gasp or cough." Underlying such statements was the understanding that pregnant women could be expected to make sacrifices for their fetuses not only because of their private interest in doing so but also because of public assumptions about their obligations to the unborn. The question of maternal sacrifice turned on ethical and legal interpretations of women's duty to care. Some claimed that once a woman made a decision not to abort a fetus she was obligated to do no harm, and could be threatened with loss of liberty for failing to act on behalf of her fetus. One legal scholar interpreted this position as an assertion of a duty to "keep baby safe from mom." Others argued that such an obligation made women into mere fetal containers and that the policies that derived from this position ultimately targeted poor women and members of minority groups.[38]

Publishers of women's magazines in the 1970s and 1980s could safely assume that the overwhelming majority of readers, and indeed the overwhelming majority of pregnant women, were already committed to acting in ways that supported the health of their fetuses. Women likely turned to magazine articles in part to confirm their decisions and in part to learn more about how to produce healthy babies. They looked to their doctors for this information as well. However, when it came to problem drinking and pregnancy, some practitioners lacked answers.

Doctors, Patients, and Drinking

As FAS moved from hypothesis to diagnosis it became vital for physicians to learn about the syndrome, to inquire about their patients' drinking habits, and to find ways of helping those who needed assistance in halting their abusive drinking. In many cases, of course, physicians never had the opportunity to intervene; often severely alcoholic women arrived at the hospital intoxicated and in labor, having received no prenatal care. In these circumstances doctors could do little besides direct the patients to alcoholism treatment in the hope that they would conquer a problem that threatened to end their lives and blight the lives of their children. Not all delivery-room encounters led to diagnosis and referrals to treatment, however. One case report noted that a woman who gave birth to six children was not diagnosed as an alcoholic until after delivering her fourth child. Among the indications that her doctors had overlooked were abnormal liver function, tremulousness or agitation after each delivery, and intoxication during delivery.[39]

Studies found that doctors hesitated to ask about women's drinking for many reasons, including lack of training, time limitations, lack of interest, fear of giving offense, and an assumption that FAS did not occur among the children of their patients. An illustration of this appeared in a report on an alcoholic woman in recovery. Her physician, apparently reluctant to demand that she quit drinking altogether, had recommended she cut back from her daily consumption of two cases of beer. The patient complied and reduced her consumption to two to three six-packs daily. (When she gave birth to twins with FAS, they were removed from her custody).[40]

Practitioners who overcame their reluctance and carefully questioned their patients about drinking probably encountered troublesome responses, from denial, which is common among substance abusers, to requests for help that could not easily be met. Not all physicians knew how to effectively counsel women abusing alcohol, nor did they know where to refer them for treatment. Women found it difficult to enter alcoholism treatment because of a lack of funds, family responsibilities, the fear of losing their children to foster care, and the presence of other problems that required intervention if they were to successfully recover from alcoholism. Although the NIAAA made a concerted effort to expand treatment options, a 1988 article in the professional literature reported that there were no alcohol detoxification units specifically designed to meet the needs of the pregnant women. A facility that opened that year in Washington State had strict rules for admission and only four beds. The headline of a story about the new unit—"Maternal Detox Treats the Fetus"—indicates how pregnant women struggling with alcohol problems were viewed.[41]

Pediatricians also found themselves on the front lines, and like obstetricians, they too felt uncomfortable raising the subject of alcohol treatment and FAS, despite their familiarity with the diagnosis. As one explained it in a letter to a pediatrics journal, clinicians were bound to do no harm and therefore had little incentive to tell a mother, "You damaged your child." It was the job of obstetricians, he argued, to help women minimize their drinking during pregnancy. A joint reply came from an obstetrician, a family practitioner, and a pediatrician, who noted that they had little to offer because many women did not seek prenatal care until well after the fetal damage had occurred. Preventing FAS was an issue of lifestyle, they concluded, not "obstetrical services rendered." Reading between the lines of the conversation, it is apparent that practitioners in various specialties felt powerless—unable to prevent FAS in many instances, unable to treat it in all cases.[42]

Dead Ends and New Paths

Between 1973 and 1985 almost 2,000 articles on FAS and related disorders appeared in professional journals. During this time, the federal government funded scientific studies of alcohol teratogenesis and based on the findings issued two successively stronger warnings against drinking during pregnancy. Subsequently, medical textbook authors and popular health writers began emphasizing to their respective readers the need to abstain from drinking when pregnant. In the case of FAS, it had been a relatively quick trip from medical discovery to medical certainty.[43]

The journey from warning to prevention would prove to be far longer. Initially, the signs along the way were positive. Surveys indicated that people quickly learned about FAS, although their perceptions of what it was were not always accurate. Women who gave birth in Los Angeles County over a three-month period in 1979 were mailed a questionnaire about alcohol and pregnancy. Ninety-six percent of respondents said they knew the risks of alcohol, listing their sources of information as the media, health care providers, personal contacts, posters, and pamphlets. Notably, fewer than half had discussed alcohol consumption with their physician or a nurse. Most worrisome was the fact that many respondents thought that FAS could be cured. Despite their knowledge of the risks, 59 percent of the women recalled drinking wine, beer, or hard liquor during their most recent pregnancy, and about 20 percent reported drinking at levels researchers deemed risky. The Bureau of Alcohol, Tobacco, and Firearms (ATF), a division of the U.S. Treasury Department, released data from a national survey that also indicated a high level of public awareness about the risks of drinking during pregnancy. Two out of three individuals surveyed reported knowing about the effects of alcohol on the fetus, with eight in ten stating that pregnant women should not drink. Other studies also showed knowledge of FAS to be widespread, if incomplete. Gallup surveys conducted in New York City in 1984 and 1985 and nationally in 1987 revealed that a significant number of adults knew about the risks of drinking during pregnancy, although a number mistakenly believed that hard liquor posed a greater risk than beer or wine.[44]

Despite the findings indicating growing levels of public awareness, from the vantage point of policy makers the glass proved to be only half full. A 1984 study from the National Center for Health Statistics reported that only about 30 percent of married mothers were heeding the warning and not drinking during pregnancy. A demographic portrait of those who continued to drink while pregnant revealed that they were likely to be heavy drinkers, smokers, unmarried, nonwhite, over thirty-five, and of low income. Perhaps the failure to comply reflected a public skepticism mirroring that of clinicians, who continued to doubt that to produce a healthy baby women had to shun alcohol altogether. More likely, survey results indicated that government warnings failed to reach or to convince particular demographic groups.[45]

The promise of preventability proved alluring, but elusive. Despite the warnings some women continued to drink heavily while pregnant, and the United States continued to see several thousand alcohol-affected children born each year, joining the thousands of other individuals already diagnosed with FAS. Stronger warnings, some concluded, were necessary. In 1977, the year the NIAAA issued its first warning, FDA commissioner Donald Kennedy wrote to the ATF asking it to consider placing warning labels on alcoholic beverages. "Quite frankly," Kennedy noted, "if the FDA retained jurisdiction . . . it would waste no time in commencing proceedings to require warning labels."[46]

Kennedy's call for warning labels garnered little attention—except from those who scoffed at his demand for government intervention into private decision making. An editorial in the *Wall Street Journal* ridiculed the proposal, remarking that "it passes all sensible bounds." Even if Kennedy's recommendation had passed the sensibility test, it seemed to have no chance of being implemented. The FDA lacked jurisdiction over alcohol labeling; that was the responsibility of the ATF, which was created in 1972 to carry out the Treasury Department's responsibilities for halting the production and sale of untaxed alcohol, along with other taxation and enforcement efforts. The ATF would soon make clear that its mission did not include protecting fetuses from birth defects caused by maternal alcohol abuse. Only Congress could change its mandate.[47]

5

◆◆

"According to the Surgeon General":
Warning Women against Drinking

The handwritten letter sent to the Bureau of Alcohol, Tobacco, and Firearms in 1978 was short and to the point: "A glass (of wine) with spaghetti is good and makes me feel good." Another letter, from public television's *French Chef* star, Julia Child, also protested proposed warning labels on alcoholic beverages, proclaiming them "foolish" because "anything is dangerous to one's health when taken in excess, such as beef, pork, even cornflakes." Many shared her view that labels, which were being considered as a means of "preventing pregnant women from consuming alcohol in amounts that might prove detrimental to their unborn infants," were "typical government poppycock!" The writers' succinct and witty efforts to prevent federal officials from affixing warning notices to alcoholic beverages ultimately proved futile. By 1989, more than a decade after the impassioned letters poured into the ATF, all packaged alcohol beverages sold in the United States would bear a warning label.[1]

Sounding the theme of protecting the innocent, advocates for labeling succeeded against beverage-industry groups and those individuals who, like the gentleman who favored wine with spaghetti, saw government efforts to direct private behavior as misguided or even dangerous. Their victory, however, was not entirely of their own making. A ruling by the U.S. Supreme Court in a tobacco case, product liability claims brought on behalf of children with FAS, efforts to pass labeling laws in individual states, and growing public alarm about drug abuse together led the beverage industry to rethink its resistance and gave labeling proponents new ammunition for their cause.[2]

Between 1977, when the NIAAA issued its first warning about drinking in pregnancy, and 1989, when the labeling law went into effect, FAS moved from the scientific arena into the domain of public health. Politicians, government officials and educators assumed growing responsibility for preventing children from being born with FAS. Laboratories, medical schools, clinics, examination rooms, and delivery floors ceased to be critical sites of engagement in the war on FAS and became instead field stations where physicians diagnosed or, ideally, prevented the syndrome. Now the theaters of action were government hearing rooms, statehouses, city hall chambers, and classrooms, where public health advocates, educators, and elected officials tried to respond to the newly discovered public health crisis. Even marriage licensing bureaus, bars, and liquor stores became part of the battleground once the crusade to warn women got under way.

The campaign for labeling legislation focused on FAS rather than other consequences of heavy drinking. Millions of women and men suffered from their abuse of alcohol, and the individual and social costs of abusive drinking were enormous. The third *Alcohol and Health* report, issued in 1978, estimated that alcohol-related deaths numbered as high as 205,000 per year and accounted for approximately 11 percent of the deaths in 1975. Later reports listed alcohol-related deaths and illnesses according to such categories as cirrhosis of the liver and alcoholic psychosis, as well as accidents and homicides. Reports to Congress explored the economic costs of alcohol abuse. In 1985, the overall mortality costs were estimated at $24 billion and productivity losses were said to be $27 billion, while cost estimates for FAS ranged from $75 million to $3.2 billion. Compared with to other alcohol-related problems, the economic and social costs of caring for individuals with FAS seemed small. Yet, in the halls of Congress, FAS mattered. Their interest in warning women and protecting fetuses led some elected officials to take on the powerful alcoholic beverage industry and to declare drinking in pregnancy a risk to be combated.[3]

Letters about Labeling

On 16 January 1978 the *Federal Register* contained an advanced notice of proposed rule making and asked for comments on the possibility that warning labels would be put on alcoholic beverage containers. The notice, which came from the ATF, posed four questions:

What type of specific warning label, if any, should be placed on containers of alcoholic beverages?

What would be the impact on consumers, primarily women, as a result of such a warning?

a) Would the warning be effective in preventing pregnant women from consuming alcohol in amounts that might prove detrimental to their unborn infants?

What other possible alternatives are available to disseminate information to the public on possible health hazards resulting from alcoholic intake?

a) Should these alternatives be in place of or in addition to a warning label? and

What other medical research is available documenting or refuting the existence of fetal alcohol syndrome?[4]

More than 3,000 organizations and individuals responded. Mobilized by the alcoholic beverage industry, labeling opponents sent the ATF preprinted postcards and boilerplate letters as well as personal correspondence. One individual wrote that if a pregnant woman were getting medical advice from liquor bottles rather than doctors, "There isn't much hope for her." Some feared that the specter of Prohibition was again haunting America, regarding labels as the first step down a slippery slope leading inexorably to a ban on the sale of alcoholic beverages. Others voiced economic arguments—probably copied from industry literature—claiming that labels would waste taxpayer dollars, raise the cost of beverages for consumers, and hurt a valued industry.

Another set of correspondents reasoned that labels would prove futile because cigarette warnings had failed to stop Americans from smoking. A few writers even marshaled theological justifications for their position. Wrote one opponent, "It's a good thing you weren't around when Jesus turned water into wine. He would have had to label it." A common theme was government meddling in private affairs—a favorite argument of business groups opposed to regulation. One angry individual encapsulated the sentiment with a proposal for a label reading, "If you drink anything that contains alcohol you may grow two heads. You could use the second head working for the Government minding other people's business."[5]

Collectively, the letters illustrated the power of the alcoholic beverage industry, and the California wine industry in particular, to mobilize large numbers of partisans. Their allies included unions representing workers in the alcoholic beverage industry, grape growers, beverage industry journals,

hospitality groups, and overseas confederates in the wine and spirits industries. Protests came as well from the owners of taverns, package stores, restaurants, and entertainment venues. Three trade groups spearheaded the
opposition: the United States Brewers Association, the Wine Institute, and
the Distilled Spirits Council of the United States (DISCUS). In far-ranging
critiques, they offered extensive rebuttals to proponents of labels, noting
their ineffectiveness and cost, which DISCUS estimated to be approximately one cent per bottle. At that rate, the group argued, producers would
spend $22 million per year, or $24.44 for each of the possible pregnancies
that would be affected. Industry groups appeared to be equally concerned
about opening the door to greater government oversight and also feared
admitting that their products could have detrimental effects.[6]

Letters from consumers and physicians offered compelling evidence that
the initial warning from the NIAAA had done little to shake public confidence that moderate drinking in pregnancy was safe or even advisable.
Again and again correspondents declared that they, or someone they knew,
had drunk alcohol during pregnancy with no resulting problems. "I have
three normal children (2 well above average in intelligence)," wrote one
woman who recalled that she "drank 4 oz minimum, sometimes more,
in pregnancy." Some women reported drinking during pregnancy on the
advice of their doctors. One said her physician had "suggested a glass of
wine during my pregnancy and nursing months." Physicians verified these
claims, writing that they told patients to enjoy a relaxing drink with dinner
during their pregnancies. Almost all of the doctors—many of them obstetricians—withheld judgment about the risks of abusive drinking. Nevertheless, the majority remained certain—based on their observations—that
light or moderate consumption posed no danger.[7]

Other health care professionals took a different stance. "As nurse coordinator in a Birth Defects Clinic," one wrote, "I see the results of the foetal alcohol syndrome and therefore recommend the use of warnings on the labels of alcoholic beverage containers." Many labeling supporters based
their interpretations on the scientific evidence rather than on clinical observations. Groups serving the disabled, including local branches of the
Association for Retarded Citizens, the Alcoholism Council, and others,
uniformly supported labels, seeing the potential for a damaged baby in every drink consumed by an uninformed pregnant woman.[8]

Arguments from individual labeling enthusiasts mirrored those of their
adversaries. Prohibitionists saw the FAS uproar as an opportunity for reig-

niting the movement to ban alcohol. A San Antonio, Texas, woman re-marked that it would be better to "abolish the alcohol and save money on labels." A few figured that since cigarettes bore labels, alcoholic beverages should do so as well. The fiscally minded wrote that their tax dollars paid to care for individuals with FAS, and pragmatists claimed that saving even a few babies would make labeling a worthwhile endeavor. As did opponents, those supporting labeling sometimes enclosed news clippings that supported their arguments. One letter contained a copy of a survey taken of readers of the *Tribune* of Grand Haven, Michigan, showing that 78.4 percent of respondents favored the label. The matter did not come up for a popular vote, however; elected officials were the ones who would decide whether alcohol, like tobacco, would carry an official government warning.[9]

Alcoholism: From Disease to Problem

The clash over warning labels involved a contest of ideas as well as interest groups. The alcoholic beverage industry buttressed its position by invoking a disease model of alcoholism, asserting that problem drinking occurred only among a small number of troubled individuals. Public health advocates rebutted this claim, arguing that alcohol consumption and alcohol problems were related and asserting that measures to control drinking were as vital as programs to assist severe chronic alcoholics. The debate between the two camps helped shape the fight over warning labels as well as other measures designed to prevent FAS. Proponents of the disease model argued that calls to warn all women against drinking were unnecessary; alcoholic women were the ones who needed to refrain from drinking during pregnancy, and they were unlikely to be dissuaded by a warning label. Supporters of a public health perspective advocated warning all consumers, believing that the information might reduce or halt drinking by pregnant women.

Groups espousing the disease model were in an advantageous position. In the decades after World War II Americans rapidly embraced this paradigm, seeing it as both socially compassionate and scientifically valid. In 1946 only 20 percent of those surveyed considered alcoholism a disease; by the 1990s, 90 percent of Americans described it as such. The surge in public credibility came in the wake of professional and governmental endorsement of the disease model. Between the mid-1950s and the mid-1960s, the American Medical Association, the American Hospital Association, and the American Psychiatric Association all passed formal resolutions naming alcoholism a disease and calling for medical treatment for those diagnosed with the disorder. In 1966 the federal government established the National Center for the Prevention and Control of Alcoholism, and in 1970 it created the NIAAA. As funds began to be directed to medical services for alcoholics, the treatment industry expanded as well.[10]

Medicalization of alcoholism resulted in a contraction of alcoholism policing. The assertion that criminalizing public drunkenness led to the punishment of individuals for a status rather than for their actions found favor in a number of lower courts. The U.S. Supreme Court, however, chose not to follow their lead. In 1968, in a five-to-four decision in *Powell v. Texas,* it refused to overturn the conviction of a chronic alcoholic arrested for public intoxication, although five of the justices acknowledged alcoholism as a disease. Despite the court's ruling in *Powell,* a number of states began steering alcoholics into detoxification and treatment programs instead of jail.[11]

Critics charged that the disease concept of alcoholism rested on shaky scientific ground or perhaps no ground at all. Alcoholism, they said, fit neither the biomedical model of disease nor the standard psychiatric diagnosis; it was simply an assertion that some people differed from normal drinkers physically and mentally because of their unique susceptibility to liquor. Other critics took aim at the consequences of the disease concept. While it replaced moral censure and criminal punishment with compassion and medical care, some believed it also undermined personal responsibility by failing to stigmatize destructive behavior.[12]

Another challenge to the disease paradigm grew out of the work of French demographer Sully Ledermann, who argued that as per-capita consumption of alcohol increased, heavy drinking increased as well. Rather than its being the case that a fixed number of people were susceptible to the disease of alcoholism, the use and abuse of alcohol shifted according to social, cultural, and economic factors that shaped consumer behavior. By implication, an overall reduction in the use of alcohol would improve the collective health of the nation. To achieve this reduction, supporters of the public health model argued for what they termed "harm reduction" or "harm minimization" measures, including limitations on hours of sale, banning of "happy hours," an increase in the drinking age, education measures aimed at deterring drinking and driving, restrictions on advertising, and, most important, higher taxes on alcoholic beverages.[13]

For a long time the alcoholic beverage industry and its allies had successfully repelled efforts to raise federal excise taxes on alcohol. After an increase in 1951 to help pay for the Korean War, they remained at the same level until 1985 in the case of distilled spirits and until 1991 for beer and wine. Because the taxes failed to keep pace with inflation, the cost of drinking diminished over time, helping to boost consumption. But the alcoholic beverage industry was not invulnerable. It lost a critical battle in 1984, when Congress passed legislation directing highway funds to states that raised their drinking age. It would lose another when warning labels were required on its cans and bottles.[14]

Congressional Consideration

In early 1978, two weeks after the ATF began opening letters, the Senate Subcommittee on Alcoholism and Narcotics held hearings on the topic "Alcohol Labeling and Fetal Alcohol Syndrome." South Carolina Republican senator Strom Thurmond called for requiring that alcoholic beverages exceeding 24 percent alcohol by volume carry an official warning notice. Thurmond had first introduced alcohol warning-label legislation in 1967; FAS gave his initiative a new urgency.[15]

Experts and advocates descended on Capitol Hill to testify. Echoing arguments made in letters to the ATF, some lambasted labels as lacking scientific justification and public value; others praised them as an effective contribution to the public-health campaign to warn women about FAS. Morris Chafetz, a psychiatrist and the NIAAA's first director, argued against labels, citing the failure of Prohibition and claiming that excessive liquor consumption was "only one among many factors contributing to birth defects. Tension, anxiety, caffeine and tobacco are potential hazards as well." Chafetz warned that labels would frighten "normal pregnant women" while failing to convince alcoholic women to change their drinking habits. Henry Rosett, a psychiatrist from the Boston University School of Medicine who had conducted research on FAS prevention by identifying and aiding alcoholic pregnant women, described his findings and his support for labels. He believed women would "heed such a caution since most are motivated by their desire for a healthy baby," and he enumerated other benefits from labels, among them the enhanced awareness of health professionals and the education of family members who could help motivate women to reduce their drinking.[16]

Federal officials similarly presented conflicting testimony. The Treasury Department sent assistant secretary and ATF director Rex D. Davis to oppose labels; the Department of Health, Education, and Welfare made its support for labeling clear through the appearance of Secretary Joseph A. Califano, Jr. The clash of cabinet-level agencies meant very little, though. As the Treasury Department made clear, it was the only agency with responsibility for regulating alcohol, and until more medical evidence was available, it would not take that step. With the government on their side, beverage industry officials felt little need to take a public stance. Instead they sent the subcommittee written comments on the proposed regulations.[17]

While labeling supporters and opponents testified in congressional hearing rooms, the ATF gathered information. It appointed three experts, analyzed the evidence about FAS, and considered the possible benefits of labels. After a review, it resolved to conduct a public awareness campaign in tandem with other federal agencies and the alcoholic beverage industry. The agency promised to assess the effectiveness of its educational efforts through public opinion polling.[18]

Consult Your Doctor

Saved from the threat of labels and told to find other means of warning women, the alcoholic beverage industry created an advertising campaign in the 1980s. Under the leadership of the Beverage Alcohol Information Council (BAIC), a consortium of ten trade associations, it wrote a script to suit its needs. The industry told women to "become informed" about drinking during pregnancy and advised them "to avoid excessive or abusive drinking," eschewing the abstinence message favored by numerous public health officials and embraced by the surgeon general in 1981. It ran one-time advertisements carrying this more modest message in three magazines, *Baby Talk, American Baby,* and *Essence,* and sent physicians a reprint of an article by Jack H. Mendelson, MD, former chief of the National Center for Prevention and Control of Alcohol. Mendelson opposed labels and had written to the ATF that "there are no adequate data which would permit reliable judgment about critical dose or duration of drinking with respect to fetal abnormalities or derangements." Mendelson "granted that no physician would encourage heavy drinking by pregnant women," but he rejected the one-size-fits-all message of abstinence. The BAIC later arranged for his taped remarks about drinking and pregnancy to be fed to radio stations in various urban areas.[19]

The education campaign made allies of the government and the bev-

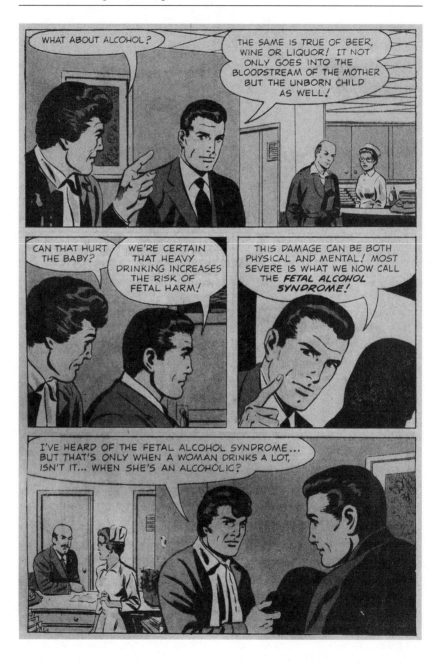

Figure 3. Pages from *Rex Morgan, M.D., Talks about Your Unborn Child*. Pamphlet produced by the Bureau of Alcohol, Tobacco, and Firearms, 1980.

erage industry, with the ATF cosponsoring televised public service announcements developed by the BAIC. Spots in English and Spanish informed viewers that "excessive drinking during pregnancy can cause serious problems for the newborn baby," yet avoided a definition of excessive, failed to explain what the resulting serious problems might be, and neglected to acknowledge that FAS was not just a problem in newborns but a lifelong condition. Challenged to enhance the warning, the BAIC stuck to its position, declaring that the decision about how much to drink was to be left to doctors; it would not tell women how much alcohol they could safely consume. The emphasis on telling women to consult their physicians was described in 1982 Senate hearings by Rex D. Davis, chairman of the Licensed Beverage Information Council and former director of the ATF.[20]

In the 1980s the public got mixed messages. The surgeon general recommended abstinence. The ATF and BAIC said, "See your doctor." The March of Dimes Birth Defects Foundation, which once recommended abstinence, joined the BAIC to produce a leaflet titled *Pregnant? Before You Drink, Think . . .* that omitted the abstinence message, and some complained that the organization had come under the influence of the alcoholic beverage industry. The NIAAA produced an educational brochure and poster—*Alcohol and Your Unborn Baby,*—and made information for available use in professional education and community outreach. It also joined with the ATF and the March of Dimes to produce the pamphlet *Rex Morgan, M.D., Talks about Your Unborn Child. Rex Morgan, M.D.,* a popular syndicated comic strip, was written by psychiatrist Nicholas P. Dallis, who also wrote the strip *Apt. 3-G,* which had included a storyline involving FAS.[21]

New Efforts

Undaunted by their failure to enact warning-label legislation in 1978, partisans kept up the fight and secured Senate support as part of a bill renewing funding for the NIAAA in 1979. Their political maneuverings caught beverage industry lobbyists off guard, but the industry recovered quickly, lined up its allies, and halted the effort. The House companion to the bill did not include a warning-label provision and, after going to a House-Senate conference committee, the labeling question was referred for study. Democratic senator Donald Riegel, Jr., of Michigan, chair of the Senate Subcommittee on Alcoholism and Drug Abuse, posed a series of questions for public comment:

Would warning labels be effective?

Would they decrease attention to health hazards not mentioned in the label text?

Should a rotating system of labels be considered?

Should labels be required on beer and wine containers?

Should the containers indicate alcohol content by volume?

Should advertisements for alcoholic beverage products carry warning labels?

The subcommittee received more than 250 replies, with supporters of the labels in the majority. The subcommittee staff prepared a report that supported labeling, and after the report came out, staffer and coauthor of the report Nancy Olson recalled, "all hell broke loose."[22]

The 1979 Senate subcommittee hearings on labeling went over well-plowed ground, but each side now dug in a little deeper, having learned from the previous encounter what the opposition was likely to say. Labeling supporters spoke about the problems of FAS and the public's right to know about health risks. Opponents deemed evidence about the risks of drinking during pregnancy incomplete and called labels a threat to the beverage industry. The counsel to the Wine Institute alleged that labels would "subject our industry to a severe, crippling governmental action far more serious than drought or flood." DISCUS's president eschewed the dramatic disaster images and spoke about the industry's record in fighting alcohol abuse and its pledge to work with the ATF to provide information about drinking and pregnancy.[23]

Letters responding to Senator Riegel's questions and testimony before the committee invoked many of the arguments made earlier, along with a new one: guilt. Would warnings cause women to feel guilty about every problem suffered by their children because they had consumed alcohol before learning they were pregnant? Would fear of lifelong guilt lead women to abstain? Nancy Lee Hall, a recovered alcoholic, the author of *A True Story of a Drunken Mother,* and the mother of seven children—none of whom had FAS—asked why a woman should be made to feel guilty if she had a couple of drinks and then gave birth to a child with a defect. Pointing out the possibility that all birth defects, whatever their cause, would be attributed to the behavior of women because of the warning labels, she wrote, "Deformities used to be the mark of the devil. Are they to become the legacy of the drinking woman? When will women be free in a free land?" An implicit reply came from David Smith, the codiscoverer of FAS. He described a woman who drank and smoked heavily, and visited her doctor before becoming pregnant. Her physician encouraged her to quit smoking cigarettes and she did, but since no one knew about the risks of heavy drinking, she did not get the word to cut back or abstain from alcohol. Doctors later diagnosed FAS in her baby and, Smith reported, she was "severely upset and guilt-ridden."[24]

Several articles in the *New York Times* later spotlighted the emerging issue of guilt. A 1983 story with the title "A Disabled Baby, a Mother With Guilt" described how two "FAS mothers"—a new locution—learned to cope with the handicapped children they had borne and to "live with the guilt that their drinking was responsible for their child's birth defects." Five years later the paper printed "Remorse over a 'Drinking Binge,'" in which a woman attributed her son's heart problems and less-than-normal IQ to a night on the town and her failure to understand what her doctor meant by "a little." While the subject of blame and contrition was only one of many being raised in the debate over warning labels, the rhetoric of guilt had clearly begun to permeate discussions of FAS. If manufacturers failed to warn women, would they be guilty if a child had FAS? Would physicians be held accountable if they failed to properly educate their patients? Or, if women were warned, would they be the guilty parties if their children had FAS? These questions would be louder after the labeling debate quieted down.[25]

The second round of legislative combat ended with another victory for labeling opponents. In a compromise with the House, the Senate agreed to hand over the matter to the Departments of Treasury and Health and Human Services for further study. The scope of the inquiry was broadened to include all health hazards associated with alcohol. When the findings of the joint study were handed back to Congress and the president in November of 1980, labels were once again rejected in favor of public information campaigns. The final report concluded that the risks of alcohol consumption were too complex and too varied among individuals to be conveyed by a label. Additionally, the report's authors questioned whether Americans had been "overwarned" by labels and should instead to get health information from doctors.[26]

Warning label advocates continued to press their agenda, meeting with little success until the reauthorization of the NIAAA came before Congress in 1986. The Senate Labor and Human Resources Committee included an amendment to the reauthorization bill to require four rotating warning labels on all alcoholic beverages:

> Warning: The Surgeon General has determined that the consumption of this product, which contains alcohol, during pregnancy may cause birth defects.
> Warning: Drinking this product, which contains alcohol, can impair your ability to drive a car or operate heavy machinery.
> Warning: This product contains alcohol and is particularly hazardous in combination with some drugs.
> Warning: The consumption of this product, which contains alcohol, can increase the risk of developing hypertension, liver disease and cancer.

According to the coalition of supporters who eventually succeeded in passing the 1988 labeling law, this bill languished and died after Kentucky's two senators kept it from reaching the Senate floor for a vote. In its place, Congress called for yet another study, this time by the Public Health Service, to evaluate the "educational impact of health warning labels."[27]

Local Initiatives

Government efforts to alert women extended well beyond the capital Beltway. Alarmed by what they learned about drinking and pregnancy and urged on by public health activists, some lawmakers began pushing for local initiatives. In December 1983, New York City mayor Edward Koch signed into law the first municipal ordinance requiring establishments selling alcohol to post warnings. The signs, which read "Warning: Drinking alcoholic beverages during pregnancy can cause birth defects," won city council approval by a wide margin. Vehement opposition and heavy lobbying against the measure came from expected adversaries, including the alcoholic beverage industry, restaurant association, the Chamber of Commerce, and from a new opponent—feminists, who identified the signs as both patronizing and discriminatory.[28]

Efforts to post warning signs and educate women about the risks of drinking during pregnancy resembled in some respects earlier health initiatives led by women fighting for consumer education and for laws assuring the purity of food and drugs. These movements, ironically, had their roots in the expansive temperance crusade of the late nineteenth and early twentieth centuries that endeavored to provide women with the knowledge needed to protect their families by arming the government with new regulatory tools. This time around, the fight for public health education evoked an angry response from activists who believed it was a thinly disguised attempt to assert the moral claims of the fetuses over the rights of pregnant women. Leaders of the *Women's Rights Law Reporter* explained their view in a letter to the *New York Times,* saying that the proposed New York City law "places the onus for healthy fetuses only on women when in fact a father's exposure to certain chemicals, foods, and drugs can lead to damaged sperm and ultimately to miscarriages and birth defects in his children." Using a related argument, the president of the New York City chapter of the National Organization for Women (NOW) urged Mayor Koch to reject the warning law. It could lead, she wrote, to the "harassment of pregnant women" and constituted a step toward "protecting the unborn at the expense of women's freedom." Her prediction ultimately came true. Feminist scholar Barbara Katz Rothman later wrote that, while "pregnant women sipping a wine spritzer have been harassed by total strangers," a man "lurching out of a bar looking for his car keys certainly poses a greater threat to the health of children." Feminist groups reiterated their assertions in 1991, when New York State began considering a statewide law requiring such signs in taverns, restaurants, and package stores. The president of the state chapter of NOW explained to legislators that warning posters were an attack on women's right to choose—a direct appeal to abortion rights advocates. "To warn of fetal damage in the absence of other health warnings," she argued, "is purely and simply an attempt by anti-choicers to establish a vocabulary of fetal rights in excess of the rights of the women in whose bodies these fetuses rest."[29]

Other feminists allied with the public health community refused to see FAS solely in the context of abortion rights, charging the beverage industry with being antifeminist for refusing to inform women about drinking and pregnancy. Sheila Blume, a physician and alcoholism expert and commissioner for alcoholism for the state, testified at the city council hearings in New York in 1983. Later she recalled her resentment of the male political leaders who claimed to speak on behalf of women when they opposed the labels. Labels, she said, informed consumers and transformed medical knowledge into public knowledge, adding that "you do not have to teach people that if you eat too much you get fat. Everybody knows it. It's part of public knowledge. If the public accepted that alcohol in pregnancy created birth defects, then you wouldn't have to shill the idea ever again. People wouldn't push drinks on pregnant women." But where was that public acceptance to come from? Warnings in bars? Health care providers? Or labels on alcoholic beverages?[30]

As the crusade to warn gathered momentum, municipal authorities jumped on the bandwagon, enacting ordinances requiring that warnings be posted to alert consumers to the risks of drinking during pregnancy. Among the cities passing such measures were Washington, Columbus, Philadelphia, and Jacksonville, Florida. Los Angeles mayor Tom Bradley signed a warning law in 1986, and the surrounding area, Los Angeles County, followed with an ordinance of its own, as did other California cities. The Los Angeles ordinance met with a court challenge when the California Restaurant Association argued that the municipal legislation usurped state authority, but the law was upheld.[31]

For the most part, opponents of labeling laws focused on preventing passage of warning laws rather than fighting expensive court battles to have them overturned. Deploying arguments ranging from the sanctity of the doctor-patient relationship to the suggestion that warnings insulted women, opponents defended the status quo. Doctors, not signs posted in grocery stores, they argued, needed to educate women about prenatal health. Proponents responded that many poor women never saw a physician prior to delivery. As in earlier encounters, each side read the scientific evidence to its own advantage—proponents saw potential disaster in every drink sipped by a pregnant woman; opponents argued that only severely alcoholic women gave birth to babies with FAS and that this kind of drinker would hardly be deterred by a sign in a barroom.[32]

State Programs

Unlike municipalities, which possessed few options for responding to the newly perceived threat of FAS, states had many remedies. Education proved to be the easiest and least controversial, because responsibility could be handed off to existing bodies such as schools or agencies running alcoholism programs. Education programs could also serve as showcases for political leaders—and their spouses—who used them to demonstrate their concern for women and for children's health. In the late 1990s Minnesota's first lady, Susan Carlson, adopted FAS as her special issue and pushed for state programs for prevention, case finding, education, and an expansion of services. Eventually she took the more drastic step of calling for involuntary treatment of pregnant women who abused alcohol, if they did not voluntarily seek help.[33]

South Dakota enacted one of the most ambitious FAS prevention programs, combining professional education and community initiatives. In 1983 the South Dakota Department of Health revised the state's birth certificate to include a space for indicating a diagnosis of FAS, and in 1986 retail establishments selling liquor were required to post warning signs. Special attention was given to Native Americans living on tribal lands. The federal Indian Health Service also directed funds to FAS prevention in the state, and several tribal codes were amended to outlaw the sale to or use of alcohol by pregnant women.[34]

Public service announcements proved to be a popular option for states wanting to inform citizens about FAS. Beginning in 1981 New Yorkers learned from radio and television spots as well as pamphlets and posters that "alcohol may be dangerous to your unborn baby." Educational efforts commenced the following year in Michigan under the sponsorship of local and private professional groups, including the state chapter of the National Council on Alcoholism. Texans got the message in 1988 when the symptoms of drug use in teenagers and of FAS appeared on 35 million paper bags distributed by more than thirty supermarket chains throughout the state.[35]

Messages on paper bags were one thing; messages in bars were another. Proposals for signs in places serving alcohol brought together the familiar throngs of hospitality and alcoholic-beverage industry advocates, public health officials, and feminists, who continued their quarrel over the appropriate dividing line between private behavior and public responsibility. Utah became the first state to pass a law requiring warning labels in establishments selling alcoholic beverages. Several tavern owners responded by printing the warnings on T-shirts that were worn by "curvaceous waitresses," an effort the Liquor Control Commission said did meet the legislature's intent. On-going debates in Massachusetts received national television coverage in 1988 as part of a story about the rise of product liability lawsuits against alcoholic beverage manufacturers. On the *CBS Evening News* Massachusetts state legislator Suzanne Bump asked, "Why should we treat the drug alcohol any differently than over-the-counter prescription drugs, which are clearly labeled so the people can know the consequences of abuse?" In response, James Saunders, president of the Beer Institute, said labels were ineffective and a false solution to a real problem.[36]

Figure 4. Posed picture of a waitress in a warning shirt. From *Bottom Line on Alcohol and Society* 2, 1978.

Californians faced the question of labeling in two stages. In 1986, as a number of counties considered mandating warning signs, the state legislature examined the issue. Beverage industry representatives made their way to Sacramento to square off against the California Medical Association, the PTA, the Consumers Union, and the March of Dimes. Kenneth Lyons Jones testified in support of a labeling law; Morris Chafetz called it "a cheap buyoff." Ultimately, the public rather than elected officials decided the matter. California voters passed a ballot initiative—Proposition 65, the Safe Drinking Water and Toxic Enforcement Act—requiring the governor to publish a list of reproductive toxins and carcinogens. When a scientific advisory panel voted unanimously to place alcohol on the list, the beverage industry quickly agreed to the posting of warning signs in liquor and grocery stores.[37]

Just as the medical, scientific, and public health communities embraced the scientific findings about alcohol and pregnancy, so too did political leaders. Their responses reflected the difficult political dance they needed to perform in order to inform consumers without alienating business allies. School health-education programs and public service announcements allowed elected officials to stand up for healthy babies and safe pregnancies and the protection of fetuses, and exposed them to little political risk. Efforts to place signs in bars, restaurants, and supermarkets proved controversial; opponents framed them as harming business and as government interference in a private matter. Little discussed was the possibility of funding detoxification and social support programs for alcoholic women.

The Alcoholic Beverage Labeling Act

After vigorously fending off federal labeling legislation for a decade, the beverage industry took a dive. In the wake of the U.S. Supreme Court ruling in *Cippolone v. Liggett Group* in 1987, the industry suddenly saw labels as providing protection against lawsuits. In the *Cippolone* case, the Supreme Court upheld the finding of a lower court that the federal requirement of a warning label preempted state tort claims. It followed that the alcoholic beverage industry could limit its liability if its products bore a federally mandated label. The industry already faced several lawsuits from parents claiming manufacturers' failure to warn them against drinking during pregnancy had led to birth defects in their children. Moreover, complying with individual state-mandated label requirements would prove more difficult and expensive than meeting a single federal requirement.[38]

The legislative endgame proved swift. In 1988 the Senate Committee on Commerce, Science, and Transportation held hearings on proposed labeling legislation, with Senator Thurmond again calling for warning labels. The legislation passed in each chamber, and a compromise version was negotiated that excluded warnings from advertisements—a key industry demand. The beverage industry also got its way on several other matters: there would be a single warning message rather than a set of rotating warnings, and the law preempted all state-mandated warning labels. As of 18 November 1989, all alcoholic beverages sold in the United States would carry a label that read:

GOVERNMENT WARNING:

1. According to the Surgeon General, women should not drink alcoholic beverages during pregnancy because of the risk of birth defects.

2. Consumption of alcoholic beverages impairs your ability to drive a car or operate machinery, and may cause other health problems.

Victory proved less sweet than many had anticipated. The small size of the print on the warnings angered some, and sent Tennessee's democratic senator Albert Gore, Jr., before the television cameras to call for further legislation to deal with the matter. The ATF issued new rules in 1990 requiring that the words GOVERNMENT WARNING be printed in bold type and setting a limit on the number of characters per inch. However, it rejected a proposal to require that the warnings be placed on the front of the containers. Later, labeling supporters moved to put warnings on advertisements. In 1990 the House Subcommittee on Transportation and Hazardous Materials held hearings on the proposal for a sensible advertising and family education act, which would have directed the Federal Trade Commission to develop regulations regarding alcoholic beverage advertising. The beverage industry geared up for a fight, with the beer industry threatening to halt sponsorship of major sports events. The legislation did not pass.[39]

Despite the weaknesses in the 1988 bill, advocates applauded when labels appeared on bottles and cans the following year, and they sounded a second ovation when social scientists determined that consumers read and in many cases responded to the message. A telephone survey of a random sample of adults six months before and six months after the implementation of the labeling law found that the messages were seen by heavy drinkers, women of childbearing age, and young men, who were most at risk for drunk driving. The ovation soon died down, however, as it became apparent that rates of FAS continued to climb and that drinking during pregnancy remained common. A study by the CDC found that alcohol consumption among pregnant women increased from 12.4 percent in 1991 to 16.3 percent in 1995, while frequent drinking, defined as having at least seven drinks a week or five drinks on one occasion, increased even more, from 0.8 percent in 1991 to 3.5 percent in 1995. It is not clear whether increased surveillance and reporting spurred by an awareness of FAS influenced the findings. Nevertheless, it seemed that severe chronic alcoholic women continued to lack access to treatment for their drinking and that some significant number of moderate drinkers were not following the advice of public health authorities.[40]

Meanwhile, other women worried needlessly. One pregnant woman called an FAS education program, concerned because, while she had had nothing to drink, early in her pregnancy she had eaten Kahlua ice cream. Others became deeply concerned about having had one or two drinks in the course of their pregnancies. One woman recalled that when she was five weeks pregnant her doctor warned her off alcohol and she "started to cry" because she had been having a few drinks a week before she learned of her pregnancy.[41]

When hailing the Senate's adoption of the labeling legislation, Richard M. Narkewicz, president of the American Academy of Pediatrics, remarked that "alcohol problems are rampant in America today, and our innocent children are paying the price." By invoking a discourse of innocence, Narkewicz left unspoken its corollary: the need to find and punish the guilty.[42]

6

◆◆

"Tempest in a Cocktail Glass": Pregnancy Policing and the Media

In the spring of 1991 the *NBC Evening News* carried a one-minute story about a bartender and a waitress at the Red Robin restaurant in Seattle, both of whom were fired for trying *not* to serve a drink to a pregnant woman. Anchor Tom Brokaw set the tone of the piece by asking, "What about the rights of the unborn when it comes to a pregnant mother who orders an alcoholic drink?" After Brokaw's lead-in the local correspondent picked up the story, interviewing the two fired employees, who were now urging the state government to bar restaurants from serving alcohol to pregnant women. Interviews followed with another bartender, a psychologist, and two attorneys with differing views on the proposed ban. In the final seconds, the correspondent offered a postscript: the woman whose request for a daiquiri had sparked the event in question had given birth to a healthy baby boy.[1]

Four days later, the *CBS Evening News* presented the same story, devoting nearly two and one-half minutes—a relatively large amount of air time—to its segment. The piece commenced with anchor Dan Rather mentioning "how a simple request for a drink tested the moral and legal limits of our obligations to one another." The on-site correspondent then recounted the details of the incident. Next came the moral issues. A lawyer from the Northeast Women's Law Center asked whether women were going to have to provide proof that they were not pregnant before being allowed to order drinks. Finally the on-site correspondent, calling the incident a "tempest in a cocktail glass," reported that local commentators were "reflecting on a society where individualism is now so rugged that the concern of strangers just isn't tolerated." He concluded: "In Seattle there are laws that promote the public's responsibility to protect things far less important than pregnancy. On the roads people are urged to watch for drivers who cheat in car pool lanes. That's 'approved meddling.' But as two young restaurant workers discovered, there is no reward for unapproved meddling." After seeming to argue for meddling in the lives of pregnant women, the story closed with the same denouement as the NBC segment: the unnamed woman had given birth to a healthy child.[2]

The two news segments followed an "arbitration formula": the reporters posed as detached observers and interviewed experts with opposing viewpoints. Unlike narrative accounts, the stories unfolded with a dialectical rather than an expository structure, in this instance posing the question of whether it was a private matter or a public concern if pregnant women drank. Both of the segments finished without a clear resolution. There was a healthy baby, and also lingering apprehension about pregnant women's drinking. There was a concern for privacy coupled with fear about the possible harm to vulnerable future citizens.[3]

The Red Robin story appeared in newspapers and on the newswires, as well as on television. In letters to the Seattle Times, opinion appeared to be divided: most, tired of hearing pregnant women being told what to do, were glad the servers got fired; a few applauded their efforts and called for more warning signs. The widespread coverage suggested that interest in drinking and pregnancy had reached a new level in the early 1990s, stimulated perhaps by the appearance of warning labels on alcoholic beverages. The Red Robin waitress had, in fact, torn a label off a beer bottle and handed it to the customer after she failed in her first attempt to discourage the woman from drinking. Much as public health advocates might have wished, members of the community, it seems, learned about FAS and took it upon themselves to inform or even to attempt to police pregnant women.[4]

A more powerful motivation for reporting the story may have been the way it fit so neatly into the much-discussed conflict between the private rights of pregnant women and those advocating "fetal protection." Both news broadcasts raised the matter, as did the woman who had ordered the drink. She claimed, as the headline in one newspaper put it, that she had been made to feel "like a child abuser" when she had, in fact, abstained from drinking until that night, late in her final weeks of pregnancy.[5]

Her choice of words seemed appropriate; America was in the midst of a drug panic over crack cocaine use by women. Crack use, associated with poor, urban, African Americans, had been blamed for numerous social problems, including rising crime rates, the decline of the family, and, beginning in the late 1980s, the births of damaged and cocaine-addicted babies. In a few localities prosecutors had begun going after the mothers of newborns who tested positive for cocaine exposure and charging them with delivering an illegal substance via the umbilical cord, something they called prenatal child abuse or fetal endangerment.[6]

As vigilance over pregnant women's use of illicit substances heightened, it seemed to be only a matter of time before the legal right of adult pregnant women to consume alcohol came to be viewed with suspicion. A Gallup poll in 1988 revealed that nearly half of those surveyed agreed with holding women legally liable for the effects that drinking and smoking during pregnancy had on their offspring. With the rise of the crack panic, discussions of FAS moved beyond guilt and into the realm of blame and later coercion, as pregnant women began to face arrest for posing a threat to their fetuses.[7]

The meaning of FAS was manufactured in many domains and shifted over time. Initially physicians and researchers defined it as a birth defect caused by heavy alcohol exposure in utero; later, public health and government officials provided an additional designation, calling it a public health problem requiring that women stop drinking when pregnant. As concern broadened, the media, and in particular television news broadcasts, reported on each of these constructions of FAS and then helped to fashion a third: FAS was what happened to innocent babies when their mothers performed criminal acts.

Alcohol and Television

Americans learned a lot about alcohol from watching television. They saw it being happily consumed on entertainment programs, they watched numerous advertisements for beer, and on occasion they looked at brief news segments that highlighted particular problems of alcohol abuse. While these formats—entertainment, advertising, and news—differed in terms of purpose and content, they shared an important perspective: alcohol was not a drug. Although public health leaders described alcohol as America's number one drug of abuse and detailed the enormous health, economic, social, and institutional consequences of that abuse, the news media and others reserved the word *drug* for illegal substances or for pharmaceuticals obtained for illegal use. For example, the Partnership for a Drug-Free America, a nonprofit organization formed in 1986, offered numerous public service announcements targeting hard drug use as dangerous while ignoring the problems associated with alcohol and tobacco products and accepting support from corporations manufacturing them. As one policy expert noted, "With alcoholism we pay attention to 'bad users,' with other drugs we talk about 'bad substances.'"[8]

Brewers spent hundreds of millions of dollars on advertising, aiming commercials at heavy drinkers and at young people in order to maintain brand loyalty and cultivate future consumers. One critic termed the advertising "anti-health education," and media expert Neil Postman reported that children saw as many as 100,000 beer commercials before they reached the legal drinking age. Other alcoholic beverage producers stayed off the airways (distilled and blended spirits producers voluntarily refrained from television advertising) and promoted their products through other media. At the opening of 1976 hearings before the Senate Subcommittee on Alcoholism and Narcotics, committee chair Senator William Hathaway quoted the figures of $100 million spent on advertising by the beer industry in 1974 and $160 million by the distilled spirits industry.[9]

While Congress responded to the critics of alcoholic beverage advertising with periodic hearings, it refrained from instituting controls. Industry representatives adeptly countered efforts at regulation with appeals to the First Amendment and to the public purse—claiming that regulations would be costly to a valued industry that represented significant tax revenues. They touted their self-developed advertising code as a model of corporate responsibility that forbade commercials encouraging underage or abusive drinking, and pointed to their public service announcements supporting safe drinking.[10]

Messages about alcohol delivered on entertainment programming dovetailed neatly with those presented by advertisers. Alcoholic beverages topped the list of drinks consumed on the shows, and the characters who drank were prosperous and used alcohol to enhance their social interactions. Occasionally, individual episodes dealt with abusive or underage drinking, and by the late 1970s the topic of drinking in pregnancy appeared on the airwaves. *Dallas,* an extremely popular prime-time soap opera in the late 1970s and early 1980s, presented a lead character, Sue Ellen, the wife of a wealthy Texas business magnate, who drank heavily during her pregnancy. On one show she received a warning from her physician to stop drinking. However, the failure of the episode to mention directly the possibility of fetal harm irked one nursing professor, who commented, "If such television characters could turn down a drink once in a while with the comment, 'No thanks, I'm pregnant,' many people could learn something from that." However, prime-time television was not in the business of health education.[11]

News programming ostensibly stood apart from the entertainment division of the networks and from commercial advertisers. One media insider claimed that "an impenetrable wall of separation" stood between the news and the advertising portions of the business. Advertisers could not stop the networks from broadcasting news stories about FAS or from reporting on government warnings about drinking in pregnancy. Nevertheless, brewery industry executives and their counterparts in the wine and distilled spirits industries could rest assured that their products would be portrayed in a positive light during hours of entertainment programming. For every few seconds of news touching on problems related to alcohol, there would be many hours of beer commercials.[12]

Television news programs mattered because they influenced viewer opinions about social problems and their solutions. Although the three networks' share of viewers and revenues declined with competition from new networks and cable news programs, major network broadcasts were identified in various surveys as the most common and the most trusted source of information, and they played a substantial role in determining which issues were of national importance. While there is no evidence that discussions of alcohol and pregnancy on the network news directly influenced any legislative measures, to the extent that political systems responded to public interests, they responded to interests shaped in a significant way by the television news industry.[13]

FAS and Television: The Early News

Television news coverage of alcohol and pregnancy began in 1977, four years after the initial research findings about FAS appeared in the English-language medical literature and several years after information about drinking in pregnancy began to be disseminated in news and women's magazines. The reports were part of revolving menu of alcohol stories that also included discussions of teenage drinking, the health effects—both positive and negative—of alcohol, and the disease of alcoholism.

Between 1977 and 1986, twenty-three segments on alcohol and preg-

Television Evening News Segments on Alcohol and Pregnancy, by Network, Date, and Subject

ABC	04/22/77	NIAAA warning about drinking and pregnancy
CBS	04/22/77	NIAAA warning about drinking and pregnancy
NBC	05/31/77	FAS: mother, child, experts
ABC	06/01/77	Official warning about drinking and pregnancy
NBC	06/01/77	Official warning about drinking and pregnancy
CBS	06/01/77	Official warning about drinking and pregnancy
CBS	01/13/78	Warning labels proposed
CBS	01/31/78	Senate hearings on FAS
NBC	06/26/78	FAS and debate over bottle labeling
CBS	08/31/78	Alcohol's effect on rat brain, and FAS
CBS	10/17/78	NIAAA report on alcohol and health, and FAS
ABC	02/07/79	ATF won't require warning labels
ABC	02/08/79	ATF: labeling issue and FAS
NBC	02/08/79	ATF won't require warning labels
ABC	05/07/79	Senate votes for warning labels
CBS	05/07/79	Senate votes for warning labels
CBS	10/29/79	Evidence of birth defects caused by alcohol
ABC	11/05/82	Animal data: risks of moderate drinking in pregnancy
NBC	11/05/82	Animal data: risks of moderate drinking in pregnancy
ABC	10/20/83	Women and alcohol; mentions birth defects
ABC	04/02/84	One drink can be harmful to a fetus
ABC	10/11/84	Risks of moderate drinking in pregnancy
CBS	10/11/84	Risks of moderate drinking in pregnancy
NBC	10/11/84	Risks of moderate drinking in pregnancy
NBC	09/04/87	National Institute of Child Health and Human Development says two drinks or less not harmful
CBS	06/14/88	Labeling legislation, FAS court cases
ABC	08/04/88	Benefits and problems of alcohol for women
NBC	05/17/89	Jury finds for Beam in failure-to-warn case
NBC	08/16/89	Alcohol in breast milk may be harmful
ABC	11/14/89	Bottle labeling begins
NBC	11/21/89	FAS on Pine Ridge Reservation
ABC	01/10/90	Women's drinking: warning about FAS
NBC	05/25/90	New warning proposed for bottle labels
NBC	03/28/91	Red Robin case
CBS	04/02/91	Red Robin case
CBS	04/16/91	Studies show FAS major cause of retardation
CBS	08/04/92	Woman arrested for drinking while pregnant
ABC	05/10/93	Academy of Pediatrics warns against drinking in pregnancy
CBS	04/06/95	Government finds increase in FAS births
NBC	04/06/95	Government finds increase in FAS births

nancy appeared on the national evening news, beginning with the story of Melissa, the little girl who was presented as the "face" of FAS. The early accounts varied in length and focus, but by placing the issue before the public, the news programs helped to make drinking and pregnancy a national concern. Eight of the early segments dealt with warning labels, five focused on government warnings to women, four reported research findings, and three discussed the risks of moderate drinking in pregnancy reported in the medical literature. In addition, there were individual segments about alcohol and women, about a report by the NIAAA, and about FAS. Coverage centered on white, middle-class women who were warned by scientific authorities not to drink when pregnant.

Hard news segments typically consisted of brief announcements read by the anchors, often regarding recent findings or statements released by government agencies. In-depth human interest stories often ran for a minute or more, presenting viewers with brief narratives that, on close viewing, seem to have been drawn from the "damsel in distress" stories favored in silent movies. Innocent women discovered to be drinking while pregnant were saved in the nick of time when valiant scientists and government officials stepped forward to warn them about the risks their infants faced if they kept on imbibing. There were no villains in these pieces. Instead, the drama hinged on whether women ought to be warned by labels on bottles or in some other fashion.[14]

Among the earliest television presentations was a broadcast on 1 June 1977, following the first government warning. CBS anchor Walter Cronkite informed viewers: "As we reported here recently, there's been increased concern over the danger of drinking during pregnancy. Studies have shown that excessive drinking can lead to abnormal children. Today the government said the danger increases with more than two drinks daily." ABC carried a similar announcement the same evening, as did NBC, which had run the Melissa story the previous night. Six months after reading the government's warning, Cronkite discussed the issue once again, reporting with some jocularity that "the government is preparing steps to protect pregnant women and elephants," noting that one federal agency proposed banning ivory imports while another wanted warning labels on alcoholic beverages.[15]

Labels were no laughing matter to federal agencies, Congress, medical scientists, or the beverage industry. As they staked out competing positions amid ongoing Capitol Hill debates, their various representatives appeared on the news to make their opinions known and to influence the public. Viewers learned that most of the interest groups, with the exception of the beverage industries, concurred with federal officials that heavy drinking could cause birth defects. The matter in question, and thus the story presented to viewers, was the disagreement over the usefulness of warning labels. The news broadcasts gave each side a say, albeit in quick sound bites. An NBC segment in 1978 showed Morris Chafetz, the NIAAA's first director, arguing that labels would "terrify normal pregnant women" and the rebuttal of Ernest Noble, his successor, who raised the subject of guilt directly in arguing that the need to prevent the birth of mentally and physically damaged children outweighed "a little guilt."[16]

Human interest stories offered a somewhat different message, turning the question away from the role of the government and toward the issue of women's behavior. Vivid personal narratives, media experts report, are not as powerful as lead stories in influencing the public agenda. However, by dramatizing public problems they bring new subjects into the stream of cultural consciousness. And depending on the race and racial attitudes of the viewer and the race of the television subject, the narratives can evoke sympathy or victim blaming. In the inaugural period of alcohol and pregnancy reporting, the broadcasts clearly sought to evoke sympathy.[17]

Melissa, the child "star" of this era who was first introduced to TV viewers when she was three years old, appeared on the *NBC Evening News* four times in a period of six years, always as a tragic victim, a role she shared with her mother. Watching Melissa's mother in 1977, viewers saw a well-dressed white woman who apparently lived in comfortable surroundings with her damaged child. Despite the silhouette lighting that hid her identity, she appeared to be young, thin, and pretty, a sympathetic figure whose personal tragedy conveyed the urgency of the FAS problem. While the subject of FAS was a new one, the narrative style was familiar—it was a "disease story" that reached viewers because it sounded a culturally resonant theme: protecting children. The Melissa story carefully directed viewers' sensibilities by personalizing the victims and valorizing the medical authorities. The segment also provided a neat resolution in the form of an easy lesson: don't drink heavily when pregnant.

One year later Melissa served as the focus of a lengthy four-and-a-half-minute special segment about FAS, prompted by the labeling debate. Her mother, her identity concealed once again, also appeared on camera, and compassion for both of them was evoked by an opening shot of them outdoors, picking daisies in a field. In a voice-over, correspondent Betty Furness slowly intoned: "Melissa is four-and-a-half years old. She's not quite like other children and never will be." Again Melissa's mother received an opportunity to explain her actions: "At the time I was—that Melissa was conceived and I was carrying her—I was heavily drinking and I did not know any damage could be done to my child because of my drinking." Scientific authorities and past and current government officials then discussed beverage labeling.

Melissa appeared on NBC two more times. In one appearance, the initial footage of Melissa, evidently pulled from the tape archives, was used to illustrate a segment on warning labels, although the segment did not give her name or discuss her story. She made a final appearance in 1982 when images from NBC's second story about Melissa were run again as background visuals while government researchers discussed their findings regarding the effects of alcohol fed to pregnant monkeys. The segments, like those appearing on the other networks, helped to make the problem of alcohol and pregnancy visible and to suggest its value as "news."[18]

In October 1984 *JAMA* published an issue entirely devoted to the subject of alcohol, sending an important signal from the medical community. All three networks reported it, and all chose to report on a single article—one that discussed maternal alcohol consumption and infant birth weight. On ABC, anchor Peter Jennings and medical editor Dr. Tim Johnson discussed the findings for almost two minutes. Johnson reported that the *JAMA*'s editor had written an editorial saying women should not drink during pregnancy. Jennings responded with a question: "Well, we have undoubtedly just scared a lot of women who are pregnant and drinking now. What about them?" Johnson answered with a brief discussion of risk and then offered his own opinion: "What they're saying, I think, is it is not worth taking any chance at all, even small, and I go along with the advice. When you can plan for it, you should not drink at least during those nine months of pregnancy." It was a surprisingly frank position for a television news commentator to take.[19]

The NBC response to the story featured two women: one drank, the other didn't. After the anchor's lead-in, the segment opened in a crowded barroom with a band playing in the background. The ambient sound continued as the camera turned to Sandra Ramirez, shown well lit and in close-up as she put a glass to her lips and took a drink. Correspondent Robert Bazell provided her name and told viewers that she was two months pregnant and liked to drink when she went out with friends. In the next shot viewers met another pregnant woman, Phyllis Levine, who was sitting at the dinner table with her husband in her quiet home. Levine, Bazell announced, had stopped drinking even before trying to get pregnant. Levine then explained: "I feel that I'm sharing my body with my baby and if I could possibly hurt the child in any way, I wouldn't want to take a chance of doing it." After moving to the federal National Institute of Child Health and Human Development, the segment concluded back in the bar, where the music still blared and several women sat drinking. Visually and with its use of sound, the NBC segment cued viewers that the alcohol-and-pregnancy narrative was moving from a disease story to one about deviance. Bazell's closing lines echoed earlier ones, as he offered indulgence to those who erred unknowingly: "The doctors say the greatest chance for damage occurs in the first three months of pregnancy, often before a woman even knows she is pregnant." However, viewers could easily recall that Rameriz, although only two months pregnant, knew her status and chose to drink. Using race, class, and ethnicity, NBC displayed pregnant drinkers as "different." Ramirez had a Hispanic surname and drank in a noisy, smoke-filled bar even when she knew she was pregnant. The segment also introduced a new "FAS child." Replacing the very young, white Melissa—who had no last name—was a ten-year-old African American girl identified as Simone Anderson.[20]

Children from minority groups were becoming the new faces of FAS. One reason may have been the simultaneous transformation of the cocaine story, which had undergone a major shift in its presentation on the evening news from being about a recreational drug used by wealthy white Americans to an illegal substance plaguing the black community. The stories often featured African American infants who had been exposed to cocaine in utero. Sympathy for women caught up in a cycle of poverty and addiction began evaporating as images of damaged "crack babies" filled the airwaves and Americans began to view them as a social burden, draining resources, filling jails, and threatening the social order.[21]

Crack

Public panic over crack cocaine use by poor African Americans and the War on Drugs that it spawned transformed the televised narrative of pregnancy and substance abuse, tugging its orbit from the sphere of public health into one revolving around accounts of crime and punishment. Prior to 1987, television news broadcasts presented cocaine use in pregnancy as a problem involving mostly white, middle-class women who repented their actions and worried about having harmed their children. Among the first "cocaine mothers" shown on television were "Cindy," a white, middle-class housewife, and "Linda," a remorseful, white, Chicago woman shown with her jittery baby, who was undergoing cocaine withdrawal. They were the counterparts to Melissa's mother. Following the media's discovery of crack cocaine and its link to inner-city violent crime, the profile of pregnant users changed: they became poor, African American women who, rather than overcoming their addiction, succumbed to the siren call of the crack pipe. Crack, television news journalists reported, conquered women's "maternal instincts," and stories soon followed about law enforcement officials bringing felony charges against new mothers whose babies tested positive for cocaine exposure.[22]

NBC alone offered 400 separate stories on crack and cocaine in the seven months preceding the 1986 elections. In 1988 and again in 1989, the issue of drugs surpassed all others mentioned in a poll asking Americans to name the nation's leading problem, suggesting the power of the media to shape public impressions. Hyperbole about crack filled the news. On NBC, anchor Tom Brokaw declared crack cocaine "America's drug of choice" and told viewers it was "flooding America," despite the fact that heroin, another illegal drug, was used by more individuals on a daily basis than crack cocaine. Brokaw ignored altogether Americans' favorite drugs, tobacco and alcohol.[23]

Media reporting about crack stimulated public interest in what was certainly a serious health and crime problem, and as interest grew, the media fed the public more stories. The networks offered dueling special reports; on CBS it was the prime-time special *48 Hours on Crack Street;* on NBC it was *Cocaine Country.* In print as well as broadcast journalism the presentation of crack stories reached a feverish pitch. According to one study, over an eleven-month period the *New York Times, Washington Post, Los Angeles Times,* the wire services, *Time, Newsweek,* and *U.S. News & World Report* printed more than one thousand articles featuring crack.[24]

Initially the media portrayed "crack babies" as innocent victims of their mothers' misdeeds. Later these infants stepped into a new role, cast as damaged citizens who would one day threaten the public. Extrapolating from an early small study of the prevalence of drug-exposed babies, one researcher estimated that 375,000 babies annually were exposed prenatally to drugs or alcohol. Newspapers soon began using this figure, while social commentators began alleging that "crack children" could not pay attention in school, lacked a social conscience, and were on the pathway to lives of crime and deviance. In a *Newsweek* editorial titled "A Desperate Crack Legacy," writer Michael Dorris, who had gained fame for a book detailing the life of his adopted Native American son who had FAS, referred to crack-exposed children as "remorseless" and "without a conscience."[25]

Careful longitudinal studies failed to demonstrate differences between crack-exposed children and those reared in similarly poor social and economic circumstances, and they exposed the methodological flaws in the early investigations, which had not controlled for prenatal exposure to other harmful substances, particularly alcohol. The new findings, however, offered no reassurance to the public, because the media paid no attention to them. Bad science remained the foundation of most reporting about crack cocaine.[26]

Public discourse about pregnancy and substance abuse in the crack era reached a crescendo with calls for jailing pregnant addicts. In a 1989 article in the *Washington Post,* conservative columnist Charles Krauthammer vividly recounted the imagined threat posed by the "bio-underclass, a generation of physically damaged cocaine babies whose biological inferiority was stamped at birth." Echoing early twentieth-century advocates of colonies for the unfit, he later proposed institutionalizing substance-abusing pregnant women: "We can either do nothing, or we can pass laws saying that any pregnant woman who takes cocaine will be sent until delivery to some not uncomfortable, secure location (boot camp, county jail, house arrest—the details are a purely technical matter) where she can do anything except leave or take drugs." A year later, federal "drug czar" William Bennett advocated the creation of orphanages and youth camps to shelter children removed from drug-infested homes.[27]

While alcohol-using women were not swept up in this particular rhetorical whirlwind (perhaps because drinking is legal), they began to be understood and stigmatized in similar ways, and eventually there would be calls to jail them as well. An editorial by *Chicago Tribune* columnist Joan Beck that was widely reprinted included the statement: "The next time a judge tries to jail a pregnant woman because she won't stop drinking, I hope some children with fetal alcohol syndrome are in the courtroom." Assertions that fetuses had claims on the liberty interests of pregnant women would continue to be made in the media and later by law enforcement officials.[28]

Melodramatic crack-mother stories shrouded all discussions of substance abuse in pregnancy with the aura of criminality. The pregnant woman who exercised her right to consume alcohol became indistinguishable from the pregnant woman who engaged in the criminal act of buying cocaine. Both were seen as threatening in ways that male users were not because they were perceived as jeopardizing the health of their fetuses and thus, symbolically, the future of the nation. Those who spoke up on behalf of fetuses, such as law enforcement officials and prosecutors, seemed to assume the status of protectors of the vulnerable.[29]

FAS on Television: The Late News

The torrent of crack-mother stories swept segments on alcohol and pregnancy out of the mainstream of disease and science reporting and into rougher waters of crime news. Unlike the earlier stories, which often communicated instruction about behavior in everyday life, crime and deviance stories were essentially morality tales. Their purpose, according to communications analysts, was "to teach about the normative contours of society, about right and wrong." While not all of the stories about alcohol and pregnancy in this second period of news coverage were deviance stories, the topic appeared with growing frequency.[30]

Only sixteen evening news segments on women and alcohol appeared between 1987 and 1996. Although the volume was vastly lower than that for women and cocaine, the tune sounded much the same—a ballad of innocent babies and guilty mothers, underscored by a theme of race and punishment. As in the earlier coverage, some segments consisted of "hard news" announcements read by the anchors. Viewers learned that a pregnant woman's consumption of two drinks a day or less had not been shown to be harmful to her fetus, that bottle labeling legislation had taken effect, that the Academy of Pediatrics had warned against drinking while pregnant, and that a government study had found FAS to be on the rise. Longer segments discussed an equally diverse range of topics, including the incident at the Red Robin restaurant and the finding that FAS was irreversible and the largest single cause of mental retardation. On the latter, the correspondent intoned, "Science has no solutions. Only a mother does when she chooses not to drink during pregnancy." FAS was beginning to be depicted as simply a matter of whether a woman wanted to drink and harm her baby or whether she chose to abstain for the sake of her fetus and for society.[31]

Unlike the televised reporting on crack that focused to some extent on the issue of addiction, stories of alcohol and pregnancy asked questions about women who "chose" to drink. A 1993 segment on the daytime television show *Sonya Live* made this clear with its title: "Because Mommy Drank." The show featured the adoptive mothers of individuals with FAS and their struggle to cope with the legacy of what they described as other women's decisions about drinking. The assumption that the birth mothers had chosen to drink ignored the scientific findings that FAS appeared in the offspring of chronic alcoholic women, who, according to the disease model, had lost control of their drinking.[32]

Within the cacophony of moralizing about illegal drugs came some quieter calls for limiting the rights of pregnant women who chose to drink. The former Red Robin employees, for instance, demanded new legislation that would allow waitpersons and bartenders not to serve alcohol to pregnant women. Such a measure would differ from laws requiring bars and restaurants to stop serving intoxicated patrons. Regulations about serving the intoxicated were intended to protect the public's health through the prevention of drunk driving—an established risk. Laws against serving alcohol to pregnant women would be aimed at protecting fetuses, who lacked legal status—despite the efforts of some political activists and legal theorists to assert such a claim, and despite the fact that the risk of damaging a fetus from light or even moderate drinking remained unproven.[33]

Early news reports on alcohol and pregnancy suggested that mothers and fetuses shared the same interests and that government officials and medical scientists worked to protect them both. After the crack panic, the alignment shifted. One side consisted of pregnant women, typically poor and members of minority groups, who seemed poised to harm their offspring. On the other side were professionals and law enforcement officials primed to protect innocent fetuses from guilty mothers. Thus the attorney supporting the fired Red Robin employees asserted that his clients had "in essence" been asked to "serve alcohol to a minor." The attorney's eliding of the difference between a fetus and a child employed the language of abortion opponents. And television stories soon became ensnared in this rhetorical trap.[34]

Native Americans, FAS, and the Media

One year after evening news viewers first saw a pregnant African American woman smoking crack on television, they met her alcohol-using counterparts: Carla (whose surname was not provided), Venus Redstar, and Sharon Whitecap, residents of the Sioux reservation in Pine Ridge, South Dakota, and the mothers of children damaged by alcohol use in pregnancy. A week-long NBC special report, *Tragedy at Pine Ridge* aired as part of the network's programming for the November 1989 "sweeps," a period during which audience ratings are taken in local markets.[35]

One of the NBC segments focused exclusively on FAS. It opened with shots of the desolate reservation, after which special correspondent Betty Rollin introduced three women and reviewed the status of their children. Unlike the deferential camera angle used in shooting Melissa's mother, all of the Native American mothers were shown in close-up. Viewers could not help noticing that Sharon Whitecap's nose had been broken and that her upper lip was scarred. She spoke to the camera, recalling: "I remember one time I was pregnant with Antonio, I stole a whole case of wine from a bootlegger and I drank and drank and drank." Earlier Rollin had introduced twenty-seven-year-old Venus Redstar, and had told viewers that, of Redstar's five children, "two of her boys show[ed] signs of fetal alcohol effect, a less severe condition from the same cause, drinking." This was in marked contrast to accounts of Melissa's mother, who had been described to viewers as "a reformed alcoholic who devotes much of her life to giving Melissa loving care." While Rollin defined Redstar in terms that placed her outside of middle-class norms, with her large family, her drinking, and her damaged boys, the camera closed in on Redstar's face, showing her mottled skin, damaged and missing teeth, and unkempt hair—which also marked her as an unsympathetic subject. A harsh interrogation followed. Rollin asked her, "So why did you do it?" Redstar answered, "Because I was depressed." Rollin pressed: "Why?" And Redstar replied, "I can't answer that either." The next comments from Rollin implied forthright condemnation as she explained how "the pregnant mother who drinks and poisons her baby with alcohol is often a mother who can't care for her baby once he's born." Yet Redstar, like Melissa's mother, was caring for her children. However, unlike Melissa's mother, who was white and regretful, Redstar was a poor Native American who had failed to express regret or to stop drinking. And in the interim between the airing of their two stories, FAS had gone from a discovery to a mark of maternal misbehavior.[36]

In the same segment, Rollin interviewed a physician at Pine Ridge Hospital who offered a drastic solution reminiscent of the ones proposed for crack mothers: "I've come to the point, after dealing with a lot of this, to recommend that women who can't control their drinking during pregnancy should have protective custody during the pregnancy for nine months." Rollin also interviewed Michael Dorris.

Dorris's book *The Broken Cord* (1989) received widespread attention, won a National Book Critics Circle Award, and was dramatized by ABC in a 1992 television movie. A poignant account, the book tells of Dorris's discovery of the source of his son's many physical, emotional, and developmental problems—his birth mother's drinking—and of his struggle to help the boy and, later, young man find a place in the world. Woven into the narrative are explanations of FAS drawn from Dorris's conversations with leading researchers and clinicians and an assessment of the staggering effects of FAS in Native American communities. Widely reviewed and highly praised, the book catapulted Dorris into the position of FAS spokesperson, and his anguished expression of his family's struggles resonated strongly with others grappling with the same problems. He wrote later of "wrenching letters" received from readers who experienced "heartache, grief and frustration uncannily identical to my wife's and mine."[37]

The Broken Cord also raised the question of whether an alcoholic pregnant woman should be prevented from drinking and thus be made to sacrifice her freedom for the sake of her fetus. Dorris's wife, novelist Louise Erdrich, who is herself Native American, opened the discussion with a passionate foreword to the book in which she asked, "Where, exactly, is the demarcation between self-harm and child abuse?" In the text, Dorris described speaking with a pregnant woman he spotted ordering a drink in an airport restaurant. When he informed her that "it's really not safe to drink when you're pregnant," the woman told him to mind his own business and then saluted him with a "cheers" as she lifted her drink. Elsewhere in the book, Dorris mused about more radical types of intervention, such as jailing pregnant women, a policy that, he reported, some tribal groups had already chosen. And he asked in relation to his own son: "If his mother had been locked up, prevented from even one night of drinking, how much more awareness, how many more possibilities might he now have? If she had come after him with a baseball bat after he was born, if she had smashed his skull and caused brain damage, wouldn't she have been constrained from doing it again and again? Was it her prerogative, moral or legal, to deprive him of the means to live a full life?" Translating moral outrage into legal action posed problems ranging from the threat that legal sanctions would deny women equal rights to the likelihood that they would discourage women from seeking help. Writing in *Parents* magazine, Dorris acknowledged the limits of incarceration. Most medical experts agreed that the threat of prosecution would not stop alcoholics from drinking but would merely drive them from seeking care.[38]

Pregnancy Policing

Poor mothers have never evoked much sympathy in a culture that deems self-regulation and individual effort the appropriate path out of need, and that holds women responsible for creating the right kind of families and the right kind of children. Under siege in the United States in the second half of the twentieth century because of a growing rate of out-of-wedlock births and the rising cost of public assistance, poor women soon faced new threats to their privacy and autonomy with the rise of pregnancy policing. According to one expert, by 1994 "over two hundred women in twenty-four states had been prosecuted for drug-related behavior during pregnancy." The core assumption underlying the arrests was that the state had a compelling interest in protecting fetuses and that prosecuting those who ingested illegal substances in pregnancy was the best means of achieving that goal.[39]

Others objected to the prosecution of pregnant and newly delivered women on the grounds that it denied women rights, discouraged them from seeking prenatal care and alcoholism treatment, and created an adversarial relationship between patients and health care providers. The AMA, in response to some of the arrests, examined the issue of legal interventions in pregnancy in 1990 and concluded that while women had a "moral responsibility to make reasonable efforts toward preserving fetal health," imposing a legal burden and related penalties on them for failing to do so would be wrong. The statement from the AMA's board of trustees also noted that court-ordered obstetrical interventions were most often sought for poor women and members of minority groups. Other concerns included the effects of pregnancy policing on the physician-patient relationship and the fear that state policies would ultimately lead to controls on physician's practices as well as on their patients. Addressing the problems of substance abuse, the report ultimately concluded that incarceration or detention might be counterproductive, because it would discourage women from seeking prenatal care and because prisons did not meet the medical needs of pregnant women.[40]

The AMA trustees did not address the fact that many women had no means of obtaining either treatment for their addiction or prenatal care. In 1991, when a rural Missouri woman was arrested and charged with second-degree assault and child endangerment after her newborn son was observed to be intoxicated at birth and was later diagnosed with FAS, the chief of neonatology at the hospital where the boy was born was outraged, calling the jailing of the woman "absurd." An editorial in the *St. Louis Post-Dispatch* observed that the alcohol treatment services nearest to the woman's home were more than 100 miles away.[41]

The media brought the issues of pregnancy policing into family living rooms as reporters and commentators debated whether fetal interests justified abridging women's rights. In 1992, on a four-minute story on the *CBS Evening News* "Eye on America" segment, anchor Connie Chung opened with a misleading question: "Consider this: a woman addicted to alcohol or drugs becomes pregnant. Her baby is born with health problems. Should the mother be held legally responsible?" The segment that followed did not discuss holding a woman responsible for having given birth to a damaged child; it posed the question of whether law enforcement officials should arrest pregnant women for drinking. The segment highlighted the case of Deborah Arandus of Hastings, Nebraska, whom police arrested for binge drinking while pregnant and charged with felony child abuse. Subsequently she gave birth to a premature baby that doctors suspected of having FAS. Two of her five other children had been given the diagnosis.

The Arandus segment joined the crack mother and the drinking mother into a single narrative. The piece opened with interviews with the arresting officer, the local prosecutor, and Arandus. Then the story jumped from Nebraska to Florida. Viewers met a Tampa judge who had sent pregnant addicts to drug treatment in jail on the basis of mental-health commitment laws. Protesting this was Lynn Paltrow, an attorney with the Center for Re-

productive Law and Policy, who argued that it was not a crime for an addicted woman to become pregnant. She also pointed out that referring
pregnant addicts to the criminal justice system would only drive more of
them away from prenatal care. Arandus made a different point when she
said she wondered if the authorities were going to "test you for smoking, if
you don't eat right, if you run down the street too fast." A Nebraska judge
eventually ruled there was no legislative intent to include unborn children
in the criminal statutes designed to protect minor children. Justice, he
stated, would have to triumph through other means, perhaps referring
to the fact that Arandas had lost custody of her infant and her five other
children.[42]

Drinking during pregnancy led to arrests or state supervision in cases in
several jurisdictions in the 1980s and 1990s. In 1985, following passage of a
statute in Illinois allowing children to be removed from parental custody if
diagnosed with FAS, a woman who gave birth to a daughter with the syndrome was placed in state supervision. In Ohio a newborn with FAS was
removed from his mother's care. When the mother took the child from the
hospital she was jailed on charges of child endangerment and child theft.
Five other children had been removed from her custody. In California, a
mother of three children who had FAS was forced to undergo monthly
pregnancy tests. In South Carolina, authorities arrested a woman for giving
birth to a legally drunk baby, and in a similar case in San Marcos, Texas, a
woman was charged with injuring a child after having given birth to an infant suffering from FAS and cocaine addiction.[43]

Press coverage of many of these cases was sparse, and the accounts typically focused on the women's lives and addiction problems rather than on
the legal issues involved in their arrests. The effect was to clothe shaky legal
maneuvers in the garb of moral certainty, uniting the question of whether
a woman ought to act in the best interests of a fetus with the question of
whether she could be legally coerced into doing so. The public scrutiny of
Diane Pfannenstiel of Laramie, Wyoming, was characteristic of media efforts to frame the stories in terms of maternal obligations rather than civil
rights. Pfannenstiel's arrest followed her discharge from an alcoholism-re-
habilitation program. She was assaulted by her husband, and when she
sought help from a group that aids battered women, they took her to the
hospital for treatment. There she was tested for alcohol, and because she
was pregnant, she was charged with felony child abuse. A judge later dismissed the charges, asking whether a woman could be prosecuted for in-

juring a fetus in the first trimester, when it could still be legally aborted. According to her obstetrician, Pfannenstiel later gave birth to "a beautiful, healthy 7-pound boy."[44]

Several editorials recounted Pfannenstiel's arrest and detailed her history, including the fact that she had previously lost custody of two children, at least one of whom had FAS. One of the writers quoted the foreword to *The Broken Cord*, where Erdrich wrote, "I would rather have been incarcerated for nine months and produce a normal child than bear a human being who would, for the rest of his or her life, be imprisoned by what I had done." In an article in the national newspaper *USA Today*, a pointed analysis of the Pfannenstiel case was followed by the question: "Does a pregnant woman's right to privacy outrank her unborn child's right to a healthy start in life?" The question was, to many, an updated version of the abortion rights debate.[45]

Pfannenstiel's status as a battered woman received extraordinarily little attention. Studies found that many pregnant women endured "intense battering aimed at the fetus," and that this behavior by male partners posed a significant risk to the fetus. The news media did not care. As Jean Reith Schroedel and Paul Peretz pointed out, "Between 1989 and 1991 . . . the *New York Times* devoted a total of 853.5 column inches to fetal abuse brought about by pregnant women's use of illegal drugs and/or drinking. During the same period there was not a single column inch dealing with adverse birth outcomes due to the physical abuse of women." Their findings underscored the fact that pregnancy policing was not simply about protecting fetuses, it was also about controlling women.[46]

Other arrests for drinking during pregnancy also made the news. In New Hampshire, Rosemarie Tourigny was charged with endangering the health of her unborn child when she was twelve weeks pregnant. Her case dragged on for many weeks, and the press dissected her troubled history with alcohol abuse, her loss of custody of three of her children, and her two evictions from motels where she had been living with her boyfriend. Tourigny's bail agreement called for her to attend AA meetings and to make daily contact with the police. The requirements, she charged, contradicted her physician's instructions to remain on bedrest because of pregnancy-related problems. At one point Tourigny tried to find the money to obtain a second-trimester abortion, but later she changed her mind. Two months after her arrest, the county prosecutor dropped the charges.[47]

The case of drinking during pregnancy that garnered the most attention involved charges of attempted first-degree intentional homicide and first-degree reckless injury brought against Racine, Wisconsin, resident Deborah Zimmermann in 1996. Zimmermann went on a drinking binge shortly before giving birth. In the hospital, before the delivery, a medical technician heard her scream, "If you don't keep me here, I'm just going to go home and keep drinking and drink myself to death and I'm going to kill this thing because I don't want it anyways." After being informed of her need for a cesarean section, Zimmermann refused the procedure, prompting the doctors to call a judge, who ordered her held until she was no longer intoxicated and permitted the forcible monitoring of the fetus. Later Zimmermann consented to the surgical procedure, and her daughter was delivered showing signs of alcohol toxicity. She was subsequently diagnosed with FAS and removed from Zimmermann's custody. Later, charges were filed. Responding to questions about the attempted-murder charge, an assistant district attorney explained it was time to "start holding women accountable for the harm they do their unborn children." If found guilty, Zimmermann faced a sentence of up to forty years in prison. The message to other pregnant substance abusers could not have been clearer: alcoholism was going to be considered a crime, not a disease in pregnant women.[48]

As the case inched its way through the legal system, the media paraded Zimmermann's life history before the public and used the case to argue the merits of pregnancy policing. *People,* the popular weekly magazine, profiled the case in a story that asked, "Should this woman—a chronic alcoholic who has been raped three times, who killed a man in a drunk-driving accident 13 years ago and who has a history of being physically abused—be held accountable by law for damaging her unborn child?" Other media outlets gave the story a different spin, using it to profile the problems of children with FAS and to explore the legal issues involved in holding a woman accountable for her actions during pregnancy. *Cosmopolitan* magazine asked, "Should a Pregnant Woman Who Abuses Drugs or Alcohol Be Locked Up in Rehab?" in its "Cosmo Controversy" section. The page featured a picture of Zimmermann, letters from advocates on both sides, and an opinion poll showing that 54 percent of women and 46 percent of men surveyed felt the government should step in to protect the health of the fetus.[49]

The Zimmermann case quickly became a touchstone in the debate over pregnancy policing. Television host Geraldo Rivera, airing a show on the topic, pointed out that a ruling in the Zimmermann case might set a legal precedent allowing states to punish pregnant women for behavior that endangered their fetus. Rivera asked guest Lynn Paltrow, "If a boozing pregnant woman can be charged, why not a smoking pregnant woman, why not a—a woman who does aerobics in the ninth month in a way that some expert might perceive her conduct to be dangerous?" Playing to a different audience, the National Public Radio show *All Things Considered* invited legal experts to consider whether the case might set a precedent. Racine County district attorney Joan Korb, who brought the charges, said that she hoped the case would either persuade the state legislature to pass new laws extending more rights to fetuses or convince prosecutors to pursue charges against pregnant women who intentionally engaged in behavior that might harm their fetuses. Undergirding the debate was the recent ruling by the Supreme Court of South Carolina that upheld the prosecution of pregnant women for using illegal drugs. The court determined that because the state recognized fetal personhood in the case of medical malpractice or in attacks on pregnant women, it recognized it in the case of a woman charged with child endangerment for drug use during pregnancy.[50]

In May 1999 the Wisconsin Court of Appeals dismissed the attempted murder charge against Zimmermann, ruling that the unborn child was not a human being and that there was no probable cause for charging Zimmermann with any crimes. Her actions may have been egregious, the court found, but they were not criminal under Wisconsin law. Zimmermann did serve time for a bail violation, which required her to cease drinking alcohol and undergo treatment; she was sentenced to four years in prison and nine years probation for this offense.[51]

Shortly before the ruling, Wisconsin passed a law allowing women to be ordered into treatment for abusing drugs or alcohol during pregnancy. The statute was explicit about providing services to an unborn child whose "expectant mother habitually lacks self-control in the use of alcoholic beverages, controlled substances or controlled substance analogs." In South Dakota, laws were rewritten to allow circuit court judges to commit pregnant women who abused alcohol or drugs to an approved treatment facility on the petition of a spouse or guardian, a relative, a physician, or the administrator of a facility. In 1999 nine states considered legislative proposals to punish pregnant women for behavior deemed potentially harmful to the fetus.[52]

Echoing the doctor interviewed on the NBC special on Pine Ridge, a physician on the Rosebud Sioux Reservation who had adopted a child with

FAS applauded the new South Dakota law, commenting, "They should throw those women in jail and make them get four or five months of treatment. No question about it." Another adoptive mother, describing herself as a feminist, pro–abortion rights, and in favor of civil rights, asked what "feminists and civil rights activists who are so quick to defend the rights of women who use alcohol and illegal drugs during pregnancy" would say to her son and to others with FAS. The change in the law did not result in a slew of commitments, perhaps because the costs of providing treatment were so high. Rather, they stood as powerful statements about the willingness of some elected officials to declare that the state had a compelling interest in protecting the interests of fetuses even if it meant limiting the rights of pregnant women. The laws prompted critics to disparage what they called a "gestational gestapo" bent on controlling the lives and freedoms of pregnant women in the name of fetal protection policies that, writer Katha Pollitt argued, reduced women to the status of "potting soil." While few women were arrested for their behavior during pregnancy, many who were observed smoking cigarettes or drinking alcohol were scolded by strangers who assumed the role of fetal advocates.[53]

Others attacked the constitutionality of fetal protection laws arguing that they permitted pregnant women to be incarcerated for acts that would not lead to the jailing of men. And, they pointed out, the women who would go to jail would inevitably be poor, minority women. Some feared a slippery slope that would lead inexorably from efforts to control the behavior of pregnant women to laws regulating the behavior of all women of reproductive age. The debate over pregnancy policing made its way into mainstream popular magazines ranging from *U.S. News & World Report* to *Glamour*. The matter was hardly theoretical. Interestingly, pregnancy policing was one arena in which pro-choice and anti-choice activists could find common ground, as some in the anti-choice movement recognized that threatening to jail substance-abusing pregnant women might lead to more abortions.[54]

No News

After a flurry of media reports on pregnancy and substance abuse, television news broadcasts turned away from the topic, perhaps because it had gotten stale. In 1992 the number of evening news items on women and crack started to decline, and the thematic emphasis switched from punishment to rehabilitation. Segments increasingly profiled women in recovery who were battling addiction in order to regain custody of their children. Reversing the earlier discourse, these later accounts trumpeted the enduring power of the maternal instinct, demonstrating how it led to victory over the allure of street drugs and enabled women to reclaim their children from foster homes and hospitals.[55]

FAS all but vanished from the airwaves. In 1994 it was not mentioned; in 1995 there were only two FAS news stories—both reporting on the findings of the Centers for Disease Control and Prevention that the number of babies born with FAS increased sixfold between 1979 and 1993. The increase may have reflected better diagnosis and case reporting, or it may have indicated an actual rise in the incidence of FAS. Neither possibility interested the media: the television news anchors simply read a statement to viewers and said nothing further.

A few stories about alcoholic women in recovery did begin appearing in print. The *Washington Post* profiled a homeless alcoholic woman who gave birth to a child with FAS in San Francisco's Golden Gate Park and who subsequently turned her life around after receiving inpatient care along with parenting and sobriety training. *People* magazine profiled another mother living on an Apache reservation in New Mexico who had regained custody of her son after conquering her alcoholism. Television news shows did not bother to recount these successes. As stories about crack babies dwindled, stories about alcohol and pregnancy disappeared. Substance abuse in pregnancy, the gestational gestapo, recovery from addiction—even the inner-city crack crisis—had become old news.[56]

In the space of two decades, news accounts of FAS shifted from disease stories to deviance narratives and then faded into silence, leaving in their wake images critical to the ongoing debate over pregnancy and addiction. The story of alcohol and pregnancy ceased to be framed in such a way that it would resonate with viewers on a personal level and lead them to change their behavior; it became a morality tale cloaked in the garb of public interest by seeming to be about the protection of the vulnerable. When news anchor Dan Rather alleged that "a simple request for a drink tested the moral and legal limits of our obligations to one another," he was also testing whether viewers would find it acceptable to deny to pregnant women the rights that others possessed. And when anchor Tom Brokaw asked about "the rights of the unborn," he was implicitly asking whether their "rights" might trump those of pregnant women.

As the topic of blame infiltrated discussions of alcohol and pregnancy in the late 1980s, prompting lawyers, law enforcement officials, and medical leaders to question whether addicted women needed assistance or punishment, another guilty party appeared briefly on the horizon. In 1986, a few years before the crack panic began, Kenneth Lyons Jones appeared at a national conference on substance abuse and pregnancy. He questioned the emerging discussion about criminalizing mothers and stated: "If we're talking about suing people, we should be suing the alcohol industry. They've known about it [the effects of alcohol on fetuses] for years, and they've been making millions and millions of dollars on it and walking free." A few years later, jurors in a civil court case would be asked to decide whether children with FAS might have a claim on those "millions and millions of dollars."[57]

7

◆◆

The Thorp Case:
Jim Beam on Trial

America's only "failure to warn" case brought against an alcoholic beverage manufacturer came to trial in Seattle in April 1989. Filed several years earlier, the case of *Michael Thorp v. James B. Beam Distilling Company* (commonly referred to as Jim Beam) gained national attention because of the high stakes involved. If the plaintiff prevailed, a cascade of other cases would likely follow, with parents of children with FAS rushing to court to seek compensation for expenses, lost income, and punitive damages, claiming that the willful negligence of manufacturers had caused their children to suffer serious birth defects. Other failure-to-warn claims against alcoholic beverage manufacturers were already in the pipeline. The *Seattle Post-Intelligencer* reported experts as saying that a successful suit could "redefine the limits of corporate responsibility." At least one financial adviser warned clients to reduce their holdings in Anheuser-Busch Companies, and a story in the *Washington Post* quoted an attorney and tobacco litigation theorist as calling the case "definitely winnable." Others believed that because alcoholic beverage manufacturers had never denied that their product posed a health risk, they enjoyed a measure of protection. Moreover, as one analyst noted, the women likely to bring suits "are excessive drinkers and the dangers of excessive drinking are well known," suggesting that juries would be unlikely to hold manufacturers to be at fault, even if they had placed no labels on their beverages.[1]

Thorp v. Beam tested the beverage industry's long-standing claim that adults knew they had to drink responsibly and that those who failed to do so had no one to blame but themselves; perhaps they suffered from the disease of alcoholism, but it was certainly through no fault of the manufacturer. Recognition of this was acknowledged in the *Restatement (Second) of Torts* that cited alcohol as an example of a product that did not require a warning because the risks of excessive consumption were assumed to be known. Standing behind this legal fortress, manufacturers had repelled a number of earlier assaults. Claims against alcoholic beverage manufacturers had rarely breached courtroom walls, and those that had entered had tended to be swiftly turned away.[2]

The *Thorp* case differed from earlier claims against the producers of alcoholic beverages and tobacco products because the plaintiff—a four-year-old boy—had not chosen exposure to the substance, and because it was not clear that the risks of drinking during pregnancy were indeed widely known. Successful claims had been brought against other products that damaged fetuses and did not carry warnings against use during pregnancy. Alcohol was known to be a teratogen, and the surgeon general had issued a warning against its use in pregnancy. The failure to put labels on alcoholic beverages, despite the known risk of FAS, might therefore be judged negligence. Moreover, with an innocent, damaged young child to present to the jury, the attorney might be able to make a compelling case that significant damages needed to be awarded. However, the jury first needed to be convinced that Michael Thorp's mother had had no way of knowing she was putting her fetus at risk by drinking large amounts of alcohol and that, had the manufacturer informed her, she would have abstained. With a near consensus among the public that alcoholism was a disease, manufacturers could defend themselves by arguing that alcoholics, by definition, had no control over their drinking and so a label would not have mattered. As Barry Berish, the chief executive officer of Jim Beam (as the company was commonly referred to), declared of Michael's mother, "You could put a skull and crossbones on the bottle, and she will continue to consume alcohol."[3]

Thorp v. Beam came to trial at a pivotal time, amid ongoing fights over fetal rights, alcohol warning labels, and the beginnings of a moral panic over drug abuse in pregnancy. Harvard law professor Alan Dershowitz called 1989 the "Year of the Fetus," referring to the many pending civil and criminal actions—ranging from lawsuits over frozen embryos to the *Thorp* case—all of which were influenced by the fetal rights debate raised by abortion opponents. Although *Thorp v. Beam* had been filed in 1987, before warning labels were mandated by Congress, the trial occurred during the brief period between passage of the Alcoholic Beverage Labeling Act and the appearance of labels on bottles. While the presence of warning labels would seem to preclude future failure-to-warn claims, the ruling in the *Thorp* case would be critical to those who had borne FAS children in the window between the first federal warning and the appearance of labels on bottles.[4]

Thorp v. Beam also coincided with the growing vilification of addicted women who appeared to harm their fetuses by surrendering to demon drugs. The media had begun to make clear that children with FAS were not the offspring of naive women who failed to hear the warnings being broadcast by physicians, nonprofit agencies, the media, and the government. They were, very frequently, the children of poor women—denizens of the ghetto, the reservation, and the homeless shelter, whose drinking had gone on for many years. While the courtroom issue was a simple one—who would bear financial responsibility for Michael Thorp—the trial occurred at a time of increased cultural anxiety about substance abusing women and their offspring.

Creating a Case

The Thorp suit began with a conversation between Barry M. Epstein, a New Jersey–based attorney with many years of experience defending corporations charged in product liability, birth defects, and toxic tort litigation, and physician Robert Brent, an internationally respected teratologist who had served as his expert witness in several cases and had written about birth-defects lawsuits. As Brent explained in his deposition and later on the witness stand, Epstein once asked him why he had not been involved in legal actions against environmental agents that caused birth defects. Brent answered, "I don't start legal cases." Epstein then asked him to name the agents that caused birth defects, and Brent replied that "the most common one was alcohol." Epstein quizzed him further, learned about FAS, and finally asked, "You mean there are children with FAS out there?" Brent answered, "Lots of them." He had seen them in his own clinic, and the most critical work, he told Epstein, had been done at the University of Washington by physician Sterling Clarren. The ball was soon rolling. Brent telephoned Clarren and asked him to give Epstein the names of patients who might agree to be litigants. Clarren subsequently called the Thorps and a few other families, who became clients of Epstein's in other suits filed against alcoholic beverage manufacturers. Clarren's involvement came to light during the discovery phase of the lawsuit, when the defense tried, unsuccessfully, to have him declared a biased witness.[5]

Epstein's firm made a big financial commitment when it chose to proceed with the claims against alcoholic beverage manufacturers. In addition to attorneys in his firm, there were two Seattle attorneys involved in the case, Roger Kindley and Kandice G. Tezak. Clearly Epstein and the partners in his firm hoped that in winning the case they would not only recover their expenses and a portion of a large damage award but would also be in a strong position to bring other successful cases against other manufacturers. The defense incurred similar costs. Serving as lead counsel for Jim Beam was the company's longtime attorney, Donald I. Strauber, who had extensive experience in products liability litigation, including a successful defense of the American Tobacco Company in a smoking-related lawsuit. Strauber was a member of the New York City law firm that had represented Jim Beam's parent company for more than thirty years. He was joined by local counsel Shannon Stafford and Diane Libby.[6]

Pretrial Maneuvers

In filing the case in November 1987, the plaintiff claimed that Jim Beam "placed in the stream of commerce" a product that it knew to be not reasonably safe and that did not carry a warning, although such a warning was feasible. The attorneys for the defense responded that any damages to Michael Thorp had occurred because of the risks his mother, Candance, had freely assumed. This was a product, the attorneys noted, that had been distilled and bottled according to all state and federal standards. They asked that the case be dismissed. Jim Beam's lawyers succeeded in knocking down the three causes of action asserted by the plaintiff to a single negligence claim under Washington State's product liability law. They also made a motion for summary judgment—asserting that the plaintiffs raised no legal issue and asking the judge to rule in their favor. The plaintiffs fought that motion and won. The judge found it was up to a jury to decide whether the company had a duty to warn about the risks of drinking during pregnancy or whether such a duty was obviated by common knowledge. If a duty existed, then the jury would determine whether Jim Beam's failure to warn was the cause of Michael's injuries.[7]

Initially Michael and his parents, Harold and Candance Thorp, claimed pain and suffering, economic losses, and expenses. By the time the case came to trial, only Michael sought an award—for past and future pain and suffering, costs of past and future care, and pecuniary loss. In scaling back the claim Epstein prevented the defense from questioning Candance Thorp about how much she stood to collect for having spent her pregnancy drinking. Nevertheless Epstein could not fully shield her from the assaults that he knew the defense would make on her character and behavior.[8]

From the beginning, the defense gave notice that it would argue that Candance Thorp, not Jim Beam, was the source of Michael's problems. In a joint status report to the court in 1988, the defense made this abundantly clear as it sought to learn all it could about Candance's past. At one point

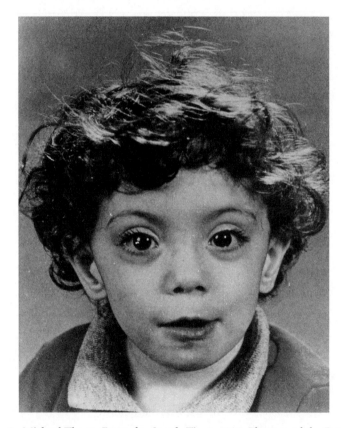

Figure 5. Michael Thorp. From the *Seattle Times,* 1989. Photograph by Peter Liddell.

the defense listed nearly 100 witnesses it hoped to call, including 36 who would address Candance's "lifestyle" and another 14 who would discuss her parenting capabilities, housekeeping, and family relationships. The defense attorneys claimed that her drinking habits, disregard for her children's welfare, and other behavioral patterns would be admissible on the issue of whether Jim Beam's failure to warn was the proximate cause of the alleged injury, and they went to court to force Washington State's Child Protective Services (CPS) and several local school districts to turn over records relating not only to Michael but also to his half siblings. The attorneys also fought to compel the Thorps to answer questions they had refused to reply to during their depositions. Finally, they asked the court to require Candance Thorp to turn over her personal address book, to enable them to locate friends who could testify about her drinking and her knowledge of the effects of heavy alcohol consumption on a fetus. The defense team also asked that she identify the father of her daughter Rebecca, as well as her contacts in AA. The court eventually ordered that the identity of the father of one of Candance's daughters "be kept secret," along with information from the police, CPS, and school records. Also excluded from the trial were medical records from a physician, now deceased, who had treated Candance. The defense claimed that his records included a note suggesting he had spoken to her about the health consequences of drinking during pregnancy.[9]

Preparing to argue that Michael's condition differed little from that of his family members, they sought the location of Harold Thorp's daughter from a previous marriage, who was the mother of two retarded children. Presumably they planned to argue that developmental disabilities ran in the Thorp family. The defense also demanded copies of all photographs of Michael and of Candance Thorp's other children, to see whether Michael's facial features reflected exposure to alcohol or simply a resemblance to his kin. Also, they asked that Candance and Harold Thorp undergo psychological examinations, because they planned to argue that Michael's intellectual and mental development reflected his inheritance—as they put it, "The acorn does not fall far from the tree."[10]

The plaintiffs tried their best to keep the case focused on Michael, the metaphorical acorn, by keeping damaging information about Candance Thorp from coming before the jury. Federal District Court judge Carolyn R. Dimmick granted some of what they asked, ordering the defense not to raise the issues of her previous marriages and boyfriends, and not to discuss the fact that her daughter Rebecca was born out of wedlock. Dimmick also kept from the jurors' ears the fact that Candance had spent time living in a women's shelter, was "missing" during part of her pregnancy, and had been cited for driving while intoxicated with Rebecca in the car. Drawing a firm line between character evidence and evidence of behavior that might have been responsible for Michael's problems proved tricky. The judge recognized that the case turned on Candance Thorp's abuse of alcohol and her awareness of its effects, and thus she allowed the defense to discuss her drinking habits and the removal of Michael from her custody.[11]

As the defense lawyers worked to learn all they could about Mrs. Thorp's past, the plaintiff's lawyers tried to uncover information about Jim Beam by aggressively pursuing evidence from the company and its advertisers. To bolster claims about alcohol teratogenesis, they tried, but failed, to convince the judge to let them introduce information from animal studies. The judge also rebuffed their efforts to inform jurors about the recently passed Alcoholic Beverage Labeling Act. Finally and most critically, the lawyers pushed hard to have the critical jury question turn on the matter of what a reasonably prudent person would have done, rather than what Candance Thorp would have done, had a label been on the bottle. Judge Dimmick refused to rule on this issue before the trial.[12]

Jury Selection and Opening Acts

After several years of wrangling over the claims, collecting evidence, and fighting over what kinds of material could be examined, the battle moved into the courtroom. Judge Dimmick allowed the attorneys for each side to make brief remarks and then asked the twenty-nine prospective jurors about their knowledge of FAS and whether they knew any of the parties involved. Six knew something about the case from the local news and several admitted to having already made up their minds. They were excused for cause, as were others who conceded that they could not be impartial. Lawyers questioned the remaining group of potential jurors. Their inquiries suggested that both sides had made use of interviews with mock jurors to identify questions that would uncover individuals predisposed to reject or accept their claims. Epstein's queries seemed designed to ferret out those biased against alcoholics. One of the defense attorneys questioned the group about health habits such as smoking and drinking diet sodas, apparently trying to identify individuals who thought it prudent to follow medical advice.[13]

Chronology of Michael Thorp v. James B. Beam Distilling Company

24 April 1989
Initial presentations before jury voir dire
Voir dire examination of prospective jurors
Opening statements on behalf of plaintiff and defendant

25 April 1989
Witness for plaintiff: Kenneth Lyons Jones, MD

26 April 1989
Witness for plaintiff: Robert L. Brent, MD

27 April 1989
Witnesses for plaintiff: Barry M. Berish, CEO, James B. Beam, by deposition; Harold Thorp, father of Michael Thorp; Candance Thorp, mother of Michael Thorp

28 April 1989
Witness for plaintiff: Candance Thorp

1 May 1989
Witnesses for plaintiff: Sterling Clarren, MD, Michael Thorp's physician; Wendy Marlowe, PhD, clinical neuropsychologist

2 May 1989
Witness for the plaintiff: Wendy Marlowe

3 May 1989
Witnesses for the plaintiff: Anthony J. Choppa, certified rehabilitation counselor; Robert T. Patton, economics consultant; Steven S. Gloyd, MD, physician to Candance Thorp; Cherie M. Peterson, alcoholism counselor to Candance Thorp

4 May 1989
Witness for the plaintiff: Cherie M. Peterson; Ceaser J. S. Pessein, chiropractor to Candance Thorp; Jack R. Morrison, MD, physician to Candance Thorp

Witnesses for the defendant: Ila J. Pound, RN, counseled Candance Thorp during pregnancy; Chris Reynolds, MD, medical director of Alcoholism Treatment Center; Andres G. Aranca, MD, physician to Candance Thorp

5 May 1989
Witnesses for the defendant: John B. Burcham, Jr., chair, Licensed Beverage Information Council; Kathleen J. Gillis, provided foster care for Michael Thorp

8 May 1989
Witnesses for the defendant: Allen Alleman, MD; George Cvetkovich, PhD, psychologist; John H. Whitney, bartender; Barbara L. Sheller, DDS, dentist to Michael Thorp; Mary M. Tolle, mother of Candance Thorp, by deposition

Chronology of Michael Thorp v. James B. Beam Distilling Company *(continued)*

9 May 1989
Witnesses for the defendant: Janina R. Galler, MD, expert in child development; Kathryn Vengler, social worker for Child Protective Services

10 May 1989
Witness for the defendant: Janina R. Galler

Rebuttal witnesses for the plaintiff: Marybell Kuehl, waitress; Linda Thompson, former social worker; Christine Lubinski, Washington, DC, representative of National Council on Alcoholism

11 May 1989
Discussion of jury instructions by lawyers and judge

12 May 1989
Instructions to jury
Argument: Barry Epstein, attorney for plaintiff
Response: Donald Strauber, attorney for defendant
Reply: Roger Kindley, attorney for plaintiff

17 May 1989
Jury finds for defendant.

Had public health advocates attended the voir dire (the interviewing of prospective jurors) they would have learned that the crusade to warn the public of the effect of alcohol on a fetus had been successful; many of the jury candidates said they knew about the risks of drinking during pregnancy, thanks to the efforts of doctors, educators, the March of Dimes, and the media. Public health advocates would not have been surprised by how many in the jury pool had been affected by alcohol in their own lives. Two were admitted alcoholics, two had alcoholic parents, one conceded that he might be becoming an alcoholic, and one had a daughter who had been hit by a drunk driver. Only one individual, other than the recovered alcoholics among the group, claimed to abstain. It remained for the lawyers to assess how knowledge of alcohol abuse and habits of imbibing would influence the judgments made of Jim Beam and Candance Thorp.

After the lawyers had used up their preemptory challenges and dismissed individuals they suspected of being unsympathetic to their case, Judge Dimmick named a civil-case jury of six—five women and one man

—as well as two alternates. After swearing them in, she reminded them not to discuss the case and to avoid news about the trial, which was being followed by local and national media. Her warning proved timely; the night before trial opened, the nationally televised PBS program *MacNeil-Lehrer NewsHour* rebroadcast a story about the case that it had aired earlier, and the judge was forced to poll the jurors on the opening day of the trial to make sure they had not seen the segment. Both Clarren and Epstein appeared in the broadcast, along with several children with FAS and the mother of one of them, who explained that she wasn't warned. Newspapers around the country had already printed articles about the case and its potential impact on the alcoholic beverage industry. An article in a newspaper in Kentucky—home of Jim Beam and nine other distilleries employing a total of 3,800 people—detailed Candance's drinking, divorces, and troubled family. Much of this information would never come before the jury.[14]

Epstein's opening statement to the jury offered a simple framework for understanding the case: Michael Thorp deserved justice in the form of a monetary award from a company whose product had damaged his mind and body. Only Michael, he made clear, would receive any award; his parents would get nothing for themselves. Epstein's statements readied the jury for the testimony they would hear and presented a simple analysis of the issues: if Jim Beam had placed a warning on its bottles, Candance Thorp would not have consumed alcohol during her pregnancy and Michael would not have FAS. Unspoken though nonetheless palpable was a familiar theme: corporate greed and deceit had blighted the life of an innocent child, and only the jury could help, by granting him a large financial award. At times Epstein veered from presenting his case to arguing his claims, drawing objections from opposing counsel and admonitions from the judge.

Defense attorney Shannon Stafford placed an entirely different set of images before the jury, preparing them to hear about Candance Thorp's alcoholism, about the many different kinds of drinks she had consumed, and about the warnings she had heard from family members and professionals. A label would have made no difference, he told the jurors. Stafford walked a fine line: he rejected a claim of FAS even as he prepared the jury to hear about Jim Beam's participation with other distillers in an educational program telling pregnant women to consult their doctors about how much to drink. He then offered a preview of the testimony jurors would hear from defense experts.[15]

The Plaintiff's Case

The case for Michael Thorp began with two expert witnesses: Kenneth Lyons Jones and Robert L. Brent. Led by Epstein, each recited his training, accomplishments, and expertise, and then proceeded to diagnose Michael's FAS. Jones, the first witness, brought some drama to the courtroom when he actually examined Michael before the jury, pointing out the physical features that indicated alcohol exposure and explaining his resulting developmental difficulties. Michael, he told them, "is not the kind of guy who is going to be able to sit in a classroom in a preschool, or regular first grade, or kindergarten, or any kind of a formal school-type setting, and be able to pay attention, be able to learn." Preparing the jury for the questions he anticipated from the defense, Epstein led Jones through a list of alternative diagnoses—malnutrition, neglect, heredity. Jones dismissed them all, repeating again and again, "Michael has FAS." As he testified, Michael sat in the courtroom in his mother's lap, smiling, saying "hi" and "hello," and blowing a kiss to one of his lawyers.[16]

Strauber, lead counsel for Beam, had worried that Michael's courtroom appearance would give a boost to the plaintiff's case. In a meeting of counsel before the judge with the jury away, he complained: "This is a four-year-old child, he's cute, he's sweet, there are unfortunate people involved, there's a defendant which obviously is a company of some size. And there's always the hope that if you can fling the case to the jury, no matter how weak your case is, no matter how absurd the claims are, there's always that hope that somehow sympathy or passion or prejudice will creep in." When he stood up to cross-examine Jones, Strauber had to make it clear to the jurors that their sympathy was unwarranted because Michael had not really been harmed by his mother's drinking. Predictably, in cross-examination he attacked Jones's diagnostic work, grilling him about his conclusions regarding alcohol teratogenesis and about his assessment of Michael. Although a cross-examination is not supposed to go beyond issues raised during the direct examination, Strauber managed to introduce different interpretations of the events in question and to present the jury with their first taste of what would be the defense's explanation for Michael's condition—bad parenting. After the plaintiffs conducted their redirect examination of Jones, Strauber got a final turn with the witness. He pounced, asking questions designed to show that Jones knew little about Michael's care. "And you have no idea whether, as a three-month-old, he stayed in the crib, or whether he sat on the floor in filthy newspapers, do you?" he asked. "No, I do not," Jones answered. "And you have no idea of whether he was fed properly, or whether a bottle was stuck in his mouth and left there for six or eight hours, do you?" Again Jones answered, "No, I do not." To leave the jury with a final negative image of Mrs. Thorp, Strauber posed his last question: "Do you know why the Child Protective Services removed Michael from his parents' home and placed him in foster care?" Epstein quickly objected and Strauber withdrew the question, but the jury must have been left wondering.[17]

Candance Thorp's life and drinking history resembled those of other mothers of FAS children, although the details did not come out in the trial. Like them, she drank, sometimes in binges; like them, she had been an abusive drinker for a long time, and like them, she had several other children—at least one of whom suffered from developmental problems. A brief for summary judgment filed by the defense detailed her decline into alcoholism and how, at one point, she had been homeless. She began drinking at twenty-one and eight years later was said to have a drinking problem. She had a child with her second husband, a child out of wedlock, and had then married a third time. At one point her sister had visited her and removed her daughter Rebecca from her care, having found Candance drinking heavily and unable to care for the girl properly in her unkempt trailer. Candance entered alcoholism treatment, and she went to live with her sister after her discharge. But she did not stay long. Her sister threw her out after she discovered beer bottles under the bed, and Candance moved into a shelter, later disappearing for several months. Eventually she was picked up on the street and was taken to a hospital. These events occurred prior to her conception of Michael and were not detailed for the jury.[18]

A new phase of her life began when she met Harold in a tavern. One newspaper account quoted Harold, who reminisced, "We took off and went up to the Hideaway and started in on our favorite whiskey, ended up in a motel with a jug of Beam, and that's how we got acquainted." A few weeks later, they began living together and conceived Michael. After helping her get a divorce, Harold became her fourth husband. Candance's drinking continued throughout her pregnancy and after Michael's birth. The jury never heard these details, but the testimony of various witnesses suggested that her life had been a troubled one. Although Michael was the plaintiff, the defense made sure that Candance Thorp was the person on trial.[19]

Figure 6. Candance Thorp and her attorney, Barry Epstein. From the *Seattle Times*, 1989. Photograph by Peter Liddell.

On the second day, the jury heard from Brent. A medical school professor, editor of the journal *Teratology,* and former president of the Teratology
Society, Brent was the author of five books and more than 500 articles
about birth defects, several of which examined the role of an expert witness. He wrote from experience, having been involved with more than 100
lawsuits or potential lawsuits, approximately 25 of which had gone to trial.
On the stand for the plaintiff, he conducted a quick tutorial on teratogens
and explained that he was not testifying for money: "All of my fees go to
the university," he told the jury. When Strauber's turn came to cross-examine, he asked Brent about his role in instigating the Thorp case and high-
lighted Brent's decision not to inquire about the Thorp household. As he
had done in his cross-examination of Jones, Strauber asked—and was
forced to withdraw—insinuating questions about Candance Thorp's history, including, "Do you have any information about any period of time in
which Mrs. Thorp had left home and was living on the street prior to the
pregnancy with Michael?"[20]

During redirect examination, Epstein tried to neutralize Strauber's queries by giving Brent the opportunity to explain his motives. Using the witness box as his platform, Brent told how he hoped to educate the public "about the dangers of alcohol, the fact that it's addictive, the fact that it causes birth defects."Litigation, he continued, is sometimes "the last resort to solve a problem." Later he added a statement about the need for politicians and government agencies to get the message out that alcohol was "addicting and that it can harm the embryo." Strauber was not about to let Brent leave the stage after this dramatic monologue. In his re-cross-examination he turned jurors' attention back to the Thorp household, asking Brent whether he had seen the records kept by CPS as well as Michael's medical records. After objections, the judge halted this line of questioning and Brent left the stand.[21]

The Thorps and Beam

Act two of the courtroom drama featured testimony from Jim Beam CEO Barry Berish and from the Thorps. Berish's testimony, taken under oath at a deposition, was read to the jury because the rules of evidence say that when employees of a company are being sued outside the jurisdiction of where they live or work, they do not have to appear at trial and their deposition can be read into evidence. Epstein needed Berish's testimony to establish the charge of negligence, and he quickly got to the heart of the matter. He asked whether Jim Beam tested its product on fetuses or asked anyone else to conduct such testing. He inquired as to whether Jim Beam monitored the scientific literature. To each question, Berish answered no. Epstein then sought to show that the company knew of the risks because it participated in the Licensed Beverage Information Council (LBIC) program to distribute information to public school districts, including a poster that said: "Drinking can harm your unborn baby. It can cause heart defects, mental retardation and other problems. These birth defects can't be changed, but they can be prevented. No one is sure how much alcohol it takes to harm an unborn baby." With this statement, Epstein tried to fashion a noose around Berish and hang him. Berish, however, proved unwilling to be choked. He agreed that pregnant women should ask their doctors about drinking; he would not agree with the claim that "drinking could harm your unborn baby" or with the statement that "no one is sure how much alcohol it takes to harm an unborn baby." Berish conceded little more than the fact that women needed to see doctors to have healthy babies. So, Epstein asked, why did the Distilled Spirits Council—in which Berish played a prominent role as a member of the executive committee and as vice chairman—sign on to the educational campaign? Berish escaped again, answering that they had not gone over the educational materials "sentence by sentence."[22]

Berish appeared to have been well prepared for the grilling he received. He gave little ground in his testimony, refusing even to concede the validity of the surgeon general's statement about alcohol and pregnancy. He sparred with Epstein over the meaning of survey data about women's knowledge of the risks of drinking during pregnancy. But when Epstein returned to the question of labels, Berish seemed to be trapped. Asked if Jim Beam regarded the health of its customers as "sacrosanct," Berish answered, "Absolutely." Reaching a crescendo, Epstein forced Berish to admit that he did not believe in FAS. Moreover, Berish explained that he would not change his mind about FAS no matter what the surgeon general, the AMA, the CDC, the March of Dimes, the Department of Health and Human Services, the NIAAA, and every pediatrics textbook written in the last ten years had to say.[23]

Having shown the jury Berish's stubborn refusal to admit that alcohol could harm an unborn child and the company's unwillingness to warn customers despite the position taken by experts, Epstein set the stage for the entrance of two people whose testimony would show the terrible results of that decision: Candance and Harold Thorp.

Harold spent a relatively short time on the witness stand, and his testimony proved both a help and a hindrance to his son's case. He testified that his wife drank Jim Beam during her pregnancy and said that when he learned about his son's condition, he was devastated. He had not heard of FAS, but, he assured the jury, had he been warned by a label, "There would have been no drinking in my home." He was certain that Candance would have stopped drinking because she was a caring person who loved her children, but he conceded that both he and Candance were alcoholics at the time Michael was conceived. Harold told the jury about holding a steady job for thirty years and "taking the cure," although he admitted to earlier cures and relapses. Guided by his attorney, he appeared as a loving father, describing how he cared for his son and worried about his future. During cross-examination, Harold was forced to discuss how he and Candance met, began living together, and conceived Michael in the space of a few weeks. Looking at Harold, the jury could undoubtedly tell he was far older—in fact, some 28 years older—than his wife. And they learned from his cross-examination that this loving father of Michael had three children from an earlier marriage whom he no longer saw.[24]

Drinking emerged as central to Harold and Candance Thorp's life together and apart. They drank despite having been told not to and despite its damaging physical effects. Harold conceded that it was hard on his liver, just as he admitted smoking despite having been told not to and suffering from coronary problems that had led him to have bypass surgery. Candance smoked too—a pack a day—and she drank throughout her pregnancy. Harold admitted that he sometimes came home from work and found her drunk. After Michael was born, Harold told jurors, Candance sometimes took her first drink at seven in the morning, before he had left for work. Even more devastating admissions followed. Candance spent a week in the hospital after drinking rubbing alcohol, leaving Michael in the care of his eighteen-year-old stepsister. After four weeks of alcoholism treatment at an inpatient facility, Candance returned home and soon relapsed. With Harold in the hospital for a gallbladder operation, CPS assumed custody of Michael and put him in foster care.

Candance Thorp's own testimony did little to polish her badly tarnished image. She admitted being an alcoholic and that she sometimes denied her condition. She acknowledged Michael's stay in a foster home during a rough period in her life. But, she argued, the experience straightened her out, and she had come out of treatment and gone to AA daily and to counseling. She had visited Michael regularly and eventually he had been returned to her care. Sympathetic jurors might have admired her for overcoming her problems, especially when she described how she helped her child cope with multiple disabilities, including profound behavioral and developmental problems.

Attorney Kandice Tezak led Mrs. Thorp through a long list of doctors she had seen, not one of whom told her not to drink when pregnant. These included a chiropractor she saw for back problems, a doctor she saw for her second pregnancy, a family physician she saw for a false pregnancy, a doctor she saw when she learned she was pregnant with Michael, and the obstetrician she saw at the end of her pregnancy. If any one of them had warned her, she assured the jury, she would have stopped drinking, just as she followed their advice on other matters. Setting the jury up for testimony they were bound to hear in cross-examination and from other witnesses, Tezak asked her about a lecture she had heard during her alcoholism treatment that included a discussion of FAS. Candance replied that she had attended every lecture; if she had missed that one portion, it was because of a visit to the restroom, a quick run for some coffee, or perhaps a late arrival.

Tezak worked hard to neutralize some of the damaging testimony that would come during the cross-examination. She asked Candance about the incident in which she allegedly drank rubbing alcohol, and Candance explained that she had not consumed it deliberately. She told the jury that it must have spilled into her drink when she was sterilizing a thermometer in order to take Michael's temperature. As for her earlier failures to stop drinking, she admitted to relapses, including one within the past six months.

When his turn came, Strauber trod cautiously. He avoided addressing Mrs. Thorp in a hostile manner that might provoke the jurors' sympathy. Instead, he approached her with a tone of incredulity. He asked her to detail her drinking and her hospitalization for alcoholism and made her report a second time on her relapses. Apparently the defense had arranged for a private detective to follow Mrs. Thorp. In the middle of the cross-examination, Strauber asked, "Haven't you been sort of stopping into a place quickly, ordering two doubles, drinking it down quickly and running out?" Candance's immediate reply was that she did not recall whether she was ordering doubles or singles. Her answer probably didn't impress the jurors. Subsequently she admitted that neither she nor her husband continued to attend AA meetings.[25]

The details of Candance Thorp's alcoholism must have left jurors wondering whether a message on a bottle would have been sufficient to get her to stop drinking. But even if they were to conclude that it would have, Jim Beam's attorneys had another escape route. Strauber got Mrs. Thorp to admit that she drank beer in taverns and in bars she consumed bar bourbon, for which no manufacturer was identified. (In Washington State, taverns serve beer only; bars serve hard liquor as well as beer). How, then, could one manufacturer be held responsible? Another weapon in the defense arsenal was Candance's selective memory. When questioned by her own attorneys, she recalled with certainty that no doctor had ever told her not to drink during pregnancy. When questioned by the defense, she found herself unable to recall that she had been thrown out of her sister's house for drinking beer.

The defense could not probe into Candance's drinking for too long, because it might underscore the assertion that Michael's problems stemmed from his exposure to alcohol in utero. Much of the cross-examination therefore focused on Mrs. Thorp's maternal lapses. Strauber forced her to tell how she had given custody of her daughter Rebecca, who was adopted by her sister. He asked her whether, during her pregnancy with Michael, she had been under a court order to participate in counseling. Candance claimed not to recall the agreement, only to have Strauber hand her the document and force her to acknowledge her signature. Having caught her in one falsehood, Strauber followed with a barrage of other questions designed to undermine her veracity. Could she recall hearing from the social worker overseeing the adoption of her daughter that she should not be drinking while pregnant? No, she explained, as an alcoholic, she was in denial about her drinking, so she would not have listened to such advice. Strauber explored the question of labeling indirectly, forcing Mrs. Thorp to admit that she smoked and also knew there were messages on packages of cigarettes. She could not recall what they said.

The plaintiff's case seemed to be unraveling. During a brief redirect examination, Mrs. Thorp asserted once again that a label on a bottle of Jim Beam would have made a difference in her drinking. Asked whether an alcoholic could stop because of a warning label, Candance answered firmly that had she seen the label she would have sought help and quit drinking. As the first week of the trial ended, the jury went off to spend the weekend pondering the credibility of this claim.

On Monday, the jury heard from Sterling Clarren, Michael's doctor, who explained that Michael's problems resulted from his mother's drinking during pregnancy. Strauber attempted to impeach him during cross-examination, quizzing Clarren about his diagnostic work, making him explain to the jury how he had been the intermediary between Epstein and the Thorps, and putting him on the spot by quoting a statement he had made on television: "Do I think that putting a warning label on a bottle of liquor, or putting a poster in a liquor store will help an alcoholic get treatment by itself? No, I don't." In redirect examination Epstein gave Clarren the opportunity to clarify his position on labeling; he told the jury that warning signs and labels were not sufficient.[26]

The next phase of the trial focused on Michael's injury and his need for compensation. Wendy Marlowe, a clinical neuropsychologist specializing in the evaluation of people with disabilities described seven meetings with Michael during which she had assessed his needs and tested his cognitive, motor, adaptive, and personality development. She had developed a "life-care plan" for him, listing the services he would require, including medical and dental care, training for his parents, special schooling and summer camps, travel and transportation services, and special equipment. During cross-examination Marlowe deftly deflected hostile questions about the substance of her conclusions. Yet she could not defend Mrs. Thorp, who came under indirect attack. The defense asked her about the CPS files, about Candance's admission into the county detox unit, and about the condition of Thorp home, which was described in the records as "extremely unsanitary and dirty." At one point, Strauber read from a report by Ann Streissguth, to whom Michael was referred to for an evaluation. "Mrs. Thorp has been drinking a fifth of hard liquor a day for many years, but during her pregnancy with Michael decreased to about half a fifth a day." The next few witnesses also answered questions about Michael's long-term needs. A certified rehabilitation counselor estimated that Michael's lifetime care would cost $2.7 million; a forensic economist estimated Michael's lifetime earnings loss because of his FAS to be $1.3 million.[27]

The plaintiff's case concluded with an effort to show that Candance Thorp had not been warned against drinking during pregnancy. Witnesses included the physician who had provided her prenatal care, an alcoholism counselor who had worked with her when she was in treatment, and the chiropractor who had treated her for low-back pain. During cross-examination of these witnesses, the defense took the opportunity to remind the jury that Candance was an alcoholic who failed to stop drinking despite many attempts to help her to do so.

After eight days of testimony, the plaintiff's attorneys rested their case and the defense moved for a directed verdict—a request that the judge order the jury to return a verdict in its favor because the plaintiff had failed to prove his case. Strauber told the court that it had been shown during cross-examination that Mrs. Thorp had been warned and that the testimony indicated a label would not have been an adequate warning. Furthermore, he charged that the burden of establishing that Jim Beam bourbon had caused Michael Thorp's FAS, as opposed to many other alcoholic beverages Candance had consumed, had not been met. Nor, he argued, had alcohol been shown to be the cause of Michael's "alleged defects." Judge Dimmick took these claims seriously and subsequently reported that she had nearly granted summary judgment for the defense. She did not, she explained, because factual issues remained for the jury to consider.[28]

Defending Jim Beam

From defense attorneys the jury heard a simple story about bad mothering and its consequences, wrapped up in a more complicated narrative about alcoholism. Three witnesses appeared at the opening of the defense to rebut Candance Thorp's claim that she had never been told not to drink when pregnant. Ila Pound, a registered nurse at the clinic where Mrs. Thorp had received prenatal care, described giving her a pamphlet on alcohol and pregnancy and discussing the matter with her. During cross-examination, Pound admitting having no proof that Candance had received or read the pamphlet. Eighty-one-year-old physician Chris Reynolds, the medical director of the alcoholism treatment center where Candance had received inpatient care, testified next. He described the one-hour lecture he delivered to all patients that included a discussion of FAS. Under cross-examination he admitted that he had never met with her individually, that the lecture covered a lot of information in a short time, and that he did not take attendance. Still, the elderly physician may have made a credible case to jurors.

Next on the witness stand was the obstetrician who had delivered Michael. He reported that Mrs. Thorp had never told him about her inpatient detoxification and that she had denied both smoking and drinking. The defense pushed him to explore other possible reasons for Michael's problems, including Candance's anemia, her age at the time she delivered Michael—thirty-four—and the speed of the delivery. He did not provide any information helpful to their case and on cross-examination stated flatly that Michael had been born at term and had not been undernourished.

Another aspect of the defense case involved Jim Beam's decision not to place a warning on its bottles. To show the company's good-faith efforts to encourage women to get information from doctors, the executive director of the National Liquor Stores Association and chairman of the Licensed Beverage Information Council, John Burcham, Jr., detailed the industry's information campaign. He described announcements in magazines, posters in health clinics, and public service messages on television and radio, and mentioned the joint programs run in cooperation with the March of Dimes, the American Council on Alcoholism, the National Urban League, and the federal government. The theme of the campaign, Burcham testified, was that "what you do makes a difference. You owe it to yourself and your unborn child to be informed about drinking and pregnancy, and not to drink abusively or excessively. You should consult your physician about health matters concerning your pregnancy."[29]

Epstein's cross-examination illuminated several points favorable to the plaintiff. Although Burcham proved happy to recite the information on the posters, like Jim Beam CEO Berish, he would not be pinned down about the content. Asked whether he would agree that drinking could harm an unborn baby, Burcham responded that he was not an expert in the field. While the LBIC happily put posters in medical offices, Burcham acknowledged that they did not consider placing the posters in places where liquor was sold so that they could be read by other interested parties. This group would include, Epstein noted, "the fathers of children whose mothers were drinking." Epstein also forced Burcham to admit that most of the LBIC's educational efforts were one-time affairs rather than ongoing programs. Asked whether the LBIC prohibited individual member companies from undertaking educational efforts on their own, Burcham said no. By implication, Jim Beam would have been free to put a warning label on its bottles. Finally, Epstein forced Burcham to admit that he had no knowledge of where the posters went or who heard the announcements. The efforts of the LBIC, Epstein's cross-examination made evident, did not meet the obligation to inform Candance of the risks she took by drinking during her pregnancy.[30]

During its redirect examination the defense reminded jurors that the federal government regulated the alcoholic beverage industry and that, had it thought warning labels necessary, it would have mandated them. Left unspoken, because of a ruling by the judge, was the fact such labels were slated to appear later that year.

Bad Mothering

Strauber had refrained from badgering Mrs. Thorp when she was on the witness stand, but when his own witnesses sat before the jury, he used them to pummel her. Kathleen Gillis, a "receiving mother" who took care of children immediately after they had been taken from their homes by CPS, had taken Michael into her care for about three weeks. She made several points for the defense, telling jurors that Michael had arrived at her home smelling "pretty bad" from cigarettes and had been "extremely thin, real pale." At first, Gillis reported, Michael cried so much when people came near him that she called him "my little coyote," but later he cried less, got used to people, and gained weight. She found him "no more active" than other children she had cared for in the past, implying that he was a normal child who had thrived under her care but suffered when living with his alcoholic parents. The logic of this assumption would have been hard for the jury to question. If the state felt it necessary to remove Michael from his alcoholic mother, how could jurors discount Gillis's testimony that in a different setting—a home with a loving, sober woman—he behaved normally? Under cross-examination, Gillis acknowledged she was neither an expert in child development nor a physician, but this may not have discredited her testimony.[31]

The next day, the defense paraded five witnesses before the jury and sifted through a number of topics. Two of those testifying addressed medical issues. A physician who had treated Michael for an ear infection discussed his notes concerning problems with Michael's height, weight, and growth. A pediatric dentist reported on his "baby bottle mouth"—cavities resulting from his being left in a crib to fall asleep with a bottle in his mouth. The plaintiff's attorney jumped on several openings in her testimony, getting her to admit during cross-examination that the problem was a common one and using the testimony to remind the jury of Michael's special needs.

With another witness, the case turned back to a critical question—was Jim Beam at fault for failing to warn Candance Thorp about drinking during pregnancy? The defense asserted that the public already knew about the risks of drinking during pregnancy, calling psychology professor George Cvetkovich to testify about the level of awareness in the local community. During cross-examination plaintiff's attorney Kindley deflated many of Cvetkovich's assertions, forcing him to review the findings from a medical group showing that women could be given help to modify their drinking and therefore needed to know about the risks. The attorney also peppered him with data that contradicted his findings, forcing him to try to account for the variations and to acknowledge that he knew little about the specifics of the surveys he interpreted. The attorney then asked him whether warnings would be of use to husbands and fathers as well as to women who consumed alcohol. Ultimately, Cvetkovich made two key concessions: that the public was entitled to know that alcohol caused birth defects and that labels on beverages would provide information at the time of purchase and at the time of use.[32]

Michael's lawyers vigorously attacked Jim Beam throughout their cross-examination of defense witnesses. Directly and indirectly they asked repeatedly why the company had not taken the simple step of putting warning labels on its products. If Jim Beam was committed to its consumers and had been a willing participant in an educational campaign, why did it refrain from this measure? Why would it assume that pregnant women and those who drank with them would not be warned by a label? The plaintiff's attorneys made the case that it was fundamentally unfair to conceal information about the risks of drinking during pregnancy. Trying to shift the spotlight away from Candance Thorp and onto a large population of women who were or might one day be pregnant, the plaintiffs argued for the right of babies to be born healthy.

Unfortunately for the plaintiff's case, the question of Candance Thorp's behavior often overshadowed the decisions made at Jim Beam corporate headquarters. A bartender who had known Harold Thorp for eight years and Candance for five described how she would take a cab or walk to his bar, sometimes in the morning, at other times in the late afternoon or evening, and then drink three or four beers in a thirty- to forty-five-minute period. At one point, he told the jury, another customer told Candance Thorp it "wasn't good to be drinking alcohol when she was pregnant." He reported that she "felt a little insulted, and finished her beer and left." His testimony did little to bolster defense claims, since more credible witnesses had already described her alcoholism and the fact that she drank other beverages besides Jim Beam. Nonetheless, it kept those issues before the jury.[33]

Perhaps the most effective witness for impeaching Candance Thorp as a "bad mother" was her own mother, Mary Maxine Tolle. Testifying by deposition, she administered the coup de grace to her grandson's case, describing Candance's alcoholism and the family's decision to call CPS to care for Michael. At several points in her testimony Tolle made devastating comments, including the statement that "if Candance was not going to provide a home for him [Michael], I wanted him to be in a good adoptive family." Although she conceded that Candance and Harold Thorp were "very good, loving, tender parents with Michael," the last line of her deposition brought the focus back to earlier years when Candance had been drinking: Tolle concluded, "You can't be a parent when you're off drinking." If Candance Thorp's own mother had felt compelled to call in state authorities, how could Candance claim that all of Michael's problems were the fault of Jim Beam?[34]

Tolle's deposition contained a few scattered remarks helpful to the plaintiff's case. She depicted Michael as "extremely hyperactive," a characterization that bolstered the claim that Michael was a damaged child. Furthermore, she remarked that she served Jim Beam to Candance when she visited and that she and her current husband also drank Jim Beam bourbon. The plaintiff's attorneys tried to impeach Tolle during cross-examination by suggesting that she too was an alcoholic. She denied this repeatedly, although she did admit that her first husband was an alcoholic who had quit drinking nine years earlier.

The Seattle jurors confronted issues being debated by many Americans in the late 1980s. To what extent were pregnant women responsible for actively promoting the health of their fetuses? Did women assume special obligations because of their impending motherhood? And if pregnant women used drugs or alcohol, should they blame the product or themselves for the problems their children later experienced? Where did the fault lie—with bad mothers or bad substances? The lawsuit did not attempt to answer these questions. Jurors were asked to assess the merits of the claims made on Michael's behalf and to determine whether his mother or his mother's favorite beverage had caused his developmental difficulties. But the six individuals sitting in judgment could not have been unaware that the issues raised in the case reached beyond the Thorps and Jim Beam.

Last Witnesses

The trial concluded as it began: with the testimony of an expert. At the opening of the trial, the jury had heard Kenneth Lyons Jones explain Michael's problems and attribute them to his mother's drinking during pregnancy. At the close, jurors heard from an expert who offered an entirely different explanation. Janina Galler, a child psychiatrist and an expert in the growth and development of disadvantaged children, described Michael as a victim of his mother's malnutrition during pregnancy and his subsequent chaotic home life. Galler had studied the effects of early malnutrition on children's behavioral development by following a group of children in Barbados who were malnourished in their first year of life. Compared with matched controls, these children had significantly more neurological problems, lower IQs, poorer social skills, and more attention deficits. When she looked at Michael, she saw the same problems and presumed the same causes.[35]

Galler's testimony clearly worried Epstein, and he demanded a voir dire to determine whether she would be raising collateral issues outside the bounds of the trial. From the questions he asked, it became clear that he hoped to keep the jurors from hearing about the problems of Michael's half siblings and to prevent Galler from testifying about her interpretation of school and CPS records. The judge overruled his objections, noting that since she had used those materials to make her judgments of Michael, she could testify about the records. With permission to examine their witness as they wished, the defense began.[36]

Galler's testimony moved swiftly from a recitation of her credentials to her conclusions about Michael's problems and their cause. A chart was shown to the jury as Galler summarized the factors shaping Michael's life. He had had an inadequate nutritional environment in utero, she concluded, because during her pregnancy Candance Thorp had suffered from iron, folate, and vitamin B-12 deficiencies, had experienced extreme variations in weight, and had conceded that when she was drinking, she did not eat. Galler also dissected Michael's emotional difficulties, recounting the many complaints to CPS, Candance's absence from home during her hospitalization for alcohol detoxification, and instances in which Candance drank until passing out. Despite the efforts of the plaintiffs to block Galler's testimony about the similarities between Michael and his half siblings, the judge allowed her to proceed, and she told the court about his resemblance to his half sister Rebecca. Both suffered from delayed speech, developmental delays, and dental problems attributed to abuse and neglect. Both had been diagnosed as hyperactive and having attention deficit disorder. Rebecca had grown out of many of her problems under the care of her adoptive mother, although other difficulties, such as a short attention span, remained. Michael too, Galler would later testify, improved when he lived away from his family in a "warm foster home setting." Galler deemed Michael's sociability abnormal for a child of his age, explaining that "indiscriminate sociability is probably the most characteristic behavioral feature of child abuse and child neglect." His short stature and low average IQ, she declared, mirrored his parents' characteristics and were not caused by FAS. Finally, she let the jury know that Michael's developmental delays could also be linked to the fact that his mother did not take him to the early-intervention program to which he had been assigned. He was absent 39 percent of the time, she reported.[37]

Had Galler stood up and pointed an accusatory finger at Mrs. Thorp, saying, "She destroyed this child," it would have been a more dramatic gesture but probably no more effective than the case she built by tossing detail after detail onto a rapidly growing stack of evidence. In the closing moments of her direct testimony, she offered one last, indelible anecdote. While examining Michael in her office, she had asked his parents about taking a break so he could have something to eat. They told her he wouldn't be interested, but when she then offered him cookies, he "wolfed" down half of four or five of them, she said (behavior she described as typical of a younger child), and also drank some milk. The court recessed for lunch, with the jurors left to ponder a family that did not think to offer food to a hungry child. The local paper summed up her testimony in its headline, "Doctor Blames Boy's Bad Home, Not Alcohol."[38]

Epstein faced an uphill battle to discredit Galler's testimony and immediately went on the offensive. He forced her to admit she knew nothing about teratology or genetics and that she rejected altogether the FAS diagnosis. Epstein aimed to show the jury that she had come to Seattle expressly to reject the diagnosis given to Michael by experts and that she lacked any knowledge of alcohol-related birth defects. He deluged her with questions designed to demonstrate her lack of knowledge about physical anomalies, dysmorphology, and alcohol teratogenesis. Early in the trial, the defense had forced witnesses for the plaintiff to admit they had not examined the records of Michael's siblings. Now the tables turned, and Galler was forced to concede she had not conducted a physical examination of Michael.

The judge interrupted the cross-examination of Galler to allow testimony from another defense witness who was not available at any other time. The timing was perfect for the defense because the witness, Kathryn Vengler, a social worker with CPS, brought the case back to the topic of Candance Thorp's problems. Vengler testified about the period when Rebecca lived as a temporary ward of the state. She did not discuss why Rebecca had been taken from her mother's custody. Instead, her testimony centered on a key fact argued by the defense: Candance's signature on a court order requiring her to participate in alcoholism counseling. In getting to the issue, references were made to the period when Candance's whereabouts had been unknown and Rebecca's case had gone to the Juvenile Court. Vengler's testimony also raised a question featured in earlier testimony—whether Candance had been warned against drinking during her pregnancy. Vengler testified that she had discussed with Mrs. Thorp her concerns about her fetus and recalled that during that conversation she "was nodding as though she was already aware of this." Vengler also stated that Candance told her that the doctor had discussed this with her.[39]

If the jury believed Vengler, then Mrs. Thorp's claim that she drank because Jim Beam had not warned her not to—and no one else had either—would evaporate. During cross-examination Epstein forced Vengler to concede that the bulk of her conversation with Candance Thorp had concerned Rebecca rather than drinking. However, in replying to his questions, Vengler found another opportunity to put Candance's past into the record. She recalled reminding her that she had "lost two other children as a result of drinking," and that unless she stopped drinking, it would happen a third time.[40]

The next day Galler returned to court and Epstein continued his effort to discredit her, using as ammunition statements in her deposition and her unwillingness to acknowledge the existence of FAS, despite its recognition by numerous government and medical groups. Epstein worked hard to undermine Galler's authority so that the jury could comfortably discard her conclusions. The defense attorneys must have felt satisfied that he had failed in this mission, because they declined the opportunity for a redirect examination. When Epstein's questioning ended, the defense rested its case.

Three rebuttal witnesses for the plaintiff appeared at the close of the case. A seventy-four-year-old waitress denied having discussed drinking during pregnancy with Candance Thorp and reported that an investigator from Jim Beam had come to her home and asked her questions regarding Candance. A former social worker, Linda Thompson, told jurors that she had arranged Michael's referral to the Children's Orthopedic Hospital because, she said, "he didn't look right." His parents, she told jurors, were "absolutely astonished" when he was diagnosed with FAS. Thompson had overseen Michael's placement in foster care and told the court that Candance and Harold had visited regularly and regained custody, describing them as "wonderful." Her testimony offered a vastly different picture of the Thorps than that painted by other witnesses, and the defense left her opinions unchallenged. Instead, during cross-examination, it focused on Candance's own admission to the hospital, her failure to adhere to some of her treatment regimen, and her failure to bring Michael in regularly for early-intervention treatment.

Finally, to rebut the claim that the alcoholic beverage industry had succeeded in warning women, the plaintiff's attorney called the Washington, D.C., representative for the National Council on Alcoholism, who termed the LBIC an advocacy group. Its message, she charged, was unclear because the notion of drinking moderately left open to individual interpretation just how much drinking was "moderate."[41]

The final few witnesses came and went quickly. Then the testimony phase ended. Once again the defense made a final request for a directed verdict, and once again the judge denied it. The case would go to the jury.

Instructing the Jury

The last courtroom firefight took place out of range of the jury, when the lawyers met with the judge to determine the wording of the jury instructions. The two sides had by this point been fighting for several years over issues relating to the discovery of evidence, the deposition of witnesses, and whether the various claims merited consideration by a jury, and throughout the trial they had continued their debates before the judge, with the jury out of the room. Now they had one last, decisive battle. Each scored a few points. The judge ruled that Candance Thorp did not have an affirmative duty to go out and inform herself about the risks of drinking during pregnancy. However, she rejected Epstein's argument that Jim Beam had a duty to warn Harold as well as Candance, because he often purchased the product for her.[42]

Judge Dimmick's instructions to the jurors began with a review of their duties and the rules of law to be applied. She gave them a series of questions to consider in sequence. Did Jim Beam have a duty to warn or instruct consumers about the risk of birth defects? Did it breach its duty to warn? Did Michael Thorp sustain injuries? Were those birth defects caused by Jim Beam's product, and were they proximately caused by the company's failure to warn and instruct? The jury needed to answer yes to each of these four questions in order to render a verdict for Michael Thorp. If it did find in his favor, then it could determine the amount of money he would receive as a damage award.[43]

When the judge concluded, Epstein offered his closing arguments, reviewing the pain and suffering that Michael would endure throughout his life because of his FAS. Confronting the problem of Mrs. Thorp's character, he reminded jurors that "alcoholics don't abandon their rights." Michael, he told them, had been "adrift in a sea of alcohol," yet Jim Beam had refused to "throw him a life line of information" and consequently he had drowned. Finally, Epstein told jurors that by awarding damages to Michael they would be sending "a message of life."[44]

Strauber's closing arguments echoed his opening statement: a warning label would have made no difference to Candance Thorp, Jim Beam had no duty to warn because knowledge of the risks of drinking were widespread, and, regardless of that, Michael's problems stemmed from his heredity and his upbringing, which "sadly left a lot to be desired." Finally, he reviewed Mrs. Thorp's drinking history and the elements of her testimony that had been refuted by other witnesses, asking who should be believed. A newspaper account of the trial pointed to two of Strauber's most compelling arguments: his statement that "everybody knows that half a bottle a day is just awful for you," and his assertion that if Candance Thorp knew that drinking at that level could cause her death, then she must have known it could cause harm to her fetus.[45]

In a brief reply, attorneys for the plaintiffs reminded jurors of CEO Berish's testimony that "no matter what, he wouldn't have put a warning label on, he wouldn't have got the words to his customers." And they sounded a patriotic theme with a stirring statement about the right of Americans "to make informed choices," which Jim Beam did not allow its consumers to do. Painting Berish as the epitome of the selfish corporate executive—a man who needlessly risked the health of innocent children—would work if the jury did not find that another person was to blame for Michael's problems—his mother.[46]

Judgments and Decisions

Long before the jury returned with its verdict, the media tried and convicted Candance Thorp. Editorial cartoonists scoffed at her claim that she had been given no warning of drinking's danger to a fetus, and that had there been one, she would not have had anything to drink. One cartoon showed Candance on the witness stand with her nose growing like Pinocchio's as she stated, "Your Honor, I was never warned about drinking when I was pregnant." A woman in the jury box was shown thinking, "I thought birth defects affected the child . . ." The *Seattle Post-Intelligencer* ran a cartoon mocking the demand for a warning label. A sign on a bottle read, "Warning: Drinking ½ bottle of this daily may harm your fetus"; another sign, on a building, read, "Warning: Jumping off the roof may harm

Figure 7. Milt Priggee cartoon about the Thorp trial, 1989. Used with permission.

your fetus"; and throughout the picture were other items carrying similar warnings.[47]

Others mocked the case as an example of litigation mania. Conservative columnist Charles Krauthammer took aim at Candance Thorp for "going chutzpah one better" by harming her child and then "asking for reparations." Several letters sent to the *Los Angeles Times* chastised the Thorps for failing to take responsibility for their choices and for lacking common sense; one suggested that they be charged with reckless child endangerment, another correspondent wrote, "I pray that the courts have the good sense to take that poor little boy away from them for good."[48]

The jury took longer to issue its finding but ultimately reached the same conclusion as the cartoonists and critics. After several days of deliberation the jurors found in favor of the distiller. In interviews, three jurors described the deliberations. The forewoman, Lynn Arthur, told reporters that they had focused on the question of whether a label would have made a difference in light of Candance Thorp's alcoholism. Another juror was widely quoted as saying, "Everybody knew that a label would not have done any good." Mrs. Thorp, she seemed to say, was caught in the grip of alcoholism, but she could not escape from the presumed responsibilities of pregnant women. The fact that she blamed Jim Beam for Michael's problems had seemed manifestly unfair to jurors, in part because she had done the drinking and in part because she drank so many different things. As a juror remarked, she "could have sued everyone." When reporters asked why the decision had taken so long, they were told there had been an immediate unanimous decision in favor of Beam, followed by a review of the evidence to be certain the initial judgment was correct.[49]

While defense attorney Strauber had worried that Michael's appearance would sway the jury's sympathy, jurors reported a far different response, suggesting, as one said, that the decision to have him appear had been a tactical mistake. One juror said they did not believe he was disabled; another noted that he looked like a normal child and did not seem to have birth defects. Their statements suggest that the lawyers' hard-fought battles over the testimony of various experts had been in vain; the medical witnesses ultimately had little influence on the decision. The panel evidently believed that alcohol caused birth defects, as Jones, Brent, and Clarren had argued, and they also believed, as Galler testified, that Michael had a bad home life. More critically, they never bothered to consider whether Jim Beam was the cause of his problems because they concluded that Candance Thorp had been warned against drinking during pregnancy. Possibly they were inclined to reach this conclusion because several of them had heard or read such warnings themselves. One reported learning about FAS from the March of Dimes; another, a twenty-two-year-old new mother, had been told by her doctor; and a third remembered reading about it in the newspaper and hearing about it on television.[50]

Trying to salvage something from the loss, Epstein initially stated that the case set no precedent and that the litigation itself "created an awareness in the public that, [sic] if it saves one child, it will all be worth it." In the immediate aftermath of the trial he refused to answer questions regarding an appeal. Nor would he answer questions about his intention to pursue the other cases that had yet to go to trial. Eventually Epstein withdrew the other cases. As *Thorp v. Beam* revealed, it was far too easy for the defense to put the mother on trial.[51]

The author of a law review article pondered whether an ideal plaintiff could be found—possibly a pregnant woman who ate her meals in restaurants, "splitting a pitcher of beer with a companion and thus drinking two or three eight-ounce glasses at lunch" and then doing the same at dinner.

These women wouldn't see a warning label. This scenario was improbable, however. The mothers of FAS children were not drinking businesswomen. They were, typically, long-term, chronic alcoholics who would easily be seen by jurors as bad mothers who, like Candance Thorp, wanted to blame alcohol manufacturers for their drinking.

As the *Thorp* case suggested, the problem of FAS was not going to go away when labels appeared on bottles. Alcoholic women needed a lot of help if they were to stop drinking, and their condition needed to be understood as chronic and relapsing rather than as something that could be resolved easily or through a single course of treatment. Moreover, while the *Thorp* trial focused attention on the mothers of children diagnosed with FAS, later court cases would shine a light on the individuals who suffered throughout their lives because of their FAS and who, because of their damaged minds, sometimes brought great suffering to others.[52]

8

◆◆

"An Argument That Goes Back to the Womb": Adoptions, Courtrooms, and FAS Today

In 1992, nineteen years after introducing Americans to Melissa and to FAS, Kenneth Lyons Jones appeared on the late-night television news show *Nightline* to plead for the life of an adult with FAS: double-murderer Robert Alton Harris. The show opened with a teaser by host Ted Koppel, who spoke of "an argument that goes back to the womb" and promised viewers a portrait of a killer who was "brain damaged as a fetus, abused as a child." This was followed by a film clip of Jones, taken from part of a video document supporting clemency for Harris that had been sent to the governor of California, Pete Wilson. Jones is heard to say of Harris, "His mother was a chronic alcoholic."[1]

The role of FAS in the Harris case signaled the beginning of a new debate over its meaning. Medical experts increasingly defined FAS as a birth defect of the mind. Using new scientific tools, they sought to elucidate how prenatal exposure to alcohol damaged portions of the brain in ways that left individuals incapable of anticipating the consequences of their actions. However, such assertions about the effects of alcohol on the developing brain often met with skepticism in the criminal courtroom. When social order rests on personal responsibility, only a very few succeed in being excused for their actions, and only when they demonstrate they lack free will. In the case of FAS, judges and juries accepted FAS as a medical diagnosis but never fully embraced its implications. Accepting what scientists were beginning to say about FAS would have meant ceding critical sociocultural ground.

Over the course of three decades FAS became first a diagnosis, then a public health problem, and next a morality tale about mothers. Now FAS would also be identified as an "abuse excuse," emblematic of the public's concern about individual responsibility and moral order, and thus it would be, in some settings, demedicalized.

Robert Alton Harris: The Child and the Man

Jones's involvement in the Harris case began when a lawyer working on Harris's death penalty appeal contacted him and sent him Harris's file. Jones opened it and saw a picture of Harris at age six. An associate who, unlike Jones, was a strong advocate for the death penalty, took a look and said, "Yes, he's got the FAS." Jones went to San Quentin State Prison, examined Harris on death row, and found that, among other features of FAS, Harris had an IQ of 61, which marked him as mentally retarded.[2]

Harris had committed a gruesome crime. While on parole for a voluntary manslaughter conviction, he kidnapped and shot two San Diego teenagers. As he watched them die, he ate the hamburgers they had just purchased. Particularly galling to the relatives of the murdered young men was that, as Harris's execution date approached, death penalty opponents rallied to save him by portraying him as a victim. The father of one of the teens, a police officer who had been the first to arrive at the crime scene and find his murdered son, was affronted when Nobel Peace Prize–winner Mother Teresa prayed for Harris and asked for clemency but did not reach out to the victims' families.[3]

Those trying to halt Harris's execution delved into his past, searching for evidence that might lead the governor to change his sentence from death to life in prison. Investigators in death penalty mitigation efforts typically construct psychobiographical accounts of the defendants' lives, detailing incidents of childhood trauma; the effects of poverty, neglect, and abuse; brutalizing encounters during earlier incarcerations in juvenile facilities; and addiction to alcohol and drugs. In many instances, careful probing reveals undiagnosed cases of FAS. That finding is then added to the list of mitigating factors, or is used in a claim of ineffective assistance of counsel when the diagnosis was not raised during trial.[4]

Investigators found much to suggest that Harris was mentally impaired. His mother, a chronic alcoholic, had served a prison term for a bank robbery committed when she was drunk. Family members reported that Harris's father had beaten him frequently, in part because he thought that Harris had been conceived in an extramarital affair. The beatings had resulted in brain damage. A newspaper story described Harris's premature birth as the result of his father's having kicked his pregnant mother, and mentioned a beating he received at fifteen months, when his father knocked him to the ground and tried to strangle him. Abandoned by his parents when he was fourteen, Harris had participated in a car theft that had landed him in prison. During his many subsequent incarcerations, Harris underwent seventeen psychological evaluations. At the age of seventeen he was said to be "a totally inadequate, institutionalized, emotionally disturbed individual." He was also found to have chronic schizophrenia, recurring hallucinations, and organic brain damage.[5]

Harris's attorneys argued that, as a result of the multiple assaults on his developing brain, he lacked the mental capacity to commit a premeditated murder. Additionally, they claimed that his initial psychiatric defense experts had done an inadequate job of presenting his condition and that he suffered from FAS. In the clemency video in which Jones appeared, another FAS expert, Ann Streissguth, testified about his condition. Most important, the video included a statement by Frank Newman, a retired California Supreme Court justice, who stated that he would not have voted to confirm Harris's death sentence if he had known about his condition and specifically his FAS. Newman's opinion was discussed on the *Nightline* broadcast.[6]

Pleas to spare Harris's life failed to move the governor, who met with both sides in the case, consulted legal and medical experts, and read up on FAS. Governor Wilson issued a lengthy statement deploring prenatal alcohol abuse as "nothing less than child abuse through the umbilical cord," and detailing his own efforts to combat and prevent substance abuse by pregnant women. Yet, he concluded, "as great as is my compassion for Robert Harris the child, I cannot excuse or forgive the choice made by Robert Harris the man." The clemency appeal foundered on Wilson's belief that "we must insist on the exercise of personal responsibility and restraint by those capable of exercising it. If we excuse those whose traumatic life experiences have injured them—but not deprived them of the capacity to exercise responsibility and restraint—we leave society dangerously at risk." FAS, Wilson seemed to say, had not diminished Harris's capacity to understand and control his impulses—a determination clearly at odds with that of the medical experts.[7]

Last-minute appeals to the Ninth Circuit U.S. Court of Appeals halted

Harris's execution for a brief time, but the U.S. Supreme Court lifted the stay. After a nearly "fourteen-year legal odyssey," Harris was executed on the morning of 21 April 1992, in the gas chamber. Harris was neither the first nor the last death-row inmate to use FAS as part of a clemency appeal. But his claim of having been a victim of prenatal alcohol exposure received significant public and media attention because of the horrific nature of his crime and because his execution was the first carried out in California since 1967.[8]

Criminals who claimed FAS in an attempt to win reduced sentences or clemency faced many obstacles. A characteristic of the syndrome is that impaired individuals sometimes have a verbal adeptness that conceals their inability to make sound and informed judgments or to understand cause and effect. In addition, adults with FAS often show no physical features of their heavy alcohol exposure in utero, having outgrown the "FAS face" that marked them as children. The claim that they suffered from invisible but nonetheless serious deficits was hard to prove to judges and juries accustomed to understanding birth defects as visible defects. Moreover, in the courtroom it proved hard to distinguish deviant behavior stemming from prenatal assaults on the developing brain, which prevented an individual from exercising free will, from behavior reflecting pathological childhood experiences that were considered potentially surmountable.[9]

Three jurors in the Harris case made this point in interviews conducted years after the trial. "We knew that [Harris's mother] drank during pregnancy," one of them told a reporter, adding, "There are lots of kids that have had bad upbringings, but they survive it, they don't go around killing." Two other jurors concurred, agreeing that Harris's childhood was miserable but not an excuse for his crimes. To them, the difference between Harris's alcoholic home and his alcohol exposure in the womb was indistinguishable, and neither excused his actions. On the night of Harris's execution, several callers to the show *Larry King Live* on CNN made the same point. One remarked, "I know too many people that have been abused and their lives are just fine."[10]

In the criminal courtroom the meaning of FAS was fluid rather than fixed. Sometimes experts argued for and jurors accepted FAS as a diagnosis of brain damage with resulting behavioral and cognitive consequences. Other times they perceived the claim as merely an effort to win sympathy for and reduce the punishment of hardened criminals. In the latter instances, FAS was demedicalized. This is not to say that FAS was purged from medical texts, nor does it imply that physicians surrendered responsibility for making the diagnosis and helping to frame its public meaning. Rather, the rejection of FAS as a mitigating factor cheapened medical authority, because while the diagnosis was accepted, the logical consequences of that diagnosis were ignored.

Diagnosis is power—the power to explain behavior and experiences. And the power of the FAS diagnosis and of those making the diagnosis was diluted when individuals said to have FAS were believed to be capable of exercising free will. Criminal law, as Judge T. Noonan, Jr., of the Ninth Circuit Court of Appeals wrote in a discussion of the Harris case, "depends on a belief in free will . . . If a human will is impaired, the human being cannot be fully responsible." For Harris and others to be judged legally responsible for their actions, medical arguments about the behavioral and cognitive effects of FAS had to be rejected. And in many cases they were.[11]

FAS as "Abuse Excuse"

By the 1990s FAS was coming under attack along with other courtroom claims of diminished culpability as part of a larger cultural critique of the nation's supposed decline in moral order. Conservatives lamented that "bad" people were being labeled "sick," which allowed them to evade responsibility for their actions, and they argued that diagnosis was undermining the rule of law. FAS and other suspect diagnoses began to be labeled "abuse excuses." The term was first used by popular commentators, cultural critics, and legal scholars. In 1994, for example, San Francisco journalist Rob Morse called diagnosis a "get-out-of-jail-free card," writing of his disgust with those who tried to escape blame for their actions by claiming tough childhoods or bad environments. He then announced his "low-life achievement awards" for the best excuses of the previous year. Number one was "Beavis & Butt-Head made me do it." The second: "I was abused as a child (optional: I had fetal alcohol syndrome)."[12]

A longer discourse on courtroom claims came from prominent attorney and Harvard Law School professor Alan Dershowitz. "Abuse excuses," he contended, were "a symptom of a general abdication of responsibility by individuals, families, groups, and even nations" and "dangerous to the very tenets of democracy." Throughout his book *The Abuse Excuse and Other Cop-outs, Sob Stories, and Evasions of Responsibility* (1994), Dershowitz placed quotation marks around the word *syndrome* and termed particular syndromes "invented," "constructed," and "concocted." FAS was just one of many suspect claims he criticized, along with "UFO Survivor Syndrome," "Chronic Lateness Syndrome" and "Failure to File Syndrome." Supporters of the medical model of FAS might have pointed out that not all claims of impairment constituted diagnoses. "UFO Survivor Syndrome" was never used in the courtroom nor could it be found in the medical literature. The source Dershowitz cited was a psychiatrist's report on Americans who believed they had been abducted. Similarly, "Chronic Lateness Syndrome" and "Failure to File Syndrome" had failed to make their way into diagnostic manuals, medical books, and scientific journals. Although each syndrome had had a day in court, none of the cases had proved successful. As for FAS, Dershowitz called it a syndrome that "seeks to explain why many children and adolescents exhibit severe behavioral problems, poor judgment, and are easily deceived by others by pointing to the fact that their mothers consumed large quantities of alcohol during pregnancy."

Dershowitz neglected to acknowledge that, unlike the many other syndromes he excoriated, alcohol teratogenesis was acknowledged in peer-reviewed medical literature around the world and had resulted in federal government warnings and support for research. Such distinctions between FAS and other syndromes made little difference to Dershowitz, however, because he viewed all of them as little more than strategies designed to transform criminals into victims. In a fundamental sense, he understood that diagnoses derived, as historian Charles Rosenberg asserted, from "a culturally available menu of alternative narratives." For Dershowitz, the FAS narrative was about escaping punishment by asserting that one's mother drank too much when she was pregnant.[13]

Critics attacked not only abuse excuses but also the experts who presented them in court. Noted public policy professor James Q. Wilson (a one-time Harvard colleague of Dershowitz) argued in his 1997 book *Moral Judgment: Does the Abuse Excuse Threaten Our Legal System?* that scientific expert witnesses in the courtroom had played a pivotal role in the triumph of sympathy over law. And just as California governor Wilson had argued earlier in the Harris case, social scientist Wilson assumed that self-control was within reach of all. It was this assumption that lawyers had to disprove if they were to win reduced sentences for clients with FAS.[14]

FAS and the Death Penalty

Attorneys representing clients with FAS were handicapped from the very beginning. Sometimes their clients lacked the capacity to understand

Miranda warnings and their right to remain silent and had offered confessions or even fabricated information that proved harmful to their case because of their desire to please the questioners. Getting the confessions and the evidence built from those confessions expunged from court records posed a challenge. Once a trial date was set, attorneys had to determine, with the help of experts, whether FAS prevented their clients from meeting the "guilty mind" requirement necessary for legal culpability, whether clients were competent to stand trial, and whether they could assist in their own defense. One Canadian attorney wrote up a list of twenty-six mistakes he had made as a lawyer for FAS clients, including, "I never asked one of my FAS clients' mothers directly about alcohol consumption." Many times the question of maternal drinking arose only after a client had been sentenced to execution and appeals were under way.[15]

It was the medicalization of FAS that led to its introduction into the courtroom setting. Attorneys employed expert witnesses, who presented the matter to the court, typically during the penalty phase of a case, when FAS was cited as a mitigating circumstance that called for a reduced sentence. In capital cases it was up to an attorney to convince jurors that, while convicted criminals with FAS ought to be punished, executing them was inappropriate. In other instances, legal appeals based on claims of ineffective assistance of counsel were made when defense lawyers had failed to raise the issue when a case was first being tried.[16]

Neither the medicalization nor the demedicalization of FAS can be measured by whether the diagnosis succeeded or failed in particular criminal cases. Each courtroom encounter was unique, and none turned entirely on a defendant's claim of FAS. The fact remains, however, that courtrooms became critical sites for negotiating the meaning of FAS—as diagnosis or as excuse—and such negotiations were not infrequent. The evidence suggested that a disproportionate number of those in the criminal justice system had been prenatally exposed to alcohol. A fact sheet on FAS posted on the Web site of the CDC reported that "teenagers and adults with FAS are more likely than those who do not have FAS to have interactions with police, authorities, or the judicial system." The reasons given were "difficulty controlling anger and frustration, combined with problems understanding the motives of others, resulting in many individuals with FAS being involved in violent or explosive situations. People with FAS can be very easy to persuade and manipulate, which can lead to their taking part in illegal acts without being aware of it." An article from the Canadian journal *Re-*

port indicated that studies found that between 23 and 50 percent of the Canadian prison population had been affected by FAS or fetal-alcohol effects, and noted that an effort was under way in British Columbia to create a special facility for prisoners with the diagnosis.[17]

Nowhere did negotiations over the meaning of FAS and criminal culpability matter more than in capital cases. Productive expert testimony, introduction of evidence about FAS early in the legal process, and effective legal counsel sometimes succeeded in winning a reduced sentence when juries and judges determined that a life sentence answered the demand for justice. But success often depended on the ability of a defense attorney to craft a story that made sense of both the crime and the claim of impairment. One attorney suggested that the jury needed to understand that the defendant was "a victim, even before birth, of society's failure to help his mother cope with alcoholism."[18]

Prior to Harris's execution but well after his conviction and sentencing, two convicted killers in California won life sentences by introducing evidence of FAS. In 1990, Ahmad Grigsby, a double murderer, was spared execution by a jury sympathetic to his prenatal alcohol exposure and manic depression. That same year, Charles Gaston escaped the gas chamber with effective expert help. His case, profiled on the evening news show *20/20*, involved FAS expert (and Michael Thorp's doctor) Sterling Clarren, who told viewers, "If you look at a baby picture of this guy, you go, 'Well that's fetal alcohol syndrome.' There's just no question about it." Gaston's case was undoubtedly aided by his status as an adopted child in an upper-middle-class home. His parents had searched for help for him but had never gotten a diagnosis. His mother recalled that none of the specialists she consulted asked her about his biological mother, and she remembered that the social worker had told her "that the night that she [the birth mother] went into labor, that she was drunk." In other instances, assertions about FAS made after sentencing were not effective in winning reduced sentences, possibly because they were viewed as desperation tactics rather than belated diagnoses.[19]

Even when FAS was accepted as a mitigating factor, it was often outweighed by the aggravating circumstances of the crime, particularly when there were many victims. Missouri executed George Gilmore, a convicted killer of five, despite evidence showing he had FAS, organic brain damage, an abusive and impoverished upbringing, and an IQ of 65, which marked him as borderline mentally retarded. Similarly, Keith Daniel Williams, a murderer of three, was executed in California in 1996, although the court heard of his FAS and mental illness. There were similar cases in Virginia, Texas, and Delaware.[20]

Perhaps the most critical acknowledgment of the medicalization of FAS occurred when courts found that defendants had a right to expert testimony about the effects of their prenatal alcohol exposure. In 1995, convicted murderer James Leroy Brett had his sentence overturned by the Washington State Supreme Court on the grounds of ineffective counsel because his attorney had failed to investigate and use expert witnesses to describe his FAS and bipolar disorder. To avoid a second trial and the possibility of being sentenced to death again, Brett pleaded guilty to aggravated murder and was given a sentence of life in prison without parole. Five years later, a Virginia death-row inmate similarly persuaded the court he had received ineffective counsel because his lawyers had failed to introduce evidence of FAS, mild retardation, and a horrific childhood. In other cases, defense lawyers who asked for funds for expert witnesses and failed to receive them made appeals on this basis and sometimes had the cases remanded (sent back to the lower court) so that expert assistance could be provided.[21]

Not all calls for expert testimony succeeded. A Massachusetts court rejected a last-minute bid for expert testimony about a convicted man's suicidal impulses and FAS. In North Carolina, the State Supreme Court rejected a request for additional expert witnesses to examine a convicted murderer for FAS, saying he had already had two evaluations by psychiatrists. Similarly, a request for an expert in FAS to find mitigating evidence was rejected by a Florida court. In some situations it was the timing of the request, or the fact that psychological experts (but not FAS experts) had already appeared on behalf of the defendant, that led appeals courts to reject it. In other instances, however, the courts clearly failed to distinguish between a defendant's alcohol abuse and FAS.[22]

Of course, expert testimony guaranteed nothing. Prosecutors had their own experts, who typically provided conflicting diagnoses. Sometimes the hostility or skepticism of judges and juries undermined the assertions of FAS experts. A judge in one Florida capital case heard testimony from a defense psychiatrist that the defendant suffered from FAS, and from a state psychiatrist, who argued that the defendant's behavior was inconsistent with that of someone who was brain damaged and that there was no conclusive evidence of FAS. The judge weighed the arguments, accepted the state's expert, and sentenced the defendant to death. In another instance, the mother of a man on death row recounted how the judge in her son's case listened to expert testimony about FAS but was "unimpressed."[23]

FAS claims entered a new phase in 2002, when the U.S. Supreme Court found in *Atkins v. Virginia* that the execution of the mentally retarded violated the Eighth Amendment prohibition against cruel and unusual punishment. The ruling removed from death row those who suffered from mental retardation because of FAS. It remains to be seen whether individuals with FAS but who are not mentally retarded become more vulnerable to execution. Having drawn a line between mental retardation and other kinds of developmental disabilities and cognitive impairments, the court may have inadvertently undermined the claims of those whose brain damage did not result in an IQ below the cutoff. Ironically, the Supreme Court's language defining the mentally retarded—"they have diminished capacities to understand and process information, to communicate, to abstract from mistakes and learn from experience, to engage in logical reasoning, to control impulses, and to understand others' reactions"—closely paralleled medical experts' descriptions of those with FAS.[24]

Behavioral Teratogenesis and Secondary Disabilities

Expert witnesses for criminal defendants argued that individuals suffering from FAS did not necessarily have funny-looking faces that marked them as damaged before birth, but they did have brains far different from those not exposed to high levels of alcohol in the womb. Their arguments rested on three related scientific developments. First, new imaging technologies appeared to reveal the precise damage done to the brain by prenatal alcohol exposure. Second, FAS was redefined: experts agreed that instead of being a single diagnosis, prenatal exposure to alcohol had a spectrum of effects, and they put in place a new system of categorization. Finally, epidemiological research suggested that those prenatally exposed to alcohol might show a range of behavioral and cognitive problems termed secondary disabilities.

Just as thalidomide had spurred research into structural teratology, investigations of alcohol-related birth defects shaped and enhanced the discipline of behavioral teratology. But while structural defects, such as the missing or truncated limbs associated with thalidomide, were easy to see and easy for scientists to link to exposure to the drug at a particular stage of development, alcohol exposure was different. In many instances, the damage it did was invisible. More important, linking particular behaviors to alcohol exposure, as opposed to environmental circumstances and other prenatal experiences and exposures, proved difficult.[25]

Behavioral teratology in humans was not a controlled science of the laboratory; it was an inexact, deductive science. Epidemiological studies suggested that many if not most individuals exposed to high doses of alcohol prenatally were also affected by maternal malnutrition, exposure to tobacco, the effects of maternal stress, obstetric complications, and low birth weight. Each condition had been shown to have behavioral effects, making it nearly impossible to tease out the precise contribution of the alcohol. Additionally, environmental factors such as poverty, abuse, neglect, and family disruption, as well as genetics, played key roles in shaping behavior. Author Michael Dorris attributed the behavioral problems and developmental delays suffered by his son to his birth mother's alcoholism. FAS researcher Ernest Abel asked whether the boy's delays might also have resulted from his treatment in "his early infancy when he was malnourished, tied to his crib and chronically ill, as well as from FAS."[26]

In the courtroom, uncertainty and ambiguity are unwelcome. Experts claiming that an individual defendant suffered from FAS knew that other detrimental life experiences also shaped behavior. During the Thorp trial, physicians Jones, Brent, and Clarren took the witness stand and declared that Michael's developmental delays resulted from his mother's drinking. Testifying for the defense, Galler argued that Michael's problems followed from his mother's poor nutrition during pregnancy and her subsequent failures as a parent. Neither side could allow that all of the factors were likely to have influenced his brain and his behavior. In criminal cases, and particularly in capital cases, juries have to weigh evidence about prenatal and postnatal harm and decide whether the individual whose life is in the balance had the capacity to act with free will or whether that ability had been taken away before birth.

Despite the inherent limitations in linking prenatal alcohol exposure to particular behavioral problems, scientific studies conducted in the late twentieth century suggested that prenatal alcohol exposure caused particular kinds of brain damage. In the 1980s, researchers offered impressionistic accounts of the behavior they observed in affected children. One group reported that children prenatally exposed to alcohol and tobacco were "less attentive, less compliant, more fidgety" than their unexposed counterparts.

Twenty years later the analysis of alcohol teratogenesis rested on data from autopsies and from advanced brain imaging techniques that showed malformations in brain tissue and the failure of particular brain regions to develop normally.[27]

The delineation of the physical features of alcohol-affected brains coincided with the development of a new classification system for effects of fetal alcohol exposure. In 1996 the Institute of Medicine presented a five-part classification scheme. Three of the categories—FAS with confirmed maternal alcohol exposure, FAS without confirmed maternal alcohol exposure, and partial FAS with confirmed maternal alcohol exposure—were characterized by growth retardation, central nervous system abnormalities, and evidence of behavioral or cognitive disorders. Another category, alcohol-related birth defects (ARBD), was distinguished by a variety of anomalies associated with maternal alcohol consumption during pregnancy. In the final category, alcohol-related neurodevelopmental disorders (ARND), the individual showed evidence of central nervous system abnormalities and behavioral and cognitive disorders. In some cases, researchers, service providers, and parents ceased referring to individuals with FAS and instead employed the term *fetal alcohol spectrum disorders* (FASD), suggesting that while an individual might not meet the diagnostic category for FAS, it was clear that alcohol had affected his or her development and behavior. The new classification scheme offered experts a way to make clear what they knew about patients and what they knew about brain development and to record a diagnosis more precise and more scientifically sophisticated that had been possible when there were fewer ways of describing those damaged by prenatal alcohol exposure. However, to those sitting in courtrooms, explanations of defendants' conditions that employed the new terminology may have sounded like obfuscations designed to confuse listeners by concealing how much the experts did *not* know.[28]

The emerging scientific evidence suggested that intelligence, learning, memory, higher-order cognitive processes known as executive functioning, attention, and motor control were affected by high levels of prenatal alcohol exposure. While studies of neuropathology in the brains of those prenatally exposed to alcohol often examined only small populations and did not compare those affected by alcohol with those who were developmentally delayed or damaged for other reasons, the findings did suggest that alcohol caused specific kinds of deficits. As with earlier studies of alcohol teratogenesis, which also came from examinations of small numbers of individuals, the results gained significance because they were replicated by groups of researchers from different countries and were supported by investigations of animal populations. Formal acknowledgement of the findings appeared in the *Tenth Special Report to Congress on Alcohol and Health,* which characterized the brains of individuals with FAS as "not developed normally," noting that "certain cells are not in their proper locations, and tissue has died off in some regions."[29]

The brain impairments researchers identified resulted in lifelong problems. As youngsters, individuals with FAS struggled to get along with peers and teachers, and were far more likely to be suspended from school, be expelled, or drop out of school than those who had no prenatal alcohol exposure. As adults, they battled to control their anger, to understand the motives of others, to refrain from substance abuse, and to resist involvement in illegal activities. Many had great difficulty living independently and keeping a job. A follow-up study of twenty-four children born to alcoholic mothers in Sweden reported that their parents and teachers described problems with "learning, impulse control and aggression" and found that many of the families relied on support services. Sixteen of the twenty-four lived in foster homes, and researchers found that effective parenting in these settings improved the lives of the children. Similarly, advocates for early-intervention programs for those with FAS reported that early diagnosis, special education, social services, and a stable and nonviolent home environment limited, but did not eliminate, the expression of secondary disabilities.[30]

Unfortunately, research found that many individuals in need of early and intensive intervention failed to receive help. And even when help was available, it could not fully erase the damage that had been done before birth. Researchers in West Berlin, a city they described as possessing a "dense social and medical infrastructure," concluded that "compensatory environmental and educational influences" did not help children with FAS achieve intellectual growth, and that in adolescence these individuals struggled with a wide spectrum of behavioral and cognitive disorders.[31]

When researchers gathered in Seattle for a conference on FAS and secondary disabilities in 1996, a team led by Ann Streissguth reported on 415 alcohol-affected individuals. Ninety percent had mental health problems, and among those over age twelve, the majority had experienced school disruption (60 percent), trouble with the law (60 percent), and confinement due to mental health and substance abuse problems or for criminal activity

(50 percent). Other conduct problems were common: half of those over twelve had exhibited inappropriate sexual behaviors, and 30 percent were said to have alcohol and drug problems. Among those over age twenty-one, 80 percent could not live alone and 80 percent had problems with employment. Twenty-eight percent of the women in the study had become mothers, and the mean age for first pregnancy was eighteen. Among them, 40 percent were found to have been drinking during pregnancy, and 17 percent had a child diagnosed with FAS while another 13 percent had given birth to a child suspected of being alcohol affected. In the majority of cases, the children had been removed from their mothers' care. Not surprisingly, the authors reiterated what had been stated for decades: the need for expanded inpatient alcoholism treatment programs for women and their children. More critically, they called for more services for those who had been diagnosed with FAS and for more efforts to diagnose in infancy or childhood those who had been damaged prenatally by alcohol exposure. Early diagnosis, their research found, was an important protective factor for secondary disabilities. While the report from Streissguth's group did not offer specific case studies of affected individuals, the stories of such individuals were appearing elsewhere—in accounts of criminal trials and in media reports of what one story called "adoption nightmares."[32]

Time Bombs and Adoption Nightmares

Among the most vigorous advocates for individuals and families coping with FAS were voluntary organizations that helped families adopt and rear alcohol-affected children. The adoption marketplace underwent a substantial change in the late twentieth century. Foreign adoptions increased and private agencies and lawyers increasingly managed domestic adoptions of infants, while the caseload of public agencies grew to include more older and special needs children. In all of these settings, the children available for adoption included a number who began to be recognized as having been affected by prenatal alcohol exposure.

In resource guides for families, adoption experts explained the needs of these children. Toddlers with FAS, one book noted, required "constant supervision because they do not comprehend boundaries and do not connect actions and consequences." Adolescents, it continued, might find it hard to keep up academically and socially, and might seek attention by "stealing, cheating, lying, and fighting." Child welfare specialists were frank but not fatalistic, urging parents to resist the negative media imagery and not give in to the sense that their children were doomed. Parents, teachers, and counselors shared suggestions for helping children live in structured environments that addressed their limitations and gave them opportunities for success. Because of these needs, adoptive parents organized to increase awareness of FAS and to find services for their children, creating organizations such as the National Organization for Fetal Alcohol Syndrome (NOFAS), which was formed in 1990. Often the message from adoptive parents contained a warning: without proper help and without a highly structured environment, individuals with FAS might harm themselves and others. Their assertions dovetailed with the arguments about FAS being voiced in criminal courtrooms, as those on trial argued they were victims as well as victimizers.[33]

In the late twentieth century, the media began highlighting the double face of FAS. Stories presented with great sympathy the innocent children who could not make friends, plan ahead, understand the consequences of their actions, or control their behavior because of the actions of their alcoholic mothers. And the media offered up portraits of hardened adult criminals who appeared to be wrapping themselves in the mantle of victimhood by offering last-ditch claims that their felonies were not their fault, because their mothers had drunk heavily during pregnancy. In between the two archetypal figures were troubled adolescents, who were often depicted as both damaged and delinquent. On the morning of Robert Alton Harris's execution, the National Public Radio show *Morning Edition* profiled a couple struggling to rear an adoptive son who was a juvenile offender. His lawyer, who was also a psychologist, explained to listeners that "young people with fetal alcohol syndrome cannot understand the consequences of their actions." Several days before the execution, the *CBS Evening News* had concluded a story about FAS with the ominous words: "Parents themselves are warning that without more recognition, FAS children will remain invisible and inevitable time bombs." In another story about a child with FAS, the serial killers Ted Bundy and David Berkowitz were mentioned and an attorney who defended murderers reported that most of his cases "involve this type of background." Vague and unsupported statements of this sort could not help but make the public wary of FAS children, hostile to their mothers, and confused about what the FAS diagnosis really meant.[34]

Media accounts made it clear that the potentially lethal youngsters were not those who were profoundly damaged by alcohol but those whose status left them in limbo. In the *CBS Evening News* story, viewers saw Danny Ibsen, a fourth-grade child with FAS who could not grasp concepts such as "time, cause and effect, reward and punishment." His mother, like other parents in her support group, wished that he had been born mentally retarded, because then "there would be services" and government help. As the report went on to explain, many children with FAS looked "utterly normal," although their behavior was not. The segment showed a seventeen-year-old girl with FAS who had twice attempted suicide and who grew catatonic, according to her mother, when she was forced to accept discipline. The segment also introduced a thirteen-year-old boy with FAS who had been attacking his sister. His mother contemplated sending him away but hesitated because she feared he would one day seek her out and kill her. To spare their children from the tragic fates that seemed to await them, the parents profiled in the story were seeking help from schools and public agencies and warning that the fuses on their children were growing short. Their advocacy put a child's face on the subject of secondary disabilities.

Michael Dorris, who had become a leading spokesperson for those with FAS and had adopted several children prenatally exposed to alcohol, repeatedly characterized individuals with FAS as incapable of knowing right from wrong. Before a Senate committee hearing testimony about FAS, he discussed his adopted children's troubled lives, which were marked by arrests for "shoplifting, sexual misconduct and violent behavior" and characterized by a lack of friendships and goals. His children, he told the senators, had "no bedrock inner values to distinguish right from wrong, safe from dangerous," because their minds had been destroyed before birth. He and others drew harsh portraits of the birth mothers and contrasted the noble and frustrating work of caring for individuals with FAS with the easy choice of walking into a bar and ordering a drink. The calls for pregnant women to become more responsible by refraining from drinking fit neatly with the emphasis on personal responsibility voiced by critics of courtroom claims of FAS.[35]

Civil cases involving adopted children with FAS often presented the same kinds of evidence about secondary disabilities that met with rejection in criminal courtrooms. Frequently the cases arose when families sought monetary relief, charging that their adoption agencies had knowingly withheld information or misrepresented their children's medical and social backgrounds, including evidence of FAS. They charged wrongful adoption and asked for damages to cover past and future costs of caring for their children. From a legal vantage point, the cases represented a step forward in family preservation. Prior to 1986, adoptive parents who believed they had been misled during the adoption process could move only to annul the adoptions. From a medical perspective, the cases involving FAS appeared to confirm its behavioral sequelae and to suggest that those with the diagnosis could be dangerous as well as damaged.[36]

The media called these cases "adoption nightmares." One newspaper story described a psychotic adopted boy who mutilated household pets and was eventually diagnosed with FAS. The family moved out of their home to a secret address after their son, who was then eighteen and no longer living with them, had threatened to kill them and another young son. A lawsuit against the social service agency that had placed the boy and withheld information about his condition was settled out of court. CBS Evening News aired a segment graphically depicting adopted children with severe problems whose conditions were kept hidden from their parents for years. One was a boy with FAS who had tried to choke a baby, and had threatened to kill other children, before he was finally institutionalized at sixteen. The adoptive family sued the county agency that had placed him, to obtain funds for his care. A story in the New York Times provided further details, including the fact that the boy had been dismissed from one facility after attempting to rape a nine-year-old girl and from another facility because he was deemed him too dangerous.[37]

Other lawsuits involving FAS and adoption also attracted newspaper and television reporters, including a claim filed in Pennsylvania by adoptive parents seeking $5 million from county officials in California who had hidden their son's condition from them, a case in California in which an adoption was severed because the county had withheld information about a child's FAS and mental illness, and the story of a Florida couple that was told their son had a heart defect when he had in fact been taken from his biological parents in part because he, like his siblings, had FAS. The actions of the adoption agencies involved were labeled by one report on lawsuits in Washington State as "sins of silence." Similar claims were made about alleged mishandling of foreign adoptions. Ultimately, legal actions forced adoption agencies to take up full-disclosure policies and to require parents to sign waivers indicating they were fully informed of all that the agency knew about their child. As a result, the lawsuits abated. But the problems with FAS children did not go away.[38]

Understandably, adoptive parents, children, and support organizations became outspoken advocates for abstinence, telling women not to drink a single drop lest their children be damaged for life. This was the message in a 1990 *New York Times Magazine* article titled "When a Pregnant Woman Drinks," which suggested that a single drink on the wrong day could have devastating effects. Similarly, the coordinator of a local chapter of the Association for Retarded Citizens was quoted in a newspaper story as saying "a drink a day can make a difference between having a healthy baby and one doomed to a lifetime of learning and behavioral problems associated with FAS." Even individuals with FAS delivered the message. The *Santa Fe New Mexican* featured a story about Melissa Sullivan, an adult whose FAS had left her with learning disabilities and an inability to hold a job. She was, the paper reported, angry at her birth mother and at society for allowing "pregnant women to drink." Echoing a popular phrase, she termed it "child abuse before birth." Eighteen-year-old Christopher Duran of Las Vegas similarly detailed his struggles with FAS, telling a reporter that he sometimes spoke to pregnant customers at the market where he worked collecting shopping carts, asking if they were drinking alcohol and warning them about the consequences.[39]

Duran was making a statement about women's individual responsibility, but he was only the messenger. At the end of the twentieth century, FAS was, simultaneously, a medical diagnosis and a judgment about bad mothers, damaged offspring, and bad excuses for bad behavior.

Paradoxes: FAS Today

In civil courtrooms the behavioral effects of prenatal alcohol exposure were often treated as scientific facts. In 1990 the U.S. Supreme Court ordered federal officials to evaluate children individually to see if they qualified for disability benefits; prior to the ruling, the government had worked from a list of disabling impairments, and FAS had not been on it. Clearly the diagnosis had gained a measure of legitimacy.[40]

In many criminal courtrooms, however, behavioral teratogenesis was a hypothesis and open to debate. On some occasions, convicted death-row criminals said by experts to have FAS were nevertheless executed; in other cases, they were taken off death row to live out their remaining days in prison. The status and meaning of their diagnoses entailed complex negotiations, and the outcomes were shaped by the skills of lawyers and experts on both sides, as well as by the determinations of jurists at different points in the proceedings.

Since its naming in 1973, FAS has had many meanings. It emerged from the medical literature, set in motion an international research program, provided the momentum for a public health crusade that led to legislation mandating warning labels on alcoholic beverages, became embroiled in a media-fueled moral panic over pregnant women's substance abuse, and made its way into courtroom battles over services for the disabled, compensation for those harmed by maternal drinking, and claims of diminished capacity in criminal trials. In each arena, perceptions of FAS were shaped by disciplinary interests: FAS was, at once, a medical problem, a public health concern, an impairment that limited one's ability to understand cause and effect, a symbol of maternal misbehavior, evidence of moral decay, and an abuse excuse. Each definition overlaid but did not fully obscure the others, as the meaning of the syndrome was negotiated again and again.

Perhaps the best way to think about FAS and to understand the path it has traveled in the past thirty years is to see where, literally, it resides today. One can peer into a civil courtroom and observe families fighting for and winning services for their children diagnosed with FAS and then enter a neighboring criminal courtroom to watch individuals diagnosed with FAS being sentenced to death despite claims of impairment. One can walk down the aisles of a bookstore and pick up a volume written by a respected medical expert explaining that FAS is a birth defect of the mind and go to a different corner of the store and pull from the shelves a book written by a respected legal scholar suggesting that FAS is a fiction cooked up by highly paid expert witnesses bent on keeping brutal criminals from being punished for their crimes. One can sit in a restaurant and watch a pregnant woman ordering a glass of wine and being scolded by a stranger, or watch a man get up from a barstool and stumble drunkenly out the door to his car without a word from anyone. On television, one can see a public service announcement warning pregnant women not to drink, followed soon after by beer commercials. Finally, one can enter a hospital emergency room and see a pregnant alcoholic woman being handcuffed and arrested for fetal endangerment or, in a few places, being assisted with her request for inpatient detoxification.

At the heart of these paradoxes lies our profound cultural ambivalence about women's obligations as mothers, about the status of the fetus, about personal responsibility, and about alcoholism. If women are viewed as legally obligated to protect fetuses, then their drinking can be policed in ways that men's drinking cannot be. If fetuses are viewed as potential future citizens, then they will be seen as having rights and claims on the state that can conflict with those of pregnant women. If chronic heavy drinking is viewed as a personal failing, representing a loss of will, then it will be treated as something an individual must acknowledge and overcome alone, without social support and inpatient care. And so long as the ifs remain, the diagnosis of FAS will be "an argument that goes back to the womb," and its meaning will continue to be negotiated but not fully resolved.

Notes

1. "We Realized We Were onto Something"

1. Telephone interview, Kenneth Lyons Jones, MD, 1999.
2. Keith L. Moore and T. V. N. Persaud, *The Developing Human: Clinically Oriented Embryology,* 5th ed. (Philadelphia: W. B. Saunders, 1993), p. 143.
3. David W. Smith and Kenneth Lyons Jones, *Smith's Recognizable Patterns of Human Malformation,* 4th ed. (Philadelphia: W. B. Saunders, 1988).
4. "Festschrift in Honor of David W. Smith," *Journal of Pediatrics* 101 (1982): 798–804; and W. E. N. "The Legacy of David W. Smith," *Journal of Pediatrics* 98 (1981): 909–910. Smith is also the author of *Recognizable Patterns of Human Deformation: Identification and Management of Mechanical Effects on Morphogenesis* (Philadelphia: Saunders, 1981).
5. William Grigg, "The Thalidomide Tragedy—25 Years Ago," *FDA Consumer* 21 (1987): 14–17; and Dr. Herxheimer, quoted in *Suffer the Children: The Story of Thalidomide/The Insight Team of the Sunday Times of London* (New York: Viking, 1979), p. 48.
6. Christy N. Ulleland, "The Offspring of Alcoholic Mothers," *Annals of the New York Academy of Sciences* 197 (1972): 167–169. See also, Anon., "Alcoholic Mothers' Babies Fail to Thrive," *JAMA* 213 (1971): 1429–1450, which describes Ulleland's research. Jones discussed Ulleland's work as it related to the discovery of FAS in his testimony in *Michael Thorp v. James A. Beam Distilling Company,* U.S. District Court, Western District of Washington, Docket C871527D, vol. 2, 24 April 1989, pp. 43–44, NAS.
7. Kenneth L. Jones et al., "Pattern of Malformation in Offspring of Chronic Alcoholic Mothers," *Lancet* 1 (1973): 1267–1271.
8. Kenneth L. Jones and David W. Smith, "Recognition of the Fetal Alcohol Syndrome in Early Infancy," *Lancet* 2 (1973): 999–1001.

9. P. Lemoine et al., "Les enfants de parents alcooliques: Anomalies observées: A propos de 127 Cas." *Ouest Médical* 25 (1968): 476–482. Another important article discussing the effects of alcohol abuse in pregnancy was published a year earlier: see M. Alexandre Lemarche, "Réflexions sur la descendance des alcooliques," *Bulletin de L'Académie Nationale de Médicine* 151 (1967): 517–521. Lemarche studied infants with physical or mental anomalies, observing that many were the offspring of alcoholics and noting that maternal alcoholism was a critical factor.

10. Paul Lemoine, "An Historical Note about the Foetal-Alcohol Syndrome: A Letter from Professor Lemoine," *Addiction* 89 (1994): 1021–1023. Lemoine cites a 1957 thesis: Jacqueline Rouquette, "Influence de l'intoxication alcoolique parentale sur le dévelopment physique et psychique des jeune enfants," Paris, 1957.

11. Bryan D. Hall and Walter A. Orenstein, "Noonan's Phenotype in an Offspring of an Alcoholic Mother," *Lancet* 2 (1974): 680–681; Josette W. Bianchine and Bruce D. Taylor, "Noonan Syndrome and Fetal Alcohol Syndrome," *Lancet* 2 (1974): 933; Charles F. Johnson, "Does Maternal Alcoholism Affect Offspring?" *Clinical Pediatrics* 13 (1974): 633–634; and R. C. Sneed, "The Fetal Alcohol Syndrome: Is Alcohol, Lead, or Something Else the Culprit?" *Journal of Pediatrics* 90 (1977): 324.

12. P. E. Ferrier et al., "Fetal Alcohol Syndrome," *Lancet* 2 (1973): 1496; R. Heather Palmer et al., "Congenital Malformations in Offspring of a Chronic Alcoholic Mother," *Pediatrics* 53 (1974): 490–493; and R. G. Barry and S. O'Nuallain, "Case Report: Foetal Alcoholism," *Irish Journal of Medical Science* 144 (1975): 286–288.

13. Olli P. Heinonen, Dennis Slone, and Samuel Shapiro, *Birth Defects and Drugs in Pregnancy* (Boston: John Wright and Publishing Science Group, 1977). On alcoholism in the postwar era, see Lori Rotskoff, *Love on the Rocks: Men, Women and Alcohol in Post–World War II America* (Chapel Hill: University of North Carolina Press, 2002).

14. Kenneth L. Jones et al., "Outcome in Offspring of Chronic Alcoholic Women," *Lancet* 1 (1974): 1076–1078. For a detailed account of the research method, see Ann Streissguth, *Fetal Alcohol Syndrome: A Guide for Families and Communities,* (Baltimore: Paul H. Brookes, 1997), pp. 41–42. For a critique of this study, see Ruth H. Neugut, "Epidemiological Appraisal of the Literature on the Fetal Alcohol Syndrome in Humans," *Early Human Development* 5 (1981): 418–419; and for a reply, see Ernest L. Abel and Robert M. Sokol, "Commentary: Fetal Alcohol Syndrome: How Good Is the Criticism?" *Neurobehavioral Toxicology and Teratology* 5 (1983): 491–492.

15. Ann Pytkowicz Streissguth, Sterling Keith Clarren, and Kenneth Lyons Jones, "Natural History of the Fetal Alcohol Syndrome: A 10-Year Follow-up of

Eleven Patients," *Lancet* 2 (1985): 85–91; and "Wesley Was First Baby Diagnosed with FAS" *Seattle Times* 28 August 1996, Lexis-Nexis Academic Universe (LNAU). See, also H.-L. Spohr, "Follow-Up Studies of Children with Fetal Alcohol Syndrome," *Neuropediatrics* 18 (1987): 13–17.

16. Lemoine, "An Historical Note," p. 1022. The follow-up study was reported in P. Lemoine and Ph. Lemoine, "Avenir des enfants de mères alcooliques (Étude de 105 cas retrouvés a l'age adulte) et quelques constatations d'intérêt prophylactique," *Annales de Pédiatrie* 39 (1992): 226–235. After his retirement Lemoine offered to give a paper at a meeting of the French Congress of Pediatrics that was partially devoted to the subject of FAS. His offer was rejected. However, shortly thereafter he won the Jellinek Prize from the International Congress on Alcoholism and Toxicomania and presented his findings at that meeting. See also Streissguth, *Fetal Alcohol Syndrome*, p. 45, and Alexander Dorozyaski, "Maternal Alcoholism: Grapes of Wrath," *Psychology Today* 26 (1993): 18. On the congruence of the French and Seattle findings, see Neugut, "Epidemiological Appraisal," pp. 411–429.

17. Charles E. Rosenberg, "Framing Disease: Illness, Society, and History," in Charles E. Rosenberg and Janet Golden, eds., *Framing Disease: Studies in Cultural History* (New Brunswick: Rutgers University Press, 1992), p. xiii. See also Robert A. Aronowitz, *Making Sense of Illness: Science, Society, and Disease* (Cambridge: Cambridge University Press, 1998); and Charles E. Rosenberg, "The Tyranny of Diagnosis: Specific Entities and Individual Experience," *Milbank Quarterly* 80 (2002): 237–260. Alan M. Dershowitz, *The Abuse Excuse: And Other Cop-Outs, Sob Stories and Evasions of Responsibility* (Boston: Little, Brown, 1994), p. 19.

18. A recent clash of viewpoints occurred during debates over the Americans with Disabilities Act. Some fought to curtail protections for addicts and alcoholics, while others supported the disease concept of addiction. Ultimately, addiction was defined as a disability and recovered addicts received protection under the law, but those still using illegal drugs were excluded. See, "Groups Waging Last-Ditch Battle for Rights of Addicts and Alcoholics," *Alcoholism and Drug Abuse Week* 1 (1989): 1.

19. For an overview of medicalization and its discontents, see both Roy Porter, *The Greatest Benefit to Mankind: A Medical History of Humanity* (New York: W. W. Norton, 1998), and Michel Foucault, *The Birth of the Clinic: An Archeology of Medical Perception,* trans. by A. M. Sheridan Smith (New York: Viking, 1975). On the cultural authority of American medicine, see Paul Starr, *The Social Transformation of American Medicine* (New York: Basic Books, 1982). The classic sociological analysis can be found in Peter Conrad and Joseph W. Schneider, *Deviance and Medicalization: From Badness to Sickness* (St. Louis: Mosby, 1980), which consists of case studies of medicalization. See also Naomi

Aronson, "Science as a Claims-Making Activity: Implications for Social Problems Research," in Joseph W. Schneider and John I. Kitsuse, eds., *Studies in the Sociology of Social Problems* (Norwood, NJ: Ablex, 1984), pp. 1–30; Joseph R. Gusfield, "On the Side: Practical Action and Social Constructivism in Social Problems Theory," in ibid., pp. 31–51; and Joseph R. Gusfield, *Contested Meanings: The Construction of Alcohol Problems* (Madison: University of Wisconsin Press, 1996).

20. Renee C. Fox, "The Medicalization and Demedicalization of American Society," *Daedalus* 106 (1977): 9–22; David J. Rothman, *Strangers at the Bedside: A History of How Law and Bioethics Transformed Medical Decision Making* (New York: Basic Books, 1991).

21. Allan M. Brandt, "Behavior, Disease, and Health in the Twentieth-Century United States: The Moral Valence of Individual Risk," in Allan M. Brandt and Paul Rozin, eds., *Morality and Health: Interdisciplinary Perspectives* (New York: Routledge, 1997), pp. 53–77; Howard M. Leichter, "Lifestyle Correctness and the New Secular Morality," in ibid., pp. 559–378.

22. Good personal accounts can be found in Judith Kleinfeld and Siobhan Westcott, eds., *Fantastic Antone Succeeds! Experiences in Educating Children with Fetal Alcohol Syndrome* (Fairbanks: University of Alaska Press, 1993); Brenda McCreight, *Recognizing and Managing Children with Fetal Alcohol Syndrome/Fetal Alcohol Effects: A Guidebook* (Washington, DC: CWLA Press, 1997); Liz Kulp and Jodee Kulp, *The Best I Can Be: Living with Fetal Alcohol Syndrome/Effects* (Brooklyn Park, MN: Better Endings New Beginnings, 2000); and Judith Kleinfeld, ed., *Fantastic Antone Grows Up: Adolescents and Adults with Fetal Alcohol Syndrome* (Fairbanks: University of Alaska Press, 2000). For fiction, see Nasdijj, *Blood Runs Like a River through My Dreams: A Memoir* (Boston: Houghton Mifflin, 2000). See also the Web site of the National Organization on Fetal Alcohol Syndrome, www.nofas.org.

2. "Conceived in Gin"

1. Personal interview with Sheila Blume, MD, 1999.

2. Rebecca H. Warner and Henry L. Rosett, "Effects of Drinking on Offspring: An Historical Survey of the American and British Literature," *Journal of Studies on Alcohol* 36 (1975): 1395–1420. Ernest L. Abel, *Fetal Alcohol Syndrome and Fetal Alcohol Effects* (New York: Plenum, 1984); Ernest L. Abel, *FAS: An Annotated Bibliography* (New York: Praeger, 1986); Ernest L. Abel, comp. *New Literature on Fetal Alcohol Syndrome and Effects: A Bibliography, 1983–1988* (New York: Greenwood, 1990); and Peter L. Petraikis, *Alcohol and Birth Defects: The Fetal Alcohol Syndrome and Related Disorders* (Rockville, MD: U.S. Dept. of Health and Human Services, National Institute of Alcohol Abuse and Alcoholism, 1987), p. 2.

3. Ralph I. Fried and James G. Ravin, "Fetal Alcohol Syndrome," *Journal of Pediatric Ophthalmology and Strabismus* 15 (1978): 394–395; Friedrich Wilhelm Kielhorn, "The History of Alcoholism: Bruhl-Cramer's Concepts and Observations," *Addiction* 9 (1996): 121, 126. Popular writers also embraced the idea that FAS had been seen before. One cited the character Betsy Martin in *The Pickwick Papers*, who had one eye because her mother drank bottled stout, and *Brave New World's* description of how children grown in bottles of alcohol were small. Lucy Barry Robe, *Just So It's Healthy: Drinking and Drugs Can Harm Your Unborn Baby* (Minneapolis: Compcare Publications, 1982), p. 51. Owsei Temkin, *The Falling Sickness: A History of Epilepsy from the Greeks to the Beginnings of Modern Neurology*, 2nd ed. rev. (Baltimore: Johns Hopkins University Press, 1971). See also Charles E. Rosenberg, "What Is Disease? In Memory of Owsei Temkin," *Bulletin of the History of Medicine* 77 (2003): 491–505.
4. Barbara W. Tuchman, *A Distant Mirror: The Calamitous 14th Century* (New York: Knopf, 1978), pp. 92–125.
5. The standard account of the gin epidemic appears in M. Dorothy George, *London Life in the 18th Century*, 2nd ed. (New York: Capricorn Books, 1965). For a critique of George, see Jessica Warner, "In Another City, In Another Time: Rhetoric and the Creation of a Drug Scare in Eighteenth-Century London," *Contemporary Drug Problems* 21 (1994): 485–511. Warner calls the responses to the gin epidemic a "drug scare" comparable to the one leading up to Prohibition in the United States. See also Ernest L. Abel, "Gin Lane: Did Hogarth Know about Fetal Alcohol Syndrome?" *Alcohol and Alcoholism* 36 (2001): 131–134, 401–405; and Ernest L. Abel, "The Gin Epidemic: Much Ado about What?" *Alcohol and Alcoholism* 36 (2001): 401–405.
6. Warner and Rosett, "Effects of Drinking on Offspring," p. 1397; Robert A. Welch, Mitchell P. Dombrowski, and Robert J. Sokol, "Maternal Chemical Dependence," in Mark I. Evans, ed., *Reproductive Risks and Prenatal Diagnosis* (Norwalk, CT: Appleton and Lange, 1991), p. 84. T. G. Coffey, "Beer Street: Gin Lane; Some Views of 18th-Century Drinking," *Quarterly Journal of Studies on Alcohol* 27 (1966): 669–692.
7. Henry Fielding, *An Enquiry into the Causes of the Late Increase of Robbers and Related Writings*, ed. Malvin R. Zirker (Middletown, CT: Wesleyan University Press, 1988), p. 90.
8. Warner, "In Another City."
9. Bénédict Auguste Morel, *Traité des dégénérescences physiques, intellectuelles et morales de l'espèce humaine et des causes qui produisent ces variétés maladives* (Paris: J. B. Baillière, 1857). For another description of alcoholic degeneration and the effects of alcohol on offspring, see Louis François Etienne Bergeret, *De l'abus des boissons alcooliques: Dangers et inconvénients pour les individus, la famille, et la société, moyens de modérer les ravages de l'ivrognerie* (Paris: J. B. Baillière et fils, 1870). See also William F. Bynum, "Chronic Alcoholism in the

First Half of the Twentieth Century," *Bulletin of the History of Medicine* 42 (1968): 160–185, and "Alcoholism and Degeneration in 19th-Century Medicine and Psychiatry," *British Journal of Addiction* 79 (1984): 59–70.

10. August Forel, *Hygiene of Nerves and Mind in Health and Disease,* trans. by Herbert Austin Aikins from the 2nd German ed. (New York: G. P. Putnam's Sons, 1907), pp. 192, 211. See also August Forel, "The Effect of Alcoholic Intoxication upon the Human Brain and Its Relation to Theories of Heredity and Evolution," *Quarterly Journal of Inebriety* 12 (1893): 203–221.

11. Michel Foucault, *Discipline and Punish: The Birth of the Prison,* trans. Alan Sheridan (New York: Vintage Books, 1979).

12. James H. Cassedy, *American Medicine and Statistical Thinking, 1800–1860* (Cambridge, MA: Harvard University Press, 1984), pp. 40–51. S. G. Howe, *On the Causes of Idiocy, Being the Supplement to a Report by S. G. Howe and the Other Commissioners Appointed by the Governor of Massachusetts . . .* (repr., New York: Arno, 1972). The case of Connecticut is cited in William Hargreaves, *The Total Abstinence Reader; Alcohol and Man, or, the Scientific Basis of Total Abstinence . . .* (New York: National Temperance Society and Publication House, 1881), p. 174.

13. Dom. Bezzola, "A Statistical Investigation into the Role of Alcohol in the Origins of Innate Imbecility," *Quarterly Journal of Inebriety* 23 (1901): 346–354; M. Bourneville, "Note sur l'influence de la syphilis héréditaire, de l'alcoolisme et de quelques professions insalubres sur la production des maladies chroniques du système nerveux chez les enfants (idiotes, épilepsies, aliénation mentale)," *Archives de Neurologie* 12 (1901): 331–334; and Henry Smith Williams, *Alcohol: How It Affects the Individual, the Community, and the Race* (New York: Century Co., 1909), p. 46.

14. Alexander MacNicholl, "A Study of the Effects of Alcohol on School Children," *Quarterly Journal of Inebriety* 27 (1905): 113–117. See, also T. A. MacNicholl, "Alcohol a Cause of Degeneracy" *Quarterly Journal of Inebriety* 24 (1902): 330–335. Warner and Rosett, "Effects of Drinking on Offspring," 1402–1408. On heredity and disease, see Charles E. Rosenberg, "The Bitter Fruit: Heredity, Disease, and Social Thought," in Charles E. Rosenberg, *No Other Gods: On Science and American Social Thought* (Baltimore: Johns Hopkins University Press, 1961), pp. 25–53. The problem of children's drinking also raised concern in late nineteenth-century Britain. A group of Edwardian medical advocates of temperance seized on a report by a government-appointed committee on national physical decline that linked infant mortality to maternal drinking to support their call for temperance. They also worked to pass laws expelling children from public houses. See David W. Gutzke, "'The Cry of the Children': The Edwardian Medical Campaign against Maternal Drinking," *British Journal of Addiction* 79 (1984): 71–84.

15. James H. Cassedy, "An Early American Hangover: The Medical Profession and Intemperance, 1800–1860," *Bulletin of the History of Medicine* 50 (1976): 405–419.

16. Barbara Leslie Epstein, *The Politics of Domesticity: Women, Evangelicism and Temperance in Nineteenth-Century America* (Middletown, CT: Wesleyan University Press, 1981); Ruth Borodin, *Women and Temperance: The Quest for Power and Liberty, 1873–1900* (New Brunswick: Rutgers University Press, 1990); and Lori D. Ginzberg, *Women in Antebellum Reform* (Wheeling, IL: Harlan Davidson, 2000), pp. 33–39.

17. N. S. Davis, "Are the Questions Relating to the Nature, Effects, Uses and Abuses of Alcohol as Existing in Fermented and Distilled Liquors Political Questions to be Settled by Votes at Ordinary Elections, or Are they True Questions concerning the Public Health and Morals, and Therefore to Be Dealt with by the Sanitary Authorities and Courts of Justice?" *Quarterly Journal of Inebriety* 25 (1903): 228. On infant mortality, see Richard A. Meckel, *Save the Babies: American Public Health Reform and the Prevention of Infant Mortality, 1850–1929* (Baltimore: Johns Hopkins University Press, 1990), pp. 101–104, and Samuel H. Preston and Michael R. Haines, *Fatal Years: Child Mortality in Late Nineteenth-Century America* (Princeton: Princeton University Press, 1991).

18. W. C. Sullivan, "A Note on the Influence of Maternal Inebriety on the Offspring," *Journal of Mental Science* 45 (1899): 489–503. As Abel noted, in prison the women may have had a better diet and better medical care than they would have otherwise been able to obtain. Ernest L. Abel, *Fetal Alcohol Abuse Syndrome* (New York: Plenum, 1998), p. 37.

19. W. C. Sullivan, *Alcoholism: A Chapter in Social Pathology* (London: James Nisbet and Co., 1906); and Sullivan, "A Note on the Influence," pp. 489–503.

20. John Harley Warner, *The Therapeutic Perspective; Medical Practice, Knowledge and Identity in America, 1820–1885* (Cambridge, MA: Harvard University Press, 1986). William Leishman, *A System of Midwifery*, 3rd American ed. (Philadelphia: Henry C. Lea, 1879), p. 214. See also A. F. A. King, *A Manual of Obstetrics*, 4th ed. (Philadelphia: Lea Brothers and Co., 1889), p. 118.

21. William Thompson Lusk, *The Art and Science of Midwifery*, 3rd ed. (New York: D. Appleton, 1889), p. 703; and Fordyce Barker, *The Puerperal Diseases*, 4th ed. (New York: D. Appleton, 1880), p. 157.

22. George H. Napheys, *The Physical Life of Woman: Advice to the Maiden, Wife, and Mother* (Philadelphia: George MacLean, 1870), p. 223; and W. S. Playfair, *A Treatise on the Science and Practice of Midwifery*, 2nd American ed. from the 2nd British ed. rev. (Philadelphia: Henry C. Lea, 1878), p. 259. On the general benefits of beer, see Bradford S. Thompson, "Malt Liquors and Their Therapeutical Action," *Medical Record* 4 (1869): 241–243. Rodney Glisan, *Text Book of Modern Midwifery* (Philadelphia: Prisley Blakiston, 1881), p. 569.

23. H. R. Storer, "Appendix" in Albert Day, *Methomania: A Treatise on Alcoholic Poisoning* (Boston, 1867) repr. in Gerald N. Grob, ed. *Nineteenth-Century Medical Attitudes toward Alcoholic Addiction: Six Studies 1815–1867* (New York: Arno, 1981), p. 62; William C. Sullivan, "The Causes of Inebriety in the Female and the Effects of Alcohol on Racial Degeneration," *British Journal of Inebriety* 2 (1904):62–64; and M. L. Holbrook, *Parturition without Pain: A Code of Directions for Escaping from the Primal Curse,* 8th ed. enlarged (New York: M. L. Holbrook, 1878), pp. 150–51.

24. John S. Fairbairn, *A Text-Book for Midwives* (London: Henry Frowned, 1914), p. 208; and W. Lewis Howe, *A Treatise on the Care of the Expectant Mother during Pregnancy and Childbirth and Care of the Child from Birth until Puberty* (Philadelphia: F. A. Davis, 1920), pp. 6–7.

25. H. T. Webber, "Eugenics from the Point of View of the Geneticist," in Morton A. Aldrich et al., *Eugenics: Twelve University Lectures* (New York: Dodd, Mead and Co., 1914), p. 139. On eugenics, see Daniel J. Kevles, *In the Name of Eugenics: Genetics and the Uses of Human Heredity* (Berkeley: University of California Press, 1985).

26. Victor Vaughn, "Eugenics from the Point of View of the Physician," in Aldrich, *Eugenics,* p. 53.

27. Nicole Hahn Rafter, ed., *White Trash: The Eugenic Family Studies, 1877–1919* (Boston: Northeastern University Press, 1988). Henry Herbert Goddard, *The Kallikak Family: A Study in the Heredity of Feeble-mindedness* (New York: MacMillan, 1912). On Goddard, see Leila Zenderland, *Measuring Minds: Henry Herbert Goddard and the Origins of American Intelligence Testing* (New York: Cambridge University Press, 1998).

28. Robert J. Karp et al., "Fetal Alcohol Syndrome at the Turn of the 20th Century; An Unexpected Explanation of the Kallikak Family," *Archives of Pediatrics and Adolescent Medicine* 149 (1995): 45–48, and Robert Karp, "An Immense Consequence from the Suppressed Recognition of Alcohol-Related Birth Defects," unpublished paper.

29. Ethel M. Elderton and Karl Pearson, "A First Study of the Influence of Parental Alcoholism on the Physique and Ability of Offspring," *Galton Eugenics Laboratory Memoirs* no. 10 (London, 1910); and Karl Pearson and Ethel M. Elderton, "A Second Study of the Influence of Parental Alcoholism on the Physique and Ability of the Offspring: Being a Reply to Certain Medical Critics of the First Memoir and an Examination of the Rebutting Evidence Cited by Them," *Galton Eugenics Laboratory Memoirs* no. 13 (London, 1910). For an analysis of this controversy, see Lawson Crowe, "Alcohol and Heredity: Theories about the Effects of Alcohol Use on Offspring," *Social Biology* 32 (1985): 146–161.

30. Philip J. Pauly, "How Did the Effects of Alcohol on Reproduction Become Scientifically Uninteresting?" *Journal of the History of Biology* 29 (1996): 28.

31. S. J. Holmes, *The Eugenic Predicament* (New York: Harcourt, Brace, 1933), p. 114; Paul Popenoe and Rosewell Hill Johnson, *Applied Eugenics* (New York: MacMillan, 1933), pp. 95–96.

32. Molly Ladd-Taylor, "'Fixing' Mothers: Child Welfare and Compulsory Sterilization in the American Midwest, 1925–1945," in Jon Lawrence and Pat Starkey, eds., *Child Welfare and Social Action in the Nineteenth and Twentieth Centuries: International Perspectives* (Liverpool: Liverpool University Press, 2001), p. 219; Kevles, *In the Name of Eugenics,* pp. 107–112. Pauly, "How Did the Effects of Alcohol," pp. 1–28.

33. Brian S. Katcher, "The Post-Repeal Eclipse in Knowledge about the Harmful Effects of Alcohol," *Addiction* 88 (1993): 729–744; and Crowe, "Alcohol and Heredity," p. 159.

34. Ronald Peter Boris William Roizen, "The American Discovery of Alcoholism, 1933–1939," PhD diss., University of California, Berkeley, 1991; William L. White, *Slaying the Dragon: The History of Addiction Treatment and Research in America* (Bloomington: Chestnut Health Systems, 1998).

35. "Conversation with Mark Keller," *British Journal of Addiction* 80 (1985): 5–9.

36. E. M. Jellinek, "Heredity of the Alcoholic," in Yale Center of Alcohol Studies, *Alcohol, Science and Society: Twenty-Nine Lectures with Discussions as Given at the Yale Summer School of Alcohol Studies* (New Haven: Quarterly Journal of Studies on Alcohol, 1945), pp. 105–114. See also E. M. Jellinek and N. Jolliffe, "Effects of Alcohol on the Individual: Review of the Literature, 1939," *Quarterly Journal of Studies on Alcohol* 1 (1940): 110–181, esp. pp. 162–164; and E. M. Jellinek, "Heredity of the Alcoholic," *Quarterly Journal of Studies on Alcohol,* special issue (1945); Howard M. Haggard and E. M. Jellinek, *Alcohol Explored* (Garden City, NY: Doubleday, Doran and Co. 1942), pp. 204–214.

37. Raymond G. McCarthy and Edgar M. Douglass, *Alcohol and Social Responsibility: A New Educational Approach* (New York: Thomas Y. Crowell and the Yale Plan Clinic, 1949), pp. 96–97; Anne Roe, "Children of Alcoholic Parents Raised in Foster Homes," in *Alcohol, Science and Society,* pp. 115–127. The full study was published as Anne Roe and Barbara Burks, *Memoirs of the Section on Alcohol Studies, Yale University, No. 3: Adult Adjustment of Foster Children of Alcoholic and Psychotic Parentage and the Influence of the Foster Home* (New Haven: Quarterly Journal of Studies on Alcohol, 1945).

38. "Effect of a Single Large Alcohol Intake on the Fetus," *JAMA* 120 (1942): 88. On the acceptance of alcohol in pregnancy, see David N. Danforth, ed., *Textbook of Obstetrics and Gynecology* (New York: Hoeber Medical Division, 1966), p. 273; Sol T. DeLee, *Safeguarding Motherhood,* 6th ed. (Philadelphia: J. B. Lippincott, 1969), p. 50; and Ralph C. Benson, *Handbook of Obstetrics and Gynecology,* 6th ed. (Los Altos, CA: Lange Medical Publications, 1977), p. 117.

39. Stanton Belinkoff and Orrin Hall, Jr., "Intravenous Alcohol during Labor,"

American Journal of Obstetrics and Gynecology 59 (1950): 429–432; Eugene R. Chapman and Phil T. Williams, Jr., "Intravenous Alcohol as an Obstetrical Analgesia," *American Journal of Obstetrics and Gynecology* 61 (1951): 676–679; and A. M. Fetchko et al., "Intravenous Alcohol Used for Preinduction Analgesia in Obstetrics," *American Journal of Obstetrics and Gynecology* 62 (1951): 662–664.

40. Fritz Fuchs et al., "Effect of Alcohol on Threatened Premature Labor," *American Journal of Obstetrics and Gynecology* 99 (1967): 627–637.

41. Fritz Fuchs, "Prevention of Premature Birth," *Clinics in Perinatology* 7 (1980): 11–12. On women's reluctance to consume alcohol, see Fritz Fuchs, "Plasma Levels of Oxytocin and 12,14-dihydro-15-keto Prostaglanden F2a in Preterm Labor and the Effect of Ethanol and Ritodrine," *American Journal of Obstetrics and Gynecology* 144 (1982): 758. On the risks of alcohol tocolysis, see Fuchs et al., "Effect of Alcohol"; Ioannis A. Zervoudakis, Alfred Krauss, and Fritz Fuchs, "Infants of Mothers Treated with Ethanol for Premature Labor," *American Journal of Obstetrics and Gynecology* 137 (1980): 713–718. On the effects, see Florence E. Sisenwein et al., "Effects of Maternal Ethanol Infusion during Pregnancy on the Growth and Development of Children at Four to Seven Years of Age," *American Journal of Obstetrics and Gynecology* 147 (1983): 52–56. For a critique of alcohol as a tocolytic, see Ernest L. Abel, "A Critical Evaluation of the Obstetric Use of Alcohol in Preterm Labor," *Drug and Alcohol Dependence* 7 (1981): 367–378.

3. "A Clinically Observable Abnormality"

1. Personal interview with Carrie Randall, PhD, 2001.

2. Randall interview and Gerald F. Chernoff, "The Fetal Alcohol Syndrome in Mice: An Animal Model," *Teratology* 15 (1977): 223–229.

3. Ashley Montagu, *Life before Birth* (New York: New American Library, 1964), pp. 100–101; and Ashley Montagu, *Life before Birth,* rev. ed. (New York: New American Library, 1977), pp. 105–108.

4. "Martinis and Motherhood," *Newsweek* 82 (16 July 1973): 93.

5. William Grigg, "The Thalidomide Tragedy—25 Years Ago," *FDA Consumer* 21 (1987): 14–17; and "More Deformities Laid to Thalidomide," *New York Times,* 14 September 1962.

6. "Cleared of Killing of Thalidomide Girl," *New York Times,* 11 November 1962.

7. "Mrs. Finkbine Undergoes Abortion in Sweden; Surgeon Asserts Unborn Child Was Deformed—Mother of 4 Took Thalidomide," *New York Times,* 19 August 1962.

8. "The 'Thalidomide Law,'" *Newsweek* 60 (3 September 1962): 49.

9. Pamela Taylor, *Practical Teratology* (London: Academic Press, 1986), pp. 114,

117, 135; Charles V. Vorhees, "Comparison and Critique of Government Regulations for Behavioral Teratology," in Edward P. Riley and Charles V. Voorhees, eds., *Handbook of Behavioral Teratology* (New York: Plenum Press, 1986), p. 52.

10. "Toll of Rubella Epidemic Assessed," *New York Times,* 14 November 1965; Jan van Dijk, *Persons Handicapped by Rubella: Victors and Victims, a Follow-up Study* (Amsterdam: Swets and Zeitlinger, 1991), p. 14.

11. A. L. Herbst, H. Ulfelder, and D. C. Poskanzer, "Adenocarcinoma of the Vagina; Association of Maternal Stilbestrol Therapy with Tumor Appearance in Young Women," *New England Journal of Medicine* 284 (1971): 878–881; Roberta J. Apfel and Susan M. Fisher, *To Do No Harm: DES and the Dilemmas of Modern Medicine* (New Haven: Yale University Press, 1984); David A. Edelman, *DES/ Diethylstilbestrol—New Perspectives* (Lancaster, England: MTP Press, 1986); W. Eugene Smith, "Death Flow from a Pipe," *Life* 72 (2 June 1972): 74–81; and W. Eugene Smith and Aileen M. Smith, *Minamata* (New York: Holt, Rinehart and Winston, 1975), pp. 178–192 and passim.

12. M. Susan Lindee, *Suffering Made Real: American Science and the Survivors at Hiroshima* (Chicago: University of Chicago Press, 1994); Howard Ball, *Justice Downwind: America's Atomic Testing Program in the 1950s* (New York: Oxford, 1986); and Gayle Greene, *The Woman Who Knew Too Much: Alice Stewart and the Secrets of Radiation* (Ann Arbor: University of Michigan Press, 1999).

13. National Clearinghouse for Smoking and Health, *Health Consequences of Smoking* (Atlanta: U.S. Dept. of Health, Education, and Welfare, Centers for Disease Control, 1971), p. 103; Gertrud S. Berkowitz, "Smoking and Pregnancy," in Jennifer R. Niebyl, ed., *Drug Use in Pregnancy,* 2nd ed.(Philadelphia: Lea and Febiger, 1988), pp. 173–178. See also National Clearinghouse for Smoking and Health, *Health Consequences of Smoking* (Washington, DC: U.S. Dept. of Health, Education, and Welfare, Public Health Service, 1973), p. 103.

14. *Women and Smoking: A Report of the Surgeon General* (Rockville, MD: U.S. Dept. of Health and Human Services, Office of the Surgeon General, 2001), p. 28; and *Review of the Research Literature on the Effects of Health Warning Labels: A Report to the United States Congress* (Washington, DC: U.S. Dept. of Health and Human Services, 1987), Appendix B, pp. 17–18. For a discussion of the Comprehensive Smoking Education Act of 1984, see A. Lee Fritschler, *Smoking and Politics: Policy Making and the Federal Bureaucracy,* 4th ed. (Englewood Cliffs, N.J.: Prentice-Hall 1989), p. 122.

15. "Alcoholic Babies," *U.S. News & World Report* 80 (17 May 1976): 43.

16. "Two Mothers and a Brave Doctor" and "The Agony of Mothers about Their Unborn," *Life* 58 (4 June 1965): 3, 24–31. See also "Spots All Over," *Newsweek* 63 (13 April 1964): 13. On the rubella epidemic and abortion politics, see Eva R. Rubin, *Abortion, Politics and Courts: Roe v. Wade and Its Aftermath,* rev. ed. (New York: Greenwood Press, 1987), pp. 17–29; Leslie J. Regan, *When Abortion*

Was a Crime: Women, Medicine and the Law in the United States, 1867–1973 (Berkeley: University of California Press, 1997), pp. 203–207, 240–243; and Kristin Luker, *Abortion and the Politics of Motherhood* (Berkeley: University of California Press, 1984), pp. 80–81.

17. James Mohr, *Abortion in America: The Origins and Evolution of National Policy, 1800–1900* (New York: Oxford, 1978), p. 256; Reagan, *When Abortion Was a Crime*, pp. 220–222. Edward A. Duffy, *The Effect of Changes in State Abortion Laws* (Rockville, MD: U.S. Maternal and Child Health Service, 1971); and Luker, *Abortion and the Politics of Motherhood*, pp. 80–91.

18. R. Sturdevant, "Offspring of Chronic Alcoholic Women," and response by Kenneth Lyons Jones and David W. Smith, *Lancet* 2 (1974): 349; Kenneth L. Jones and David W. Smith, "The Fetal Alcohol Syndrome," *Teratology* 12 (1975): 1–10; and Kenneth Lyons Jones, "Maternal Alcoholism," in Muriel Nellis, ed., *Drugs, Alcohol and Women: A National Forum Sourcebook* (Washington, DC: National Research and Communications Associates, 1975), p. 173.

19. "Liquor and Babies," *Time* 106 (14 July 1975): 36; Barbara Walters, *ABC Evening News*, 1 June 1977, Vanderbilt Television News Archives (hereafter cited as VTNA). On physician responses see, e.g., Richard V. Lee, "Drug Abuse," in Gerard N. Burrows and Thomas F. Ferris, eds., *Medical Complications during Pregnancy* (Philadelphia: Saunders, 1975), p. 899; Jack A. Pritchard and Paul C. MacDonald, *Williams Obstetrics*, 15th ed. (New York: Appleton-Century-Crofts, 1976) p. 258.

20. J. R. Bierich et al., "Über das Embryo-Fetale Alkoholsyndrom," *European Journal of Pediatrics* 121 (1976): 155–177, cited in Ph. Dehaene et al., "Le Syndrome d'alcoolisme foetal dans le nord de la France," *Revue de l'Alcoolisme* 23 (1977): 145–158. F. Majewski et al., "Zur Frage der Interruptio Bei Alkoholkranken Frauen," *Deutsche Medizinische Wochenschrift* 103 (1978): 895–898; Frank Majewski, "Alcohol Embryopathy: Some Facts and Speculations about Pathogenesis," *Neurobehavioral Toxicology and Teratology* 3 (1981): 143–144.

21. Sterling K. Clarren, "Recognition of Fetal Alcohol Syndrome," *JAMA* 245 (1981): 2436–2439. For the term *pregnancy termination* see, e.g., Jack A. Pritchard and Paul C. MacDonald, *Williams Obstetrics*, 16th ed. (New York: Appleton-Century-Crofts, 1980), p. 321. Aubrey Milunksy, "Genetic Counseling: Prelude to Prenatal Diagnosis," in Aubrey Milunsky, ed., *Genetic Disorders of the Fetus: Diagnosis, Prevention, Treatment*, 2nd ed. (New York: Plenum Press, 1986), p. 20. On executive-branch politics, see Karen O'Conner, *No Neutral Ground? Abortion Politics in an Age of Absolutes* (Boulder: Westview Press, 1996), pp. 55–112.

22. "Martinis and Motherhood," p. 93.

23. U.S. Dept. of Health, Education, and Welfare, *Alcohol and Health: Report from the Secretary of Health, Education and Welfare* (New York: Charles Scribner's Sons, 1973), p. 30.

24. On the convergence hypothesis, see Kaye Middleton Fillmore, "'When Angels Fall': Women's Drinking as Cultural Preoccupation and as Reality," in Sharon C. Wilsnack and Linda J. Beckman, eds., *Alcohol Problems in Women: Antecedents, Consequences, and Intervention* (New York: Guilford Press, 1984), pp. 7–36; "Alcoholism: New Victims, New Treatment," *Time* 102 (22 April 1974): 76; and Susan Cheever Cowley, "Women Alcoholics," *Newsweek* 88 (15 November 1976): 73–74. See also Roberta G. Ferrence, "Sex Differences in the Prevalence of Problem Drinking," in Oriana Josseau Kalant, ed., *Alcohol and Drug Problems in Women* (New York: Plenum Press, 1980), pp. 69–124; Eileen M. Corrigan, *Alcoholic Women in Treatment* (New York: Oxford University Press, 1980), pp. 5–7.

25. National Clearinghouse for Drug Abuse Information, *Women and Drugs: An Annotated Bibliography* (Rockville: National Institute on Drug Abuse, 1975), p. 3; Parker G. Marden and Kenneth Kolodner, *Alcohol Abuse among Women: Gender Differences and Their Implications for the Delivery of Services* (Rockville, MD: National Institute on Alcohol Abuse and Alcoholism, 1979), pp. 9–10.

26. Fillmore, "'When Angels Fall'"; Melinda Kanner, "That's Why the Lady Is a Drunk: Women, Alcoholism, and Popular Culture," in Diane Raymond, ed., *Sexual Politics and Popular Culture* (Bowling Green: Bowling Green State University Popular Press, 1990), p. 183. See also Michelle Lee McClellan, "Lady Lushes: Women Alcoholics and American Society, 1880–1960," PhD diss., Stanford University, 1999.

27. Betty Friedan, *The Feminine Mystique* (New York: Dell, 1963), pp. 20, 239.

28. Cowley, "Women Alcoholics," pp. 73–74; David Brinkley, *NBC Evening News,* 29 September 1976, VTNA; and Walter Cronkite, *CBS Evening News,* 17 December 1974, VTNA.

29. National Institute on Alcohol Abuse and Alcoholism, *Services for Alcoholic Women: Foundations for Change: Resource Book* (Rockville: U.S. Dept. of Health, Education, and Welfare, National Institute on Alcohol Abuse and Alcoholism, 1979), pp. v, 3; Vasanti Burtle, ed., *Women Who Drink: Alcoholic Experience and Psychotherapy* (Springfield, IL: Charles C. Thomas, 1979), p. xiii; "State Acts on Women Drinkers," *New York Times,* 3 November 1974; "Parley to Consider Female Alcoholism," *New York Times,* 16 November 1975; William L. White, *Slaying the Dragon: The History of Addiction Treatment and Recovery in America* (Bloomington, IL: Chestnut Health Systems, 1998), p. 279. For a further discussion of whether the AA model of helplessness is harmful to women alcoholics, see Sondra Burman, "The Disease Concept of Alcoholism: Its Impact on Women's Treatment," *Journal of Substance Abuse Treatment* 11 (1994): 121–126. On the women's health movement, see Sheryl Burt Ruzek, *The Women's Health Movement: Feminist Alternatives to Medical Control* (New York: Praeger, 1978).

30. McCambridge's testimony is cited in Harold E. Hughes, *The Man from Ida*

Grove: A Senator's Personal Story (Lincoln, VA: Chosen Books, 1979), pp. 279–281. For another account of the hearings, see Nancy Olson, *With a Lot of Help from Our Friends: The Politics of Alcoholism* (New York: Writer's Club Press, 2003), pp. 40–52. U.S. Senate, Committee on Labor and Public Welfare, Hearing, "Alcohol Abuse among Women: Special Problems and Unmet Needs," 94th Cong., 2nd sess., 29 September 1976, Washington, DC: Government Printing Office. Walter Cronkite, *CBS Evening News,* 29 September 1976, VTNA. Myra MacPherson and Donnie Radcliffe, "Betty Ford Says That She Is Addicted to Alcohol," *Washington Post,* 22 April 1978, LNAU; Peter Jennings, *ABC Evening News,* 20 October 1983, VTNA.

31. National Institute on Drug Abuse, *Final Report on Drugs, Alcohol, and Women's Health: An Alliance of Regional Coalitions* (Rockville: National Institute on Drug Abuse, 1978), p. 25. See also Stephen R. Kandall, *Substance and Shadow: Women and Addiction in the United States* (Cambridge, MA: Harvard University Press, 1996), p. 197, and *Services for Alcoholic Women,* p. 6.

32. Hughes, *The Man from Ida Grove,* p. 277; William White, Ernest Kurtz, and Caroline Acker, "The Combined Addiction Disease Chronologies, 1966–1972," http://www.bhrm.org/papers/1966–1972. Nancy K. Mello and Jack H. Mendelson, eds., *Recent Advances in Studies of Alcoholism: An Interdisciplinary Symposium, Washington, D.C., July 25–27, 1970* (Rockville: National Institute of Mental Health, National Institute on Alcohol Abuse and Alcoholism, 1971).

33. U.S. Dept. of Health, Education, and Welfare, *Second Special Report to the U.S. Congress on Alcohol and Health: New Knowledge* (Rockville, MD: U.S. Dept. of Health, Education, and Welfare, National Institute on Alcohol Abuse and Alcoholism, 1974), pp. x, 49–50; "Tribute to Mark Keller," *Alcohol Health and Research World* 19 (1995): 65.

34. Morris E. Chafetz, "Children of Alcoholics," *New York University Education Quarterly* 10 (1979): 23–29; Stephanie Brown, "Adult Children of Alcoholics: The History of a Social Movement and Its Impact on Clinical Theory and Practice," in Marc Galanter, ed., *Recent Developments in Alcoholism,* vol. 9 (New York: Plenum Press, 1991), pp. 267–285.

35. Stephen H. Dinwiddie and Theodore Reich, "Epidemiological Perspectives on Children of Alcoholics," in Galanter, ed., *Recent Developments* pp. 287–299; Kenneth J. Sher, "Psychological Characteristics of Children of Alcoholics: Overview of Research Methods and Findings," in Galanter, ed., *Recent Developments,* pp. 301–326.

36. Secretary of Health, Education, and Welfare, *Third Special Report to the U.S. Congress on Alcohol and Health* (Rockville, MD: U.S. Dept. of Health, Education, and Welfare, National Institute on Alcohol Abuse and Alcoholism, 1978). On the three studies, see A. P. Streissguth et al., "Teratogenic Effects of Alcohol

in Humans and Laboratory Animals," *Science* 209 (1980): 353–361. See also Patricia D. Mail and Elsie D. Taylor, "Alcohol, Women and the NIAAA: The First Two Decades," in Jan M. Howard, ed., *Women and Alcohol: Issues for Prevention Research* (Bethesda: U.S. Dept. of Health and Human Services, National Institute on Alcohol Abuse and Alcoholism, 1996), pp. 1–17; National Institute on Alcohol Abuse and Alcoholism, *Women and Alcohol: Health-Related Issues, Proceedings of a Conference, May 23–25, 1984,* Research Monograph 16 (Rockville, MD: National Institute on Alcohol Abuse and Alcoholism, 1984).

37. Interview with Phyllis Pedrizzetti, Italian Americans in the West Collection, Library of Congress Folklife Center, Washington, DC.

4. "Not Quite Like Other Children"

1. David Brinkley, *NBC Evening News,* 31 May 1977, VTNA. The network had probably learned from a press release that a warning was forthcoming.

2. "Alcohol and Fetuses," *U.S. News & World Report* 83 (11 July 1977): 60. "Pregnant Drinkers," *Newsweek* 89 (13 June 1977): 72; Jennifer Dunning [Information Bank Abstracts], *New York Times,* 1 June 1977, LNAU.

3. Described in Secretary of Health, Education and Welfare, *Third Special Report to the U.S. Congress on Alcohol and Health* (Rockville: U.S. Dept. of Health, Education, and Welfare, National Institute on Alcohol Abuse and Alcoholism, 1978), p. 171; Henry L. Rosett, "A Clinical Perspective of the Fetal Alcohol Syndrome," *Alcoholism: Clinical and Experimental Research* 4 (1980): 121.

4. U.S. Dept. of Health, Education, and Welfare, National Institute of Alcohol Abuse and Alcoholism, *Alcohol and Health: Report from the Secretary of Health Education and Welfare* (New York: Charles Scribner's Sons, 1973), pp. xii, xvi.

5. Margaret Marsh and Wanda Ronner, *The Empty Cradle: Infertility in America from Colonial Times to the Present* (Baltimore: Johns Hopkins University Press, 1996), pp. 210–242.

6. Barbara Katz Rothman, *The Tentative Pregnancy: Prenatal Diagnosis and the Future of Motherhood* (New York: Viking, 1986); Patricia Bayer Richard, "The Tailor-Made Child: Implications for Women and the State," in Patricia Boling, ed., *Expecting Trouble: Surrogacy, Fetal Abuse, and New Reproductive Technologies* (Boulder: Westview Press, 1995), pp. 9–24; Deirdre Mira Condit, "Fetal Personhood: Political Identity under Construction," in Boling, ed., *Expecting Trouble,* pp. 25–54; Aliza Kolker and B. Meredith Burke, *Prenatal Testing: A Sociological Perspective* (Westport, CT: Bergin and Garvey, 1998). On genetic counseling and decision making, see Rayna Rapp, "Chromosomes and Communication," *Medical Anthropology Quarterly* 2 (1988): 143–157. On fetal surgery, see Monica J. Casper, *The Making of the Unborn Patient: A Social Anatomy of Fetal Surgery* (New Brunswick: Rutgers University Press, 1998). For a cri-

tique of "quality control," see Erik Parens and Adrienne Asch, *Prenatal Testing and Disability Rights* (Washington, DC: Georgetown University Press, 2000).

7. Joan C. Callahan and James W. Knight, "Prenatal Harm as Child Abuse?" in Clarice Feinman, ed., *The Criminalization of a Woman's Body* (Binghamton, NY: Harrington Park Press, 1992), pp. 131–134; Bonnie Steinbock, *Life before Birth: The Moral and Legal Status of Embryos and Fetuses* (New York: Oxford University Press, 1992).

8. Interview with Kenneth R. Warren, PhD, 2000.

9. Robert J. Sokol and Sterling K. Clarren, "Guidelines for Use of Terminology Describing the Impact of Prenatal Alcohol on the Offspring," *Alcoholism: Clinical and Experimental Research* 13 (1989): 597–598.

10. Ann Streissguth, *Fetal Alcohol Syndrome: A Guide for Families and Communities* (Baltimore: Paul H. Brookes, 1997), p. 25; George Steinmetz, "The Preventable Tragedy: Fetal Alcohol Syndrome," *National Geographic* 181 (1992): 36–39.

11. The early case reports are discussed in Chapter 1. Peter De Chateau, "A Case of Fetal Alcohol Syndrome [translation]," *Läkartidningen* 72 (1975): 1933; A. Cahuana et al., "Fetopatía alcohólica," *Anales Españoles de Pediâtria* 10 (1977): 673–676; G. Loiodice et al., "Considerazioni cliniche intorno a due casi di malformazioni congenite in bambinu nati da madri affette da alcolismo cronico," *Minerva Pediatrica* 27 (1975): 1891–1893; H. Manzke and F. R. Grosse, "Inkomplettes und Komplettes Fetales Alkoholsydrom bei Drie Kindern Einer Trinkerin," *Medizinische Welt* 26 (1975): 709–712; H. Saule, "Fetales Alkohol-Syndrom Ein Fallbericht," *Klinische Pädiatrie* 186 (1974): 452–455; J. R. Bierich et al., "Über das Embryo-Fetale Alkoholsyndrom," *European Journal of Pediatrics* 121 (1976): 155–177.

12. Katherine K. Christoffel and Ira Salafsky, "Fetal Alcohol Syndrome in Dizygote Twins," *Journal of Pediatrics* 87 (1975): 963–967; Sterling K. Clarren et al., "Brain Malformations Related to Prenatal Exposure to Ethanol," *Journal of Pediatrics* 92 (1978): 64–67; Frank Majewski, "Alcohol Embryopathy: Some Facts and Speculations about Pathogenesis," *Neurobehavioral Toxicology and Teratology* 3 (1981): 129–144.

13. Ann Pytkowicz Streissguth and Sandra Randels, "Long-Term Effects of Fetal Alcohol Syndrome," in Geoffrey C. Robinson and Robert W. Armstrong, eds., *Alcohol and Child Family Health: The Proceedings of a Conference* (Vancouver: University of British Columbia, 1988), pp. 135–151.

14. Cahuana, "Fetopatía alcohólica," pp. 673–676; John J. Mulvihill et al., "Fetal Alcohol Syndrome: Seven New Cases," *American Journal of Obstetrics and Gynecology* 125 (1976): 937–941; Kenneth L. Jones and David W. Smith, "Recognition of the Fetal Alcohol Syndrome in Early Infancy," *Lancet* 2 (1973): 1000; Sophie Pierog, Oradee Chandavasu, and Irving Wexler, "The Fetal Alcohol

Syndrome: Some Maternal Characteristics," *International Journal of Gynaecology and Obstetrics* 16 (1979): 413.

15. Clarren, "Brain Malformations," pp. 64–67; Ernest L. Abel, "Characteristics of Mothers of Fetal Alcohol Syndrome Children," *Neurobehavioral Toxicology and Teratology* 4 (1982): 3–4.

16. Sterling K. Clarren, "The Diagnosis and Treatment of Fetal Alcohol Syndrome," *Comprehensive Therapy* 8 (1982): 45; Larry Burd et al., "Screening for Fetal Alcohol Syndrome: Is It Feasible and Necessary?" *Addiction Biology* 5 (2000): 127–139.

17. Ernest L. Abel, "An Update on Incidence of FAS: FAS Is Not an Equal Opportunity Birth Defect," *Neurotoxicology and Teratology* 17 (1995): 437–443.

18. Claire B. Ernhart et al., "Underreporting of Alcohol Consumption," *Alcoholism: Clinical and Experimental Research* 12 (1988): 506–511; Lee Ann Kaskutas and Karen Graves, "An Alternative to Standard Drinks as a Measure of Alcohol Consumption," *Journal of Substance Abuse* 12 (2000): 67–78; interview with Carrie Randall, PhD, 2001; Robert J. Sokol, "Alcohol-in-Pregnancy: Clinical Research Problems," *Neurobehavioral Toxicology* 2 (1980): 157–165.

19. G. I. Shurygin, "Ob Osobennostiiakh Psikhicheskogo Razvitiia Detei ot Materei Stradaiushchikh Khronicheskim Alkogolizom," *Pediatria* 11 (1974): 71–73, cited and discussed in Sterling K. Clarren and David W. Smith, "The Fetal Alcohol Syndrome," *New England Journal of Medicine* 298 (1978): 1063–1067. R. Olegard et al., "Effects on the Child of Alcohol Abuse during Pregnancy," *Acta Peadiatrica Scandinavia* 275, Supplement (1979): 112–121. For a further analysis of the Göteborg studies, see Marita Aronson, *Children of Alcoholic Mothers* (Department of Pediatrics and Psychiatry, University of Göteborg, Sweden, 1984). On Belfast, see Henry L. Halliday, Mark McC. Reid, and Garth McClure, "Results of Heavy Drinking in Pregnancy," *British Journal of Obstetrics and Gynaecology* 89 (1982): 892–895.

20. Henry L. Rosett et al., "Reduction of Alcohol Consumption during Pregnancy with Benefits to the Newborn," *Alcoholism: Clinical and Experimental Research* 4 (1980): 178–184; Henry L. Rosett, Lyn Weiner, and Kenneth C. Edelin, "Strategies for Prevention of Fetal Alcohol Effects," *Obstetrics and Gynecology* 57 (1981): 1–7; Gunilla Larsson and Ann-Britt Bohlin, "Fetal Alcohol Syndrome and Prevention Strategies," *Pediatrician* 14 (1987): 51–56; Erja Halmesmaki, "Alcohol Counseling of 85 Pregnant Problem Drinkers: Effect on Drinking and Fetal Outcome," *British Journal of Obstetrics and Gynaecology* 95 (1988): 243–247.

21. M. Kaminski, C. Rumeau, and D. Schwartz, "Alcohol Consumption in Pregnant Women and the Outcome of Pregnancy," *Alcoholism: Clinical and Experimental Research* 2 (1978): 155–163.

22. Jan W. Kuzma and Robert J. Sokol, "Maternal Drinking Behavior and De-

creased Intrauterine Growth," *Alcoholism: Clinical and Experimental Research* 6 (1982): 396–402; Joel J. Alpert et al., "Maternal Alcohol Consumption and Newborn Assessment: Methodology of the Boston City Hospital Prospective Study," *Neurobehavioral Toxicology and Teratology* 3 (1981): 145–201; Eileen M. Ouelette et al., "Adverse Effects on Offspring of Maternal Alcohol Abuse during Pregnancy," *New England Journal of Medicine* 297 (1977): 528–530; Robert J. Sokol, Sheldon I. Miller, and George Reed, "Alcohol Abuse during Pregnancy: An Epidemiologic Study," *Alcoholism: Clinical and Experimental Research* 4 (1980): 135–145. See also Robert J. Sokol et al., "The Cleveland NIAAA Prospective Alcohol-in-Pregnancy Study: The First Year," *Neurobehavioral Toxicology and Teratology* 3 (1981): 203–209.

23. P. J. M. Davis, J. W. Partridge, and C. N. Storrs, "Alcohol Consumption in Pregnancy: How Much Is Safe?" *Archives of Disease in Childhood* 57 (1982): 940–943; Katherine Tennes and Carol Blackard, "Maternal Alcohol Consumption, Birth Weight and Minor Physical Anomalies," *American Journal of Obstetrics and Gynecology* 138 (1980): 774–780; Moira L. Plant and Martin A. Plant, "Maternal Use of Alcohol and Other Drugs during Pregnancy and Birth Abnormalities: Further Results from a Prospective Study," *Alcohol and Alcoholism* 23 (1988): 229–233; Nabeel D. Sulaiman et al., "Alcohol Consumption in Dundee Primagravidas and Its Effects on Outcome of Pregnancy," *British Medical Journal* 296 (1988): 1500–1503 and Ann P. Streissguth et al., "The Seattle Longitudinal Prospective Study on Alcohol and Pregnancy," *Neurobehavioral Toxicology and Teratology* 3 (1981): 223–233. Another natural history can be found in a follow-up of three siblings with FAS: see Sylvia Iosub et al., "Long-Term Follow-up of Three Siblings with FAS," *Alcohol: Clinical and Experimental Research* 5 (1981): 523–527.

24. Carrie L. Randall, "Alcohol as a Teratogen in Animals," *Alcohol and Health,* Monograph 2 (Washington, DC: U.S. Dept. of Health and Human Services, Alcohol, Drug Abuse, and Mental Health Administration, 1982), pp. 291–307; and Abel, *Fetal Alcohol Syndrome and Fetal Alcohol Effects* (New York: Plenum Press, 1984), p. 145.

25. Ernest L. Abel and Robert J. Sokol, "Alcohol Use in Pregnancy," in Jennifer R. Neibyl, ed., *Drug Use in Pregnancy* (Philadelphia: Lea and Febiger, 1988), pp. 193–198; D. Duimstra et al., "Fetal Alcohol Surveillance Project in the Northern Plains," *Public Health Reports* 108 (1993): 225–229. The investigators in the Northern Plains study found a rate of 3.9 per 1,000 live births in the infants who were screened, but they estimated that if the rate had been the same in the infants who were not screened, the actual number would be 8.5 cases per 1,000 live births.

26. The CDC used the classifications "Black" "White" and "Native American." "Leading Major Congenital Malformations among Minority Groups in the

United States, 1981–1986," *JAMA* 261 (1989): 205–209. For other discussions of socioeconomic status, see Qutub H. Qazi et al., "Factors Influencing the Outcome of Pregnancy in Heavy-Drinking Women," *Developmental Pharmacology and Therapeutics* 4 (1982): 6–11; Nesrin Bignol et al., "The Influence of Socioeconomic Factors on the Occurrence of Fetal Alcohol Syndrome," *Advances in Alcohol and Substance Abuse* 6 (1987): 105–118.

27. Marcia Russell, "The Impact of Alcohol-Related Birth Defects (ARBD) on New York State," *Neurobehavioral Toxicology* 2 (1980): 277–283. On the estimated cost nationally, see Ernest L. Abel and Robert J. Sokol, "A Revised Estimate of the Economic Impact of Fetal Alcohol Syndrome," *Recent Developments in Alcoholism* 9 (1991): 117–125.

28. N. Paul Rosman and Edgar Y. Oppenhiemer, "Maternal Drinking and Fetal Alcohol Syndrome," in Shaul Harel and Nicholas J. Anastasiow, eds., *The At-Risk Infant: Psycho/Social/Medical Aspects* (Baltimore: Paul H. Brookes, 1985), p. 124; Barry S. Zuckerman and Ralph Hingson, "Alcohol Consumption During Pregnancy: A Critical Review," *Developmental Medicine and Child Neurology* 28 (1986): 649–654; Rita H. Neugut, "Epidemiological Appraisal of the Literature on the Fetal Alcohol Syndrome in Humans," *Early Human Development* 5 (1981): 411–418; Rita H. Neugut, "Commentary: Fetal Alcohol Syndrome: How Good Is the Evidence?" *Neurobehavioral Toxicology and Teratology* 4 (1982): 593–594; Eve Roman, Valerie Beral, and Barry Zuckerman, "The Relation between Alcohol Consumption and Pregnancy Outcome in Humans: A Critique," in Harold Kalter, ed., *Issues and Reviews in Teratology,* vol. 4 (New York: Plenum Press, 1985), pp. 205–235.

29. Genevieve Knupfer, "Abstaining for Foetal Health: The Fiction That Even Light Drinking Is Dangerous," *British Journal of Addiction* 86 (1991): 1063–1073; Ernest L. Abel, "What Really Causes Fetal Alcohol Syndrome?" *Teratology* 59 (1999): 4–6; Elizabeth M. Armstrong and Ernest L. Abel, "Fetal Alcohol Syndrome: The Origins of a Moral Panic," *Alcohol and Alcoholism* 35 (2000): 276–282.

30. "Surgeon General's Advisory on Alcohol and Pregnancy," *FDA Drug Bulletin* 11 (1981): 1–2.

31. "Motherly Advice: Don't Drink While Pregnant," *Time* 118 (3 August 1981): 81. For the current advice, see Fetal Alcohol Syndrome Branch of the Division of Birth Defects, Child Development, Disability, and Health of the Centers for Disease Control and Prevention, http://www.cdc.gov/nceh/programs/CDDH/fas/fasprev.htm, 13 December 1999.

32. Moira Plant, *Women, Drinking and Pregnancy* (London: Tavistock, 1985), pp. 6–17. For international comparisons, see International Center for Alcohol Policies, Report 6, "Government Policies on Alcohol and Pregnancy," January 1999, www.icap.org/publications/report6.htm; Howard M. Leichter, *Free to Be*

Foolish: Politics and Health Promotion in the United States and Great Britain (Princeton: Princeton University Press, 1991).

33. E. Stewart Taylor, *Beck's Obstetrical Practice and Fetal Medicine*, 10th ed. (Baltimore: Williams and Wilkins, 1976), p. 105; Roy M. Pitkin, "Drugs in Pregnancy," in E. J. Quilligan and Norman Kretchmer, eds., *Fetal and Maternal Medicine* (New York: John Wiley and Sons, 1980), pp. 399–400.

34. Ralph C. Benson, *Handbook of Obstetrics and Gynecology*, 8th ed. (Los Altos, CA: Lange Medical Publishers, 1983), p. 140; Joan M. Bengston et al., "Managing the Uncomplicated Pregnancy; Includes Related Information on Chorionic Villus Sampling and Bendectin," *Patient Care* 21 (1987): 56. For another discussion of the risks of failing to obtain an alcohol history, see Robert J. Sokol and Sidney F. Bottoms, "Practical Screening for Risk-Drinking during Pregnancy," in Ronald Ross, ed., *Diagnosis of Alcohol Abuse* (Boca Raton: CRC Press, 1989), pp. 251–261. For a legal analysis of medical liability, see Sandra Bolton, "Maternal Drug Abuse as Child Abuse," *Western State University Law Review* 15 (1987–1988): 281–295.

35. William D. Dolan, chairman, Report E, *Fetal Effects of Maternal Alcohol Use*, Report of the Council on Scientific Affairs, American Medical Association, 1982, pp. 29–39. From the archives of the American College of Obstetricians and Gynecologists (ACOG), Washington, DC.

36. Nancy Hughes Clark, "Birth Defects: How to Prevent Them," *Harper's Bazaar* 110 (July 1977): 109. See also Geraldine Carro, "Mothering: Pregnancy No-Nos" *Ladies' Home Journal* 94 (September 1977): 24; Nissa Simon, "Getting Ready for Pregnancy," *Parents* 57 (October 1982): 151; Paula Adams Hillard, "Drugs: Risks vs. Benefits," *Parents* 58 (July 1983): 76; Paula Adams Hillard, "Alcohol and Pregnancy," *Parents* 59 (March 1984): 122, 124.

37. Judith S. Stern, "Alcohol: Mixed Blessing," *Vogue* 175 (June 1985): 137, 139. See also "Ways to Protect Your Unborn Child," *Ebony* 41 (July 1986): 72. Ronald Gots et al., "Having a Baby—1978" *Good Housekeeping* 186 (January 1978): 70.

38. Betty Watts Carrington, "Mother-to-Be, Baby-to-Be," *Essence* 10 (May 1979): 84; Simon, "Getting Ready for Pregnancy," p. 151. On expectations of pregnant women, see Barbara Duden, *Disembodying Women: Perspectives on Pregnancy and the Unborn*, trans. Lee Hoinacki (Cambridge, MA: Harvard University Press, 1993). Condit, "Fetal Personhood"; Janet Gallagher, "Collective Bad Faith: 'Protecting' the Fetus," in Joan C. Callahan, ed., *Reproduction, Ethics, and the Law: Feminist Perspectives* (Bloomington: Indiana University Press, 1995), pp. 344–345; Deborah E. Campbell and Alan R. Fleischman, "Ethical Challenges in Medical Care for the Pregnant Substance Abuser," *Clinical Obstetrics and Gynecology* 35 (1992): 803–812.

39. Pierog, Chandavasu, and Wexler, "The Fetal Alcohol Syndrome"; Claire Toutant and Steven Lippman, "Fetal Alcohol Syndrome," *American Family Physician* 22 (1980): 113–117.

40. C. L. Donovan, "Factors Predisposing, Enabling and Reinforcing Routine Screening of Patients for Preventing Fetal Alcohol Syndrome: A Survey of New Jersey Physicians," *Journal of Drug Education* 21 (1991): 35–42; Ernest L. Abel and Michael Kruger, "What Do Physicians Say about Fetal Alcohol Syndrome: A Survey of Obstetricians, Pediatricians and Family Medicine Physicians," *Alcoholism: Clinical and Experimental Research* 22 (1998): 1951–1956; Suzanne M. Miller, "Case Studies: Profiles of Women Recovering from Drug Addiction," *Journal of Drug Education* 25 (1995): 145.

41. Eileen M. Corrigan, *Alcoholic Women in Treatment* (New York: Oxford University Press, 1980); Harriet B. Braiker, "Therapeutic Issues in the Treatment of Alcoholic Women," in Sharon C. Wilsnack and Linda J. Beckman, eds., *Alcohol Problems in Women: Antecedents, Consequences and Intervention* (New York: Guilford Press, 1984), pp. 346–368; Paul M. Roman, *Women and Alcohol Use: A Review of the Research Literature* (Rockville, MD: U.S. Dept. of Health and Human Services, Alcohol, Drug Abuse, and Mental Health Administration, 1988), pp. 38–45; "Treatment Constraints for Minority Women," *Alcoholism and Alcohol Abuse among Women: Research Issues* (Rockville, MD: U.S. Dept. of Health, Education, and Welfare, National Institute on Alcohol Abuse and Alcoholism, 1979), pp. 156–157; Jennifer Merrill, "Maternal Detox Treats the Fetus; First Unit of Its Kind: Maternal Detoxification Unit, Puget Sound Hospital," *Alcohol and Addiction Magazine* 8 (1988): 49.

42. Barbara A. Morse et al., "Pediatricians' Perspectives of FAS," *Journal of Substance Abuse* 4 (1992): 187–195. A study of doctors in Saskatchewan indicated that "many learned about FAS from the media." J. L. Nanson et al., "Physician Awareness of FAS: A Suvery of Pediatricians and General Practitioners," *Canadian Medical Association Journal* 152 (1995): 1971–1976. See also Joan M. Stoler and Lewis B. Holmes, "Under-Recognition of Prenatal Alcohol Effects in Infants of Known Alcohol Abusing Women," *Journal of Pediatrics* 135 (1999): 430–436; Abel and Kroger, "What Do Physicians Know about FAS," pp. 1951–1954. Karl W. Hess, "Fetal Alcohol Syndrome: Misplaced Emphasis," *American Journal of Diseases of Children* 145 (1991): 721, and "In Reply," ibid.

43. Peter L. Petraikis, *Alcohol and Birth Defects: The Fetal Alcohol Syndrome and Related Disorders* (Washington, DC: Dept. of Health and Human Services, National Institute on Alcohol Abuse and Alcoholism, 1987), pp. 4–5. In 1992 Abel and Sokol cite a total of more than 5,000 articles. Ernest L. Abel and Robert J. Sokol, "Consequences of Alcohol Abuse," in Norbert Gleicher, ed., *Principles and Practice of Medical Therapy in Pregnancy,* 2nd ed. (New York: Appleton and Lange, 1992), p. 79.

44. Michael J. Minor and Bernice Van Dort, "Prevention Research on the Teratogenic Effects of Alcohol," *Preventive Medicine* 11 (1982): 346–349; Opinion Research Corporation, *Public Perceptions of Alcohol Consumption and Pregnancy.* Prepared for Bureau of Alcohol, Tobacco, and Firearms (Princeton: Opinion

Research Corporation, 1979), George Gallup, Jr., "Good News and Bad on Public Awareness of FAS," *Alcoholism and Addiction* 6 (1985): 11; George C. Gallup, "Fetal Alcohol Syndrome: Public Exhibits Increased Awareness," *Alcoholism and Addiction* 7 (1987): 10.

45. Associated Press (AP), "More Pregnant Women Abstain from Liquor," *New York Times* 16 January 1984, LNAU. R. Louise Floyd, Pierre Decoufle, and Daniel W. Hungerford, "Alcohol Use prior to Pregnancy Recognition," *American Journal of Preventive Medicine* 17 (1999): 106.

46. "FDA Presses for Alcohol Warning Label," *Washington Post* 23 November 1977, LNAU; Information Bank Abstracts, *Wall Street Journal,* 14 November 1977, LNAU.

47. "Abstract," *Wall Street Journal,* 25 November 1977, LNAU. The FDA attempted to mandate alcoholic beverage labels in 1975, terminating a Memorandum of Understanding between the ATF and the FDA regarding their regulatory prerogatives. The distilled spirits and wine industries brought legal action, and the FDA was subsequently enjoined from imposing labeling regulations. In 1976 a district court ruled in *Brown-Forman Distilleries Corp v. Matthews,* 435 F. Supp. 5 (WD KY, 1976), that the ATF had labeling authority. The federal government did not appeal the decision. R. Jeffrey Smith, "Agency Drags Its Feet on Warning to Pregnant Women," *Science* 199 (1978): 748–749; "Protests Foam Up over Labeling Rules," *Business Week* 2410 (8 December 1975): 23–24.

5. "According to the Surgeon General"

1. Elliot Comeaux, letter, 11 March 1978, Bureau of Alcohol, Tobacco and Firearms (ATF); and Mrs. Paul Child, letter, 14 March 1978, ATF. I reviewed all letters sent to the ATF and cite only those from which I quote directly. The ATF's summary of the letters appears in Dept. of the Treasury, *Progress Report Concerning the Advance Notice of Proposed Rulemaking on Warning Labels on Containers of Alcoholic Beverages and Addendum* (Washington, DC: Government Printing Office, February, 1979).

2. Howard M. Leichter, *Free to Be Foolish: Politics and Health Promotion in the United States and Great Britain* (Princeton: Princeton University Press, 1991), pp. 176–177. On warning-label legislation see Lee Ann Kaskutas, "Interpretations of Risk: The Use of Scientific Information in the Development of Alcohol Warning Label Policy," *International Journal of the Addictions* 30 (1995): 1519–1548. For the perspective of a Senate staffer, see Nancy Olson, *With a Lot Help from Our Friends: The Politics of Alcoholism* (New York: Writers Club Press, 2003).

3. Secretary of Health, Education, and Welfare, *Third Special Report to the U.S.*

Congress on Alcohol and Health (Rockville, MD: U.S. Dept. of Health, Education, and Welfare, National Institute on Alcohol Abuse and Alcoholism, 1978), p. xi. Secretary of Health and Human Services, *Sixth Special Report to Congress on Alcohol and Health* (Rockville, MD: U.S. Dept. of Health and Human Services, National Institute on Alcohol Abuse and Alcoholism, 1987). Secretary of Health and Human Services, *Eighth Special Report to the U.S. Congress on Alcohol and Health* (Rockville, MD: U.S. Dept. of Health and Human Services, National Institute on Alcohol Abuse and Alcoholism, 1993), pp. 256–257.

4. *Federal Register* 43 (16 January 1978), pp. 2186–2187.

5. James C. Stubbers, letter, 1 February 1978, ATF. Mrs. M. A. LaMantria, letter, 13 March 1978, ATF. B. B. Powell, letter, 9 December 1977, ATF. The date of Powell's letter suggests that some had advance warning of the call for comments.

6. Comments submitted to the Bureau of Alcohol, Tobacco, and Firearms, from the Distilled Spirits Council of the United States. Reported in U.S. Senate, Committee on Human Resources, Hearing, *S1464, to Require a Health Warning on the Labels of Bottles Containing Certain Alcoholic Beverages,* 31 January 1978, 95th Cong., 2nd sess. Washington, DC: Government Printing Office, 1978, pp. 273–399.

7. Mrs. Albert B. Hunt, letter, 30 January 1978, ATF. Carol Chandler, letter, 14 March 1978, ATF.

8. Catherine M. Bone, letter, 13 December 1977, ATF.

9. Lillian B. Maroney, letter, 9 December 1977, ATF.

10. Jack S. Blocker, *American Temperance Movements: Cycles of Reform* (Boston: Twayne, 1989), p. 150. A chronology of the disease model of addiction and its public acceptance can be found in "Combined Addiction Chronologies of William L. White, Ernest Kurtz, and Caroline Acker," www.bhrm.org/papers/ 1942–1955.pdf, 1956–1965.pdf, 1966–1972.pdf. See also Carolyn L. Wiener, *The Politics of Alcoholism: Building an Arena around a Social Problem* (New Brunswick: Transaction Books, 1981), p. 28; William L. White, *Slaying the Dragon: The History of Addiction Treatment and Recovery in America* (Bloomington, IL: Chestnut Health Systems, 1998), p. 188.

11. On medicalization, see Lynn M. Appleton, "Rethinking Medicalization: Alcoholism and Anomalies," in Joel Best, ed., *Images of Issues: Typifying Contemporary Social Problems,* 2nd ed. (New York: Aldine de Gruyter, 1995), pp. 59–80; Blocker, *American Temperance Movements,* pp. 130–161.

12. William L. White, "Addiction as a Disease: Birth of a Concept," *Counselor* 1 (2000): 46–51; Appleton, "Rethinking Medicalization."

13. Harold D. Holder and Michael J. Stoil, "Beyond Prohibition: The Public Health Approach to Prevention," *Alcohol Health and Research World* 12 (1988): 292–297; Ernest P. Nobel, *Prevention of Alcohol Abuse and Alcoholism: Alcoholism*

and Related Problems: Issues for the American Public (Englewood Cliffs, NJ: Prentice-Hall, 1984), p. 160.

14. Louis Alan Talley and Brian W. Cashell, "RS20172: Excise Taxes on Alcohol, Tobacco, and Gasoline: History and Inflation-Adjusted Rates," 22 April 1999. The data come from the Congressional Research and were posted on the Web site of the National Council for Science and the Environment, http://cnleorg/ NLE/CRSreports/Economics/econ_21.htm. The excise tax rate on beer, for example, was set at $9.00 per barrel in 1951; the statutory rate in 1999 was $18.00. If the rate had been adjusted for inflation between November 1951 and December 1998 it would have been $55.88. For a recent analysis of the lobbying power of the alcoholic beverage industry, see Michael Massing, "Strong Stuff," *New York Times Magazine,* 22 March 1998, pp. 36–41, 48–58, 72–73; Leichter, *Free to Be Foolish,* pp. 157, 160–164. See also Robin Room, "Alcohol Control and Public Health," *Annual Review of Public Health* 5 (1984): 293–317; Holder and Stoil, "Beyond Prohibition," pp. 292–297.

15. Kaskutas, "Interpretations of Risk," p. 1523.

16. Witnesses also included Gerald L. Klerman, administrator of the Alcohol, Drug Abuse and Mental Health Association; Ernest P. Noble, NIAAA director; Donald Kennedy, commissioner of the FDA; Bennett D. Katz, chair of the Task Force on Responsible Decisions about Alcohol of the Education Committee of the States; Richard J. Davis, assistant secretary of the Treasury Department; Rex D. Davis, director of the ATF. "Invited Statement of Morris E. Chafetz, M.D.," U.S. Senate Subcommittee on Alcoholism and Narcotics, and "Testimony, Henry L. Rosett, M.D.," U.S. Senate, Committee on Human Resources, Hearing, *Alcohol Labeling and Fetal Alcohol Syndrome,* 95th Cong., 2nd sess., 31 January 1978.

17. R. Jeffry Smith, "Agency Drags Its Feet on Warning to Women," *Science* 1999 (1978): 748–749; *The Alcoholism Report* 7 (1979): 1.

18. U.S. Dept. of the Treasury and National Institute on Alcohol Abuse and Alcoholism, *Progress Report concerning the Advance Notice of Proposed Rulemaking on Warning Labels on Containers of Alcoholic Beverages and Addendum* (Washington, DC: Government Printing Office, 1979), pp. 11, 18–19. The experts were Judith Hall, director of the Division of Medical Genetics at Children's Orthopedic Hospital in Seattle; Sergio Fabro, professor and director of fetal maternal medicine at George Washington University; and Amitai Etzioni, a sociologist and director of the Center for Policy Research in New York.

19. Chris Valauri, "Fetal Alcohol Syndrome," *Modern Brewery Age* 32 (1981): 29–32. Jack H. Mendelson, letter, 22 February 1978, ATF; and Jack H. Mendelson, "The Fetal Alcohol Syndrome," *Advances in Alcoholism* 1 (1979): 1–4.

20. See U.S. Senate, Committee on Labor and Human Resources Hearing, *Effects of Alcohol Consumption during Pregnancy,* September 21 1982, 99th Cong., 2nd

sess. Washington, DC: Government Printing Office, pp. 109–119. See also U.S. Dept. of the Treasury and U.S. Dept. of Health and Human Services, *Report to the President and the Congress on Health Hazards Associated with Alcohol and Methods to Inform the General Public of these Hazards* (Washington, DC: Dept of the Treasury, 1980), Appendix C; and AP, 27 June 1979, LNAU.

21. Randolph E. Schmid, "Alcohol and Pregnancy," AP, 28 April 1980, LNAU. Beverage Alcohol Information Council, "Background Memorandum," Winter 1980, ATF; and "March of Dimes Campaigning against Alcohol," United Press International (UPI), 19 June 1988, LNAU. Olson, *With a Lot of Help,* p. 437.

22. "The Great Debate: Health Warnings for Alcoholic Beverages," *Bottom Line on Alcohol and Society* 3 (1980): 3–5. U.S. Senate Committee on Labor and Human Resources, *Report on Consumer Health Warnings for Alcoholic Beverages and Related Issues,* 96th Cong., 1st sess. (Washington, DC: Government Printing Office, 1979). Olson, *With a Lot of Help,* p. 415.

23. U.S. Senate, Committee on Labor and Human Resources, Hearing, *Labeling of Alcoholic Beverages,* 96th Cong., 1st sess. 14 September 1979, Washington, DC: Government Printing Office, p. 201.

24. Senate Committee, *Report on Consumer Health Warnings,* pp. 86–87.

25. "A Disabled Baby, a Mother With Guilt," *New York Times,* 31 July 1983, LNAU; and Jerry Cheslow, "Remorse over a 'Drinking Binge,'" *New York Times,* 19 June 1988, LNAU.

26. U.S. Dept. of the Treasury and U.S. Dept. of Health and Human Services, *Report to the President and the Congress on Health Hazards Associated with Alcohol and Methods to Inform the General Public of these Hazards,* November 1980. The Carter administration disagreed with the finding, arguing that labels were preferable to other forms of government action. Susan Okie, "Alcohol Risks Are Termed Too Complex for Coverage on Bottle Warning Labels," *Washington Post,* 26 November 1980, LNAU. Kaskutas, "Interpretations of Risk," pp. 1524–1525.

27. Testimony of Christine Lubinski, U.S. Senate Committee on Commerce, Science, and Transportation, Hearing, *Alcohol Warning Labels,* 100th Cong., 2nd sess., 10 August 1988. Philip Richardson et al., *Review of the Research Literature on the Effects of Health Warning Labels: A Report to the United States Congress, June 1987* (Washington, DC: Dept. of Health and Human Services, 1987), p. 1.

28. Bryan Miller, "Food Notes," *New York Times,* 2 November 1983; Michael Goodwin, "Council Bill Warns on Drinking during Pregnancy," *New York Times,* 16 November 1983, LNAU; Dan Collins, "'When a Woman Is Pregnant, She Never Drinks Alone,'" UPI Regional News, 8 December 1983, LNAU; "New York Requires Warning to Pregnant Women," *Washington Post,* 9 December 1983, LNAU; Alan Finder and Richard Levine, "Sober Warning to the Pregnant," *New York Times,* 20 November 1983, LNAU.

29. Mary Sue Henifin and Anne Schettino Casale, "A Biased Warning on Birth Defects," *New York Times*, 13 November 1983, LNAU; William Murphy, "Koch Signs Alcohol Warning Bill for Women," AP, 8 December 1983, LNAU. The associate director of the American Civil Liberties Union delivered a similar message. See Michael Goodwin, "Council Bill Warns on Drinking during Pregnancy," *New York Times*, 16 November 1983, LNAU. Barbara Katz Rothman, *Recreating Motherhood* (New Brunswick: Rutgers University Press, 1989), p. 61. Kevin Sack, "Unlikely Union in Albany: Feminists and Liquor Sellers," *New York Times*, 5 April 1991, LNAU.

30. Interview with Sheila Blume, MD, 1999.

31. Executive Director, Alcoholism Council of Greater New York, "Alcohol and Babies," *New York Times*, 26 February 1986, LNAU. The California Superior Court and later the State Supreme Court rebuffed the California Restaurant Association's claim. Stephanie Chavez, "Signs about Ill Effects of Alcohol on Fetuses OKD," *Los Angeles Times*, 12 June 1986, LNAU; and "Warning Signs on Drinking Ruled Valid," *Los Angeles Times*, 31 October 1986, LNAU.

32. Ted Vollmer, "County OKs Posting of Warnings on Alcohol," *Los Angeles Times*, 1 October 1986, LNAU.

33. For a discussion of state programs, see U.S. Dept. of Health and Human Services, *Program Strategies for Preventing Fetal Alcohol Syndrome and Alcohol-Related Birth Defects* (Rockville: National Institute on Alcohol Abuse and Alcoholism, 1987), pp. 13–14. On Minnesota, see KARE-TV, *KARE 11 News Today*, 28 March 1997, LNAU; WCCO-TV, *The Five O'Clock News*, 11 March 1997, LNAU; Governor Arne H. Carlson's Task Force on Fetal Alcohol Syndrome, *Suffer the Children: The Preventable Tragedy of Fetal Alcohol Syndrome* (St. Paul: State of Minnesota, 1998), p. 16.

34. Ann L. Wilson, "The History of Fetal Alcohol Syndrome in South Dakota, 1970–1992," Department of Pediatrics, School of Medicine, University of South Dakota, 1992, Appendix A-2 pp. 235–242.

35. Sheila Blume, "Drinking and Pregnancy: Preventing Fetal Alcohol Syndrome," *New York State Journal of Medicine* 81 (1981): 92. UPI Regional News, 3 August 1982, LNAU. "New Anti-Drug Program Launched by State," UPI Regional News, 9 March 1988, LNAU.

36. "Warning Labels on Alcoholic Beverages," *Bottom Line on Alcohol in Society* 2 (1978): 6–7. Charles Kuralt, *CBS Evening News*, 14 June 1988, VTNA. Bump earlier claimed that the labeling law was the first step in winning the war on drugs "by changing society's attitude toward our most widely used drug." "Booze Warning Labels Urged," UPI Regional News, 5 April 1988, LNAU.

37. California Environmental Protection Agency, "Proposition 65," http://www.calep.ca.gov; Tillie Fong, "Bill Calls for Alcohol Warning Labels," *Los Angeles Times*, 18 December 1986, LNAU. Paul Jacobs, "Alcohol as a Hazardous

Chemical: It May Make Governor's List," *Los Angeles Times,* 26 January 1987, LNAU; Leo C. Wolinksy, "Liquor Label Warning Plan Dies at Hearing," *Los Angeles Times,* 19 March 1987, LNAU; Richard C. Paddock, "Alcohol Warning Label Bill Is Derailed in Legislature," *Los Angeles Times,* 23 May 1987, LNAU; Daniels C. Carson, "Alcohol Will Go on Toxics List; Warning Signs Considered for Wine, Beer," *San Diego Union-Tribune,* 29 August 1987, LNAU; Richard C. Paddock, "State Backs Sign Posting as Warning on Alcohol," *Los Angeles Times,* 10 November 1987, LNAU; and Richard C. Paddock, "Labels to Warn Pregnant Women Urged for Liquor," *Los Angeles Times,* 11 November 1987, LNAU.

38. For an editorial favoring labels because of the tort protection they would offer, see Dirk Olin, "This Dud's for You: Alcoholic Beverage Labeling Politics," *New Republic* 199 (1988): 12–13. See also Clay Campbell, "Note: Liability of Beverage Manufacturers: No Longer a Pink Elephant," *William and Mary Law Review* 31 (1989–90): 157–196; A. Lee Fritschler, *Smoking and Politics: Policy Making and the Federal Bureaucracy* (Englewood Cliffs, NJ: Prentice Hall, 1989), pp. 23–26; Eileen Wagner, "The Alcoholic Beverages Labeling Act of 1988: A Preemptive Shield against Fetal Alcohol Syndrome Claims?" *Journal of Legal Medicine* 12 (1991): 167–198.

39. John D. McClain, "Government to Require More Legible Health Warnings," AP, 14 February 1990, LNAU. "Bills Introduced to Extend Alcohol Health/Risk Warnings to Advertisements," *Alcoholism Report,* April 1990, LNAU; William M. Welch, "Beer Institute Threatens Ax to Sports Coverage If Warnings Expanded," AP, 17 July 1990, LNAU. U.S. House Committee on Energy and Transportation, *Hearing before the Subcommittee on Transportation and Hazardous Materials to Consider H.R. 4493.* 101st Cong., 2nd sess. Washington, DC: Government Printing Office, 18 July 1990. The bill would have required a series of rotating warnings. In 1991 the Senate Committee on Commerce considered S. 664, the Alcoholic Beverage Advertising Act. In 1998 Senator Thurmond introduced a measure that called for the striking of the phrase "may cause health problems" from the beverage label and inserting in its place "may lead to alcoholism." He also wanted a third warning added: "Moderate consumption of alcoholic beverages may cause health problems such as hypertension and breast cancer." His efforts failed. In 1999 he introduced an amendment to the act that would grant authority to carry out the act to the secretary of health and human services, transferring it from the secretary of the treasury. Regarding the exclusion of warnings from advertisements, see Donna L. Polowchena, "The Right to Know," in Ruth C. Engs, ed., *Controversies in the Addiction's Field* (Dubuque, IA: Kendall/Hunt, 1990), p. 138.

40. Lee Kaskutas and Thomas K. Greenfield, "First Effects of Warning Labels on Alcoholic Beverage Containers," *Drug and Alcohol Dependence* 31 (1992): 1–14.

41. Betsy A. Lehman, "Is Any Amount Safe?" *Boston Globe,* 23 July 1990, LNAU;

Ronni Sandroff, "Happy Hour Revisted? Effects of Moderate Alcohol Use," *Health* 20 (1988): 31, LNAU.

42. "U.S. Senate Unanimously Approves Alcohol Warning Labels," P. R. Newswire, 17 October 1988, LNAU.

6. "Tempest in a Cocktail Glass"

1. Tom Brokaw, *NBC Evening News,* 28 March 1991, VTNA.

2. Dan Rather, *CBS Evening News,* 2 April 1991, VTNA.

3. Richard Campbell, *Sixty Minutes and the News: A Mythology for Middle America* (Urbana: University of Illinois Press, 1991), pp. 119–121; S. Elizabeth Bird and Robert W. Dardenne, "Myth, Chronicle, and Story: Exploring the Narrative Qualities of News," in J. W. Carey, ed., *Media, Myths and Narratives: Television and the Press* (Beverly Hills: Sage, 1988), pp. 67–86.

4. AP, "Cocktail Servers Fired for Trying to Talk Pregnant Woman Out of Drink," *Chicago Tribune,* 27 March 1991, LNAU; Michael Kinsley, "TRB from Washington: Cocktails for Two," *New Republic* 204 (1991): 6. In the *Seattle Times* see, for example, Lorraine Berry Andrews, "My Belly Isn't Public Domain," and Kevin Helwig, "No Booze for Pregnant Women," *Seattle Times,* 3 April 1991; LNAU.

5. Christy Scattarella, "Daiquiri Sour—Woman Says Red Robin Incident Made Her Feel Like a Child Abuser," *Seattle Times,* 28 March 1991, LNAU.

6. Drew Humphries, *Crack Mothers; Pregnancy, Drugs and the Media* (Columbus: Ohio State University Press, 1999).

7. The poll data were cited in Ronni Sandroff, "Invasion of the Body Snatchers: Fetal Rights vs. Mothers' Rights," *Vogue* 178 (1988): 330.

8. Cynthia Cotts, "The Partnership: Hard Sell in the Drug War," *Nation* 254 (9 March 1992): 300–302; Dan E. Beauchamp, *Beyond Alcoholism: Alcohol and Public Health Policy* (Philadelphia: Temple University Press, 1980), p. 17.

9. Charles Atkin and Martin Block, *Content and Effects of Alcohol Advertising,* (Washington, DC: Bureau of Alcohol, Tobacco, and Firearms, 1981); Charles K. Atkin et al., "The Role of Alcohol Advertising in Excessive and Hazardous Drinking," *Journal of Drug Education* 12 (1983): 313–326; Guy Cumberbatch, *A Measure of Uncertainty: The Effects of Mass Media* (London: John Libbey, 1989); William Leiss, Stephen Kline, and Sut Jhally, *Social Communication in Advertising: Persons, Products, and Images of Well-Being,* 2nd ed. rev. (New York: Routledge, 1990). On the alcoholic beverage industry, see Michael Jacobson, Robert Atkins, and George Hacker, *The Booze Merchants: The Inebriating of America* (Washington, DC: Center for Science in the Public Interest, 1983). In 1996 Seagrams proposed to break the self-imposed ban on electronic advertising of distilled spirits. Ted M. Nugent, ed., *Standard and Poor's Industry Sur-*

veys: Alcoholic Beverages and Tobacco (New York: Standard and Poor's, 1997), p. 2. See also Catherine A. Quagliania, "Malt Beverages," "Wines, Brandy and Brandy Spirits," and "Distilled and Blended Liquors," in Scott Heil and Terrance W. Peck, eds., *Encyclopedia of American Industries,* 2nd ed. (Detroit: Gale, 1998), pp. 113–133. U.S. Senate Committee on Labor and Human Resources, Hearing, *Media Images of Alcohol: The Effect of Advertising and Other Media on Alcohol Abuse,* 94th Cong., 2nd sess. 8 and 11 March 1976, Washington, DC: Government Printing Office.

10. Lawrence M. Wallack, "Mass Media Campaigns in a Hostile Environment: Advertising as Anti-Health Education," *Journal of Alcohol and Drug Education* 28 (1983): 51–63; Neil Postman et al., *Myths, Men and Beer: An Analysis of Beer Commercials on Broadcast Television* (Falls Church, VA: AAA Foundation for Traffic Safety, 1987), unpaged abstract; U.S. Senate, *Media Images of Alcohol,* and U.S. Senate Committee on Labor and Human Resources, Hearing, *Alcohol Advertising,* 99th Cong., 1st sess., 7 February 1985; Robert B. Overend, "You Can Say No to Alcohol, Government Media Campaign Tells Teens and Women," *Traffic Safety* 82 (1982): 18–20, 27–29.

11. James R. DeFoe et al., "Drinking on Television: A Five-Year Study," *Journal of Drug Education* 13 (1983): 25–38. Episode 28, Season 1, *Dallas,* 1979. See also Episodes 15 and 29. "TV Soaps Could Help Cut Down on Drinking Mothers," UPI Regional News, 30 March 1988, LNAU. The Harvard Alcohol Project persuaded some entertainment show writers to mention designated drivers and to use caution in depicting drinking in their shows. Joseph Turow, *Media Systems in Society: Understanding Industries, Strategies, and Power,* 2nd ed. (New York: Longman, 1997), pp. 152–155.

12. Richard S. Salant, *Salant, CBS and the Battle for the Soul of Broadcast Journalism: The Memoirs of Richard S. Salant,* ed. Bill Buzenberg and Susan Buzenberg (Boulder: Westview, 1999).

13. Turow, *Media Systems in Society,* p. 12. Herbert J. Gans, *Deciding What's News: A Study of CBS Evening News, NBC Nightly News, Newsweek and Time* (New York: Vintage, 1979); Joseph R. Dominick, *The Dynamics of Mass Communication,* 2nd ed. (New York: Random House, 1987), pp. 462, 484; Shanto Iyengar and Donald R. Kinder, *News That Matters: Television and American Opinion* (Chicago: University of Chicago Press, 1987). See also Neil Postman and Steve Powers, *How to Watch TV News* (New York: Penguin, 1992).

14. On television news narratives, see John Corner, *Television Form and Public Address* (London: Edward Arnold, 1995); John Hartley, *Tele-ology: Studies in Television* (London: Routledge, 1992).

15. Walter Cronkite, *CBS Evening News,* 1 June 1977, VTNA; Barbara Walters, *ABC Evening News,* 1 June 1977, VTNA; and David Brinkley, *NBC Evening News,* 31 May 1977, VTNA. Walter Cronkite, *CBS Evening News,* 13 January 1978,

VTNA. Warning-label legislation received little attention from the print media. See Paul H. Lemmens, "Coverage of Beverage Alcohol Issues in the Print Media in the United States, 1985–1991," *American Journal of Public Health* 89 (1999): 1555–1560.

16. David Brinkley, *NBC Evening News*, 26 June 1978, VTNA.

17. Iyengar and Kinder, *News That Matters*, p. 9.

18. David Brinkley, *NBC Evening News*, 31 May 1977, VTNA. David Brinkley, *NBC Evening News* 26 June 1978, VTNA; David Brinkley, *NBC Evening News*, 8 February 1979, VTNA; Roger Mudd, *NBC Evening News*, 5 November 1982, VTNA.

19. Special issue, *JAMA* 252 (1984); Peter Jennings, *ABC Evening News*, 11 October 1984, VTNA. On CBS, anchor Dan Rather simply described the scientific findings. Dan Rather, *CBS Evening News*, 11 October 1984, VTNA.

20. Tom Brokaw, *NBC Evening News*, 11 October 1984, VTNA.

21. Drew Humphries, "Crack Mothers at Six: Prime-Time News, Crack/Cocaine, and Women," *Violence against Women* 4 (1998): 45–61.

22. Drew Humphries, *Crack Mothers: Pregnancy, Drugs and the Media* (Columbus: Ohio State University Press, 1999), p. 99; Jimmie L. Reeves and Richard Campbell, *Cracked Coverage: Television News, the Anti-Cocaine Crusade, and the Reagan Legacy* (Durham: Duke University Press, 1994), p. 208; Jacqueline Litt and Maureen McNeil, "Crack Babies and the Politics of Reproduction and Nurturance," in Joel Best, ed., *Troubling Children: Studies of Children and Social Problems* (New York: Aldine de Gruyter, 1994), pp. 93–113; Henry H. Brownstein, *The Rise and Fall of a Violent Crime Wave: Crack Cocaine and the Social Construction of a Crime Problem* (Guilderland, NY: Harrow and Heston, 1996); Laura E. Gomez, *Misconceiving Mothers: Legislators, Prosecutors and the Politics of Prenatal Drug Exposure* (Philadelphia: Temple University Press, 1997).

23. Craig Reinarman and Harry G. Levine, "Crack in Context: Politics and Media in the Making of a Drug Scare," *Contemporary Drug Problems* 16 (1989): 548; Craig Reinarman and Harry G. Levine, "The Crack Attack: America's Latest Drug Scare, 1986–1992," in Joel Best, ed., *Images of Issues: Typifying Contemporary Social Problems* (New York: Aldine de Gruyter, 1989), pp. 147–185. See also Reeves and Campbell, *Cracked Coverage,* and James A. Inciardi, *The War in Drugs II: The Continuing Epic of Heroin, Cocaine, Crack, Crime, AIDS and Public Policy* (Mountain View, CA: Mayfield, 1992).

24. Inciardi, *The War on Drugs II,* pp. 106–108.

25. Reeves and Campbell, *Cracked Coverage;* Michael Dorris, "A Desperate Crack Legacy," *Newsweek* 115 (25 June, 1990): 8.

26. Gomez, *Misconceiving Mothers.*

27. Charles Krauthammer, "Children of Cocaine," *Washington Post,* 20 July 1989, LNAU. Charles Krauthammer, "Put Cocaine Babies in Protective Custody," *St.*

Louis Post-Dispatch, 6 August 1989 (LNAU). For a follow-up discussion, see Abigail Trafford, "Should Women Who Use Drugs while Pregnant Be Locked Up?" *Washington Post,* 18 August 1998, LNAU; Litt and McNeil, "'Crack Babies,'" p. 93.

28. Joan Beck, "Editorial: Women's Rights Are No Excuse for Mothers-to-Be Who Drink," *Orlando Sentinel Tribune,* 21 February 1990, LNAU.

29. Sara Kershnar and Lynn Paltrow, "Pregnancy, Parenting and Drug Use: Which Women? Which Harm?" http://www.harmreduction.org/news/summer01/kershar.htm. The authors note that more than over 80 percent of the women prosecuted were African American or Latina.

30. Bird and Dardenne, "Myth, Chronicle and Story," p. 71.

31. Dan Rather, *CBS Evening News,* 2 April 1991, VTNA. The same story was reported on a morning news segment. See Charles Osgood, *CBS Morning News,* 17 April 1991, LNAU.

32. CNN Transcript 287-2, *Sonya Live,* 30 April 1993, LNAU.

33. Genevieve Knupfer, "Abstaining for Foetal Health: The Fiction that Even Light Drinking Is Dangerous," *British Journal of Addiction* 86 (1991): 1063–1073.

34. Tom Brokaw, *NBC Evening News,* 28 March 1991, VTNA.

35. Meg Moritz, "The Ratings 'Sweeps' and How They Make News," in Gary Burns and Robert J. Thompson, eds., *Television Studies: Textual Analysis* (New York: Praeger, 1989), pp. 121–136. A critic of the series charged that it failed to place Native American alcoholism in a historical framework and stereotyped all Native Americans as drunks. Furthermore, she noted that the awarding of a Pulitzer Prize in 1989 to the *Anchorage Daily News* for a series on alcoholism and Native Americans had begun a stampede among other news organizations to chronicle the problem. Nancy Butterfield, Gannett News Service, 7 December 1989, LNAU.

36. Tom Brokaw, *NBC Evening News,* 21 November 1989, LNAU.

37. Dorris, "A Desperate Crack Legacy." For a critique of Dorris's construction of motherhood, see Maureen McNeil and Jacquelyn Litt, "More Medicalizing of Mothers: Foetal Alcohol Syndrome in the USA and Related Developments," in Sue Scott et al., eds., *Private Risks and Public Dangers* (Aldershot, England: Avebury, 1992), pp. 112–328

38. Michael Dorris, *The Broken Cord* (New York: Harper, 1989), pp. xvii, 165. Michael Dorris, "Fetal Alcohol Syndrome," *Parents* 65 (1990): 240. On prosecutions, see Lynn M. Paltrow, "Criminal Prosecutions against Pregnant Women, National Update and Overview," Reproductive Freedom Project, American Civil Liberties Union Foundation, April 1992, http://advocatesforpregnant women.org/articles/1992stat.html.

39. Loren Siegel, "The Pregnancy Police Fight the War on Drugs," in Craig Reinarman and Harry G. Levine, eds., *Crack in America: Demon Drugs and So-*

cial Justice (Berkeley: University of California Press, 1997), pp. 249–259; see also Cynthia R. Daniels, ed., *Lost Fathers: The Politics of Fatherlessness in America* (New York: St. Martin's Press, 1998); Stephen R. Kandall, *Substance and Shadow: Women and Addiction in the United States* (Cambridge, MA: Harvard University Press, 1996), p. 273. See also Ellen Marie Weber, "Alcohol- and Drug-Dependent Pregnant Women: Laws and Public Policies That Promote and Inhibit Research and the Delivery of Services," in M. Marlyne Kilbey and Kursheed Asghar, eds., *Methodological Issues in Epidemiological, Prevention, and Treatment Research on Drug-Exposed Women and Their Children* (Rockville: National Institute of Drug Abuse, 1992), pp. 349–364.

40. For discussions of these issues, see Lee A. Schott, "The Pamela Rae Stewart Case and Fetal Harm: Prosecution or Prevention," *Harvard Women's Law Journal* 11 (1988): 227–245; Deborah J. Krauss, "Regulating Women's Bodies: The Adverse Effect of Fetal Rights Theory on Childbirth Decisions and Women of Color," *Harvard Civil Rights–Civil Liberties Law Review* 26 (1991): 523–548; Marcy Tench Stovall, "Looking for a Solution: In Re Valerie D and State Intervention in Prenatal Drug Abuse," *Connecticut Law Review* 25 (1993): 1265–1300; Jean Reith Schroedel and Pamela Fiber, "Development and Trends in the Law: Punitive versus Public-Health Oriented Responses to Drug Use By Pregnant Women," *Yale Journal of Health Policy, Law and Ethics* 1 (2001): 217–235. American Medical Association, Board of Trustees, "Legal Interventions during Pregnancy," *JAMA* 264 (1990): 2663–2670.

41. Joan Little, "Woman Jailed after Baby Is Born Intoxicated . . . Charges May Be First in Missouri, Officials Say," *St. Louis Post-Dispatch*, 26 November 1991, LNAU. "Jail Won't Help This Alcohol Abuser," *St. Louis Post-Dispatch*, 9 December 1991, LNAU. The paper called for more state-funded centers to serve women and children.

42. Connie Chung, *CBS Evening News*, 4 August 1992, VTNA. Paltrow's position is further explained in Lynn M. Paltrow, "When Becoming Pregnant Is a Crime," *Criminal Justice Ethics* 9 (1990): 41–47. See also Drew Humphries et al., "Mothers and Children, Drugs and Crack: Reactions to Maternal Drug Dependency," in Clarice Feinman, ed., *The Criminalization of a Woman's Body* (New York: Harrington Park Press, 1992), pp. 203–221. District Court of Adams County, Nebraska, Memorandum Opinion and Order, 17 July 1993, *State of Nebraska v. Deborah Arandus*, Case No. 93072.

43. "Woman Challenges Fetal Alcohol Syndrome Law," UPI Regional News, 4 October 1985, LNAU; Tom Schultz, "Infant Is Safe, But Mom's in Jail; 11-Day-Old Boy Back in County's Custody," *Cleveland Plain Dealer*, 6 August 1997, LNAU. Rolland Smith and Judy Lynne, "Report," KNSD Radio, 7 June 1995, LNAU; WSOC-TV, *Eyewitness News Midday*, 24 September 1998, LNAU. Mike Todd, "Mother of Drug-Addicted Baby Faces Charges in San Marcos," *Austin American-Statesman*, 22 January 1997, LNAU.

44. "Woman Charged with Child Abuse for Alleged Drinking during Pregnancy," UPI Regional News, 17 January 1990, LNAU; "Larger Legal Questions Unanswered in the Case of Alleged Child Abuse by Drinking," UPI Regional News, 7 February 1990, LNAU; "Woman Once Charged with Abuse of Fetus Gives Birth," UPI Regional News, 18 June 1990, LNAU; and *Wyoming v. Pfannenstiel*, NO 1-90-8CR (County Court of Laramie, Wyoming, 1 February 1990).

45. Bruce Hilton, "At What Moment Does Responsibility Begin?" *Chicago Tribune*, 6 May 1990, LNAU. See also Tamar Lewin, "Drug Use in Pregnancy: New Issues for the Courts," *New York Times*, 5 February 1990, LNAU; Joan Beck, "Womb Not a Haven for the Babies of Women Who Drink," *Chicago Tribune*, 8 February 1990, LNAU; Ellen Goodman, "Being Pregnant, Addicted: It's a Crime," *Chicago Tribune*, 11 February 1990, LNAU. Andrea Stone and Chance Conner, "Courts Address Unborn's Rights: Cases Challenge Mother's Alcohol, Drug Use: Alcohol's Effects Often Long Term," *USA Today*, 2 February 1990, LNAU.

46. Jean Reith Schroedel and Paul Peretz, "A Gender Analysis of Policy Formation: The Case of Fetal Abuse," *Journal of Health Politics, Policy and Law* 19 (1994): 355.

47. Mark Hayward, "Police Charge: Unborn Child Endangered; Chesterfield Woman Arrested, Blood-Alcohol Level .21," *Union Leader*, 14 August 1996, LNAU; "Experts Doubt Fetus Abuse Charge," UPI Regional News, 15 August 1996, LNAU; Mark Hayward, "Bail Requirements Hit in Unborn Child Case: Facts on Mothers Who Drink During Pregnancy," *Union Leader*, 15 August 1996, LNAU; Mark Hayward, "Charges Dropped in Unborn Child Endangerment: Official: State Laws Don't Cover Case," *Union Leader*, 16 October 1996, LNAU. Women and men could and did have parental rights terminated because of alcoholism. See Rosemary Shaw Sackett, "Terminating Parental Rights of the Handicapped," *Family Law Quarterly* 25 (1991): 253–298; Sandra Bolton, "Maternal Drug Abuse as Child Abuse," *Western State University Law Review* 15 (1987–88): 281–295.

48. *State of Wisconsin v. Deborah Zimmermann*, Circuit Court Branch V, Racine County, 96-CF-525. *State of Wisconsin v. Deborah J. Zimmermann*, Circuit Court, Racine County, Summons, DA Complaint 96-F-368.

49. Anne Marie O'Neill, Leah Eskin, and Linda Satter, "Under the Influence: Drunk while Pregnant, A Woman Is Charged with Trying to Kill Her Baby," *People* 46 (9 September 1996): 52–55. See also *Real Life*, NBC, 29 August 1996, LNAU; *Today*, NBC, 5 September 1996, LNAU; Tom Brokaw, *NBC Evening News*, 5 September 1996, VTNA.

50. "Panel Discussion on Whether Pregnant Women Who Engage in Behavior That Might Be Dangerous to Their Unborn Child Should Be Punished Legally," *Rivera Live*, SYN News Transcripts, 12 September 1996, LNAU. *All Things Considered*, Transcript #2335-13, 13 September 1996, LNAU. *Cornelia*

Whitner v. State of South Carolina, Supreme Court of South Carolina, 328 S. C. 1; 492 S. E. 2d 777; 1997 S. C., Lexis 203, 70 A. L. R. 5th 723.

51. Court of Appeals Decision, 26 May 1999, No. 96-2797-CR, *State of Wisconsin v. Deborah J. Z.* See "Wisconsin: Woman Charged w/Feticide Violates Bail Terms," *American Political Network Abortion Report,* 26 May 1997, LNAU.

52. *Wisconsin Statutes,* Chapter 46, Social Services, 46.001 (1998); and *Wisconsin Statutes,* Chapter 48, Children's Code: Subchapter III, Jurisdiction 48.133 (1998), p. 35. On fetal protection, procreative liberty, and maternal-fetal rights, see "Symposium: Criminal Liability for Fetal Endangerment," *Criminal Justice Ethics* 9 (1990): 12–51. *South Dakota Codified Laws,* Chapter 34–20A, Treatment and Prevention of Alcohol and Drug Abuse, 34–20A-63, Emergency Commitment—Grounds, 1999. Laury Oaks, *Smoking and Pregnancy: The Politics of Fetal Protection* (New Brunswick: Rutgers University Press, 2001) p. 172. One legal scholar suggested that mental health statutes made a better alternative than civil commitment statutes because they did not have a perpetrator-victim perspective. See James M. Wilton, "Compelled Hospitalization and Treatment during Pregnancy: Mental Health Statutes as Models for Legislation to Protect Children from Prenatal Drug and Alcohol Exposure," *Family Law Quarterly* 25 (1991): 149–170. For a critique of the Wisconsin and South Dakota laws, see Lynn M. Paltrow, David S. Cohen, and Corinne A. Carey, "Governmental Responses to Pregnant Women Who Use Alcohol or Other Drugs, Year 2000 Overview," Women's Law Project and National Advocates for Pregnant Women, http://advocatesforpregnantwomen.org/articles/gov_ response_review.

53. AP, "S. D. to Order Pregnant Drinkers into Treatment," *Arkansas Democrat-Gazette,* 24 May 1998, LNAU; Alison M. Leonard, "Fetal Personhood, Legal Substance Abuse and Maternal Prosecutions: Child Protection or 'Gestational Gestapo'?" *New England Law Review* 32 (1998): 615–660; Katha Pollitt, "'Fetal Rights'; A New Assault on Feminism," in Molly Ladd-Taylor and Lauri Umansky, eds., *"Bad" Mothers: The Politics of Blame in Twentieth-Century America* (New York: New York University Press, 1998), pp. 285–298; and Oaks, *Smoking and Pregnancy.*

54. Martha A. Field, "Controlling the Woman to Protect the Fetus," *Law, Medicine and Health Care: A Publication of the American Society of Law and Medicine* 17 (1989): 114–129; Ted Gest, "The Pregnancy Police, On Patrol," *U.S. News & World Report* 106 (6 February 1989): 50; Susan Edmiston, "Here Come the Pregnancy Police," *Glamour* 88 (August 1990): 202–205; see also Richard Cohen, "Editorial: When A Fetus Has More Rights than the Mother," *Washington Post,* 28 July 1988, LNAU.

55. Humphries, "Crack Mothers at Six."

56. Sandra G. Boodman, "Alcoholic Mothers and Their Children," *Washington*

Post, 17 April 1990, LNAU; Montgomery Brower and Maria Wilhelm, "Children in Peril," *People* 33 (16 April 1990): 86–89.

57. Jim Schachter, "Criminal Penalty for Mothers Wrong, Experts Say," *Los Angeles Times,* 22 October 1986, LNAU.

7. The Thorp Case

1. Steve Miletich, "Distiller Rips Alcoholic Mother as Trial Opens," *Seattle Post-Intelligencer,* 25 April 1989. For other cases, see "Families Sue Alcohol Brewers for Children's Birth Defects," UPI, 3 December 1987, LNAU. Robert J. Cole, "Market Place: Alcohol Lawsuits and Stock Impact," *New York Times,* 26 July 1988, LNAU; Malcolm Gladwell, "Trial against Liquor Maker to Test Limits of Liability," *Washington Post,* 26 April 1989, LNAU. Andrew Wolfson, "Birth-Defect Suits May Spell Trouble for Liquor Industry," *Courier-Journal,* 24 April 1989, LNAU. See also Andrew Blum, "Alcohol Marketing under Attack: Must Drinkers Be Warned of Risks?" *National Law Journal,* 5 September 1988 p. 3, LNAU; Timothy Egan, "A Worried Liquor Industry Readies for Birth-Defect Suit," *New York Times,* 21 April 1989; Joni H. Blackman, "Alcohol on Trial: A First-of-Its-Kind Case Looks at Who Should Pay Price for Mother's Drinking," *Los Angeles Times,* 4 May 1989, LNAU; "Product Liability: Who Injured This Child?" *Time* 133 (8 May 1989): 71.

2. American Law Institute, *Restatement (Second) of Torts,* 402A, Comment i. Two important cases were *Hon v. Stroh,* 853 F.2d 510 (3rd Cir. 1987), which asserted that the dangers of regular ordinary alcohol consumption were unknown, and *Brune v. Brown Forman Corp.,* 758 S.W. 2d 827 (Tex. App. 1988), which claimed that the dangers of acute alcohol poisoning from rapid heavy consumption required a warning. See Eileen N. Wagner, "The Alcoholic Beverages Labeling Act of 1988: A Preemptive Shield against Fetal Alcohol Syndrome Claims," *Journal of Legal Medicine* 12 (1991): 167–200.

3. Gladwell, "Trial against Liquor Maker."

4. Alan Dershowitz, "Editorial: Abortion Issue Intrudes in Fetal Rights Litigation," *St. Petersburg Times,* 2 September 1989, LNAU. Rhondetta Goble, "Fetal Alcohol Syndrome: Liability for Failure to Warn—Should Liquor Manufacturers Pick Up the Tab?" *Journal of Family Law* 28 (1989–90): 71–85, suggests that the Alcoholic Beverage Labeling Act would foreclose future claims. For a different opinion, see Carter H. Dukes, "Comments: Alcohol Manufacturers and the Duty to Warn: An Analysis of Recent Case Law in Light of the Alcoholic Beverage Labeling Act of 1988," *Emory Law Journal* 38 (1989): 1189–1221.

5. *Michael Thorp v. James B. Beam Distilling Company,* No. C87-01527D, Vol. 3, 26 April 1989, pp. 86–94, National Archives in Seattle. Hereafter all records will

be from this case unless otherwise stated; all records are from the National Archives in Seattle. Volume numbers refer to the trial transcript. Epstein was a partner in the firm of Sills, Cummis, Zuckerman, Radin, Tischman, Epstein, and Gross, P.A., of New Jersey. His affidavit stated he had been involved for ten years in birth defects litigation. Affidavit of Barry M. Epstein in Support of Application to Appear and Participate, 4 March 1988. See also http://www.sills cummis.com. On Brent's earlier work, see Robert L. Brent, "Litigation-Produced Pain, Disease and Suffering: An Experience with Congenital Malformation Lawsuits," in John L. Sever and Robert L. Brent, eds., *Teratogen Update: Environmentally Induced Birth Defect Risks* (New York: Alan R. Liss, 1986), pp. 215–227; Robert L. Brent, "Medicolegal Aspects of Teratology," ibid., pp. 203–214; "Biographical Sketch, Robert Brent, M.D., Ph.D., D.Sc.(Hon.)," http://kidshealth.org/ai/staff/bio.ai.brent.robert.html See also UPI, "Families Sue Alcohol Brewers for Children's Birth Defects," 3 December 1987, LNAU; and Motion to Compel Answers to Deposition Questions and the Production of Documents, 29 December 1988.

6. Kindley and Tezak were with Ryan, Swanson, Cleveland in Seattle; Strauber was from Chadbourne and Parke; and his local associates were from Stafford, Frey, Cooper, and Stewart. Alessandro G. Olivieri, "[Big Suits] West," *American Lawyer* (1989): 26, LNAU. See also Affidavit of Donald Strauber, 8 April 1988.

7. Complaint and Jury Demand (Product Liability Claim), 5 November 1987, NAS. See *Revised Code of Washington* 7.72.030 [1988 c 94S 1; 1981 c 27 S 4] for relevant product liability law. Answer, Affirmative Defenses, and Jury Demand, 1 March 1988; Declaration of Shannon Stafford in Support of Defendant's Motion for Summary Judgment, 10 November 1988; Defendant's Memorandum in Support of Motion for Summary Judgment, 10 November 1988; Plaintiffs' Memorandum in Opposition to Motion for Summary Judgment, 5 December 1988; Defendant's Memorandum in Opposition to Plaintiffs' Motion for Partial Summary Judgment, 12 December 1988; Reply Brief in Support of Plaintiffs' Motion for Partial Summary Judgment, 19 December 1988; Defendant's Reply Memorandum in Support of Its Motion for Summary Judgment, 19 December 1988; Memorandum in Support of Motion to Strike Strict Liability and Negligence Causes of Action, 30 December 1988; Jim Beam's Memorandum in Support of Supplementing Summary Judgment Record, 23 February 1989; Order, 6 March 1989.

8. Complaint and Jury Demand, pp. 13–14.

9. Joint Status Report, 29 February 1988, p. 2; Notice of Depositions upon Oral Examination and Praecipe, 23 November 1988. This lists 32 individuals to be deposed. The complaint about the 100 witnesses is in Plaintiffs' Combined Memorandum of Law in Support of Three Motions *In Limine* regarding Character Evidence, Product Misuse and "Should Have Known" Evidence, 10 April

1989. See also Defendant's Memorandum in Opposition to Plaintiffs' Motions *In Limine* regarding What Plaintiffs Term "Character Evidence," "Product Misuse," and "'Should have Known'" Evidence, 14 April 1989; Order Compelling Production of Child Protective Service's Records, 28 November 1988; Defendant's Response to Plaintiff's Motion to Quash Subpoenas, 29 November 1988; Plaintiffs' Reply Brief in Support of Motion to Quash Subpoenas and Response to Defendant's Motion for an Order Compelling the Production of Records from Division of Child and Family Services, 29 November 1988; Order for Production of Documents, 30 December 1988; Motion to Compel Answers to Deposition Questions and the Production of Documents, 29 November 1989; Protective Order, 30 December 1988; Defendant's Memorandum in Support of the Admissibility of the Medical Records of Dr. Siverling, 8 May 1989. The issue was discussed after the trial began, in a meeting with the judge. Vol. 9, 4 May 1989, pp. 116–123; and vol. 10, 5 May 1989, pp. 4–7.

10. Motion to Compel Answers to Deposition Questions; Notice of Appeal of Defendant Beam Brands Company to Magistrate Sweigert's Minute Order Re Psychological Examination of Candance and Harold Thorp, 8 February 1989. See also Plaintiffs' Response to Jim Beam's Appeal of Magistrate Sweigert's Order Re Psychological Examination of Candance and Harold Thorp, 10 February 1989.

11. Protective Order, 30 November 1988; Defendant's Motion for Order Compelling Discovery and attached Exhibit E, Deposition of Connie Peare, 9 December 1988. Peare is Candance Thorp's sister. See also Defendant's Memorandum in Opposition to Plaintiffs' Motions *In Limine* regarding What Plaintiffs Term "Character Evidence," "Product Misuse," and "Should Have Known Evidence," 14 March 1989; Plaintiffs' Combined Memorandum of Law in Support of Three Motions *In Limine* regarding Character Evidence, Product Misuse, and "Should Have Known" Evidence, 10 April 1989; Plaintiff's Motion to Exclude Reference to Specific Acts of Conduct, 26 April 1989; Summary of Evidentiary Rulings, 27 April 1989.

12. Letter from Barry L. Shapiro to the Honorable Carolyn R. Dimmick, 4 October 1988; *Thorp v. Beam*, Stipulation Relating to Document Production, 13 October 1988; Plaintiffs' Memorandum in Opposition to Motions *In Limine* with Respect to Animal Studies, (undated, incomplete document); and Summary of Trial Rulings, 28 April 1989.

13. Vol. 1, 24 April 1989.

14. *MacNeil/Lehrer NewsHour*, 24 May 1988, Transcript 3302, LNAU. Vol. 2, pp. 3–5. Wolfson, "Birth-Defect Suits." See also "Babies and Booze," *Louisville Courier-Journal*, 26 April 1989, LNAU. The problem was raised again later; see vol. 10, 5 May 1989, pp. 7, 22.

15. Vol. 1, 24 April 1989.

16. Vol. 2, April 25, 1989, p. 73; Steve Miletich, "Boy, 4, Makes His Case," *Seattle Post-Intelligencer*, 25 April 1989.

17. Vol. 2, 25 April 1989, pp. 170–172.

18. Index to Exhibits Supporting Plaintiffs' Memorandum in Opposition to Motion for Summary Judgment, Plaintiffs' Memorandum in Opposition to Motion for Summary Judgment, 5 December 1988; Jim Beam's Memorandum in Support of Supplementing Summary Judgment Record, 23 February 1989; Plaintiffs' Memorandum in Opposition to Motion for Summary Judgment, 5 December 1988; and vol. 3, 26 April 1989, pp. 109–111.

19. Blackman, "Alcohol on Trial." Defendant's Memorandum in Support of Motion for Summary Judgment, 10 November 1988. See also: Superior Court of Washington, County of King Juvenile Court, Dependency Petition of Michael Thorp, No. 86-7-00215-2.

20. Vol. 3, pp. 17, 107. On Brent's testimony, see Stephanie Nichols, "Liquor Company's Attorney Tries to Discredit Doctor," UPI, 26 April 1989, LNAU.

21. Vol. 3, pp. 157–158.

22. Vol. 4, 27 April 1989, pp. 12, 21. The plaintiffs tried to obtain a ruling before trial precluding the admission of evidence regarding the LBIC's role in a public information campaign. See Plaintiffs' Memorandum of Law in Opposition to the Admission of Evidence Regarding the LBIC's "Public Information Campaign," 4 May 1989.

23. Vol 4, p. 58. Ironically, the day Berish testified, the State of Washington announced an aggressive campaign to warn women against drinking during pregnancy, including the posting of signs in every place that liquor was sold. Joni H. Blackmon, "Alcohol and Birth Defects: State Plans Publicity Campaign," *Seattle Post-Intelligencer*, 28 April 1989. On Berish's testimony see Steve Militech, "'I Would Have Quit Drinking,'" *Seattle Post-Intelligencer*, 28 April 1989.

24. Vol. 4, p. 94.

25. Vol. 5, 28 April 1989, p. 64.

26. Vol. 6, 1 May 1989, p. 128.

27. Vol. 7, 2 May 1989, pp. 163, 185.

28. Vol. 9, p. 85. See also Arthur C. Gorlick, "Judge Almost Dismissed Alcohol Case," *Seattle Post-Intelligencer*, 5 May 1989.

29. Vol. 10, p. 37.

30. Ibid, p. 95.

31. Ibid, pp. 164, 168.

32. Exhibit A: Curriculum Vita, George T. Cvetkovich, undated. There was a fight over the admissibility of public opinion surveys as evidence. See Defendant's Memorandum in Support of the Admissibility of Public Opinion Surveys, 5 May 1989.

33. Vol. 11, 8 May 1989, p. 152.

34. Ibid, pp. 213, 218–219.

35. See Janina R. Galler et al., "The Influence of Early Malnutrition on Subsequent Behavioral Development, I: Degree of Impairment in Intellectual Performance," *Journal of the American Academy of Child Psychiatry* 22 (1983): 8–15; Janina R. Galler, "The Influence of Early Malnutrition on Subsequent Behavioral Development, II: Classroom Behavior," *Journal of the American Academy of Child Psychiatry* 22 (1983): 16–22; Janina R. Galler, Frank Ramsey, and Giorgio Solimano, "The Influence of Early Malnutrition on Subsequent Behavioral Development, III: Learning Disabilities as a Sequel to Malnutrition," *Pediatric Research* 18 (1984): 209–213; Janina R. Galler et al., "The Influence of Early Malnutrition on Subsequent Behavioral Development, IV: Soft Neurologic Signs," *Pediatric Research* 18 (1984): 826–832. Galler published many other studies based on her long-term follow-up of this population.

36. Vol. 12, 9 May 1989.

37. Ibid, pp. 69, 72.

38. Ibid. p. 100. Steve Miletich, "Doctor Blames Boy's Bad Home, Not Alcohol," *Seattle Post-Intelligencer* May 10, 1989.

39. Vol. 12, p. 175. The question of whether Vengler would be permitted to discuss this warning was a matter of contention. See Memorandum of Law in Support of Plaintiff's Motion to Preclude the Testimony of Kathryn Vengler on Any Issue Other than That Specifically Identified in the Pretrial Order or, in the Alternative, for Leave to Depose Ms. Vengler in Advance of Her Testimony, 1 May 1989; and Defendant's Memorandum in Opposition to Plaintiff's Motion to Limit the Testimony of Kathryn Vengler or, in the Alternative, for Leave to Depose Ms. Vengler in Advance of Her Testimony, 5 May 1989.

40. Ibid, p. 182.

41. Ibid, pp. 118–119.

42. Vol. 14, 11 May 1989.

43. Vol. 15, 12 May 1989.

44. Ibid., pp. 38, 43.

45. Ibid., pp. 77, 80; Stephanie Nichols, "Jury Gets Case Tying Liquor to Birth Defects," UPI, 14 May 1989, LNAU.

46. Vol. 15, pp. 142, 151.

47. Milt Piggree cartoon, *Seattle Times,* 24 April 1989; Greenberg cartoon, *Seattle Post-Intelligencer,* 6 May 1989.

48. Charles Krauthammer, "Paying for Folly," *Washington Post,* 28 April 1989, LNAU. For other views, see Bernard Levin, "What a Bottle for the Baby: American Courts," *Times* (London), 29 June 1989, LNAU; Harry Levins, "Lawyers, Labels Leading Ladders to Lower Rungs," *St. Louis Post-Dispatch,* 12 June 1989, LNAU. Diane Silver, letter to the editor, *Los Angeles Times,* 11 May 1989, LNAU;

JoAnn Jackson, letter to the editor, ibid.; Dave and Joann Moine, letter to the editor, ibid. For comments after the verdict, see Jennifer L. Gunther, "Whiskey Trial," *San Diego Union-Tribune,* 30 May 1989, LNAU; "'Jim Beam' Verdict Is Victory for Common Sense," *Newsday,* 21 May 1989, LNAU.

49. Terry Finn, "Distiller Not Liable for Child's Birth Defects," UPI, 18 May 1989, LNAU; Katia Blackburn, "Jim Beam Cleared in Birth Defect Lawsuit," AP, 18 May 1989, LNAU. "Alcohol Cleared in Deformity Suit," *New York Times,* 18 May 1989, LNAU.

50. Steve Miletich, "Jim Beam Not at Fault in Tragedy, Jury Says," *Seattle Post-Intelligencer,* 18 May 1989.

51. Blackburn, "Jim Beam Cleared," N. A. Lang, "Will Jim Beam's Court Victory Deter Similar FAS Liability Suits?" *Insurance Review* 109 (July 1989): 9, LNAU.

52. Wagner, "Alcoholic Beverage Labeling Act."

8. "An Argument That Goes Back to the Womb"

1. Ted Koppel, *Nightline,* 15 April 1992, LNAU.

2. Kenneth Lyons Jones, "Early Recognition of Prenatal Alcohol Effects: A Pediatrician's Responsibility," *Journal of Pediatrics* 135 (1999): 405–406; telephone interview with Kenneth Lyons Jones, MD, 1999.

3. Steve Baker, "Retrospective Forum: The Robert Alton Harris Execution: Justice Not Revenge: A Crime Victim's Perspective on Capital Punishment," *UCLA Law Review* 40 (1992): 339–343.

4. On death penalty mitigation efforts, see Victoria Slind-Flor, "Against Death but for Profit," *National Law Journal,* 19 January 1998, LNAU; Craig Haney, "Mitigation and the Study of Lives: On the Roots of Violent Criminality and the Nature of Capital Justice," in James R. Acker, Robert M. Bohm, and Charles S. Lanier, eds., *America's Experiment with Capital Punishment: Reflections on the Past, Present, and Future of the Ultimate Penal Sanction* (Durham: Carolina Academic Press, 1998), pp. 351–384.

5. Dan Morain, "Video Plea Made to Save Harris: Crime: In the Tape Sent Out by ACLU, Experts Say the Killer Was Abused as a Child and Has Brain Damage. They Ask Wilson for Clemency," *Los Angeles Times,* 31 May 1992, LNAU; Houston Chronicle News Services, "Harris Suffered Abuse from Father; Abandoned," *Houston Chronicle,* 21 April 1992, LNAU. Craig Haney, "Symposium: The Social Context of Capital Murder: Social Histories and the Logic of Mitigation," *Santa Clara Law Review* 35 (1995): 547–609; Charles M. Sevilla and Michael Laurence, "The Robert Alton Harris Execution: Thoughts on the Cause of the Present Discontents: The Death Penalty Case of Robert Alton Harris," *UCLA Law Review* 40 (1992): 345–379. Sevilla was counsel for Harris

from 1982 to 1992; Laurence was counsel for Harris from 1990 to 1992. All of this information became part of his clemency appeal.

6. Harriet Chiang, "Wilson Denies Harris Clemency; ACLU Appeals the Case to State Supreme Court," *San Francisco Chronicle*, 17 April 1992, LNAU; Katherine Bishop, "California Killer Is at Center of Storm on Limiting Death Penalty Appeals," *New York Times*, 6 December 1991, LNAU. In 1985 the U.S. Supreme Court had ruled that indigent defendants in death penalty cases had a federal constitutional right to psychiatric assistance, but the Court prohibited the retroactive application of new rules of constitutional procedure. Daniel M. Weintraub, "The Trick to Getting Wilson's Ear: How Do You Make Your Case to a Man Known for Circuitous Decision-Making? The Key, Insiders Say, Is to Pique the Governor's Interest, Know Your Facts, and Make Your Idea His Idea," *Los Angeles Times*, 2 June 1993, LNAU.

7. "Excerpts from Wilson's Message on Clemency," *San Francisco Chronicle*, 17 April 1992, LNAU.

8. Howard Mintz and Richard Barbieri, "Will Ninth Circuit Fall in Line? Supreme Court's Emphatic Reaction to Repeated Stays of Harris' Execution Seen as an Attempt to 'Lessen the Nerve' of Some Judges in Death Penalty Cases," *The Recorder*, 22 April 1992, LNAU.

9. Alexander Morgan Capron, "Fetal Alcohol and Felony," *Hastings Center Report* 22 (1992): 29.

10. Lisa Stansky, "Harris Jurors Think They Did the Right Thing; Three Think New Evidence Wouldn't Persuade Them; Panel Worried That Sentence Could Be Altered," *The Recorder*, 15 April 1992, LNAU; *Larry King Live*, "Death Watch for Robert Alton Harris," CNN Transcripts, 20 April 1992; LNAU. On alcoholism as an aggravating factor, see William J. Bowers and Benjamin D. Steiner, "Choosing Life or Death: Sentencing Dynamics in Capital Cases," in Acker, Bohm, and Lanier, eds., *America's Experiment with Capital Punishment*, p. 341.

11. John T. Noonan, Jr., "Essay: Horses of the Night: *Harris v. Vasquez*," *Stanford Law Review* 45 (1993): 1011–1025.

12. Dennis Prager, "The American Tradition of Personal Responsibility," *The Heritage Lectures* 515 (Washington, DC: Heritage Foundation, 1995); and Rob Morse, "Low-Life Achievement Awards," *San Francisco Examiner*, 10 February 1994, LNAU. On FAS and diminished capacity claims, see "Court Cases on Diminished Capacity/Guilt," http://depts.washington.edu/fadu/legalissues/cc .dimcap.html.

13. Alan M. Dershowitz, *The Abuse Excuse and Other Cop-outs, Sob Stories, and Evasions of Responsibility* (Boston: Little, Brown, 1994), p. 326; Charles Rosenberg, "Banishing Risk: Continuity and Change in the Moral Management of Disease," in Allan M. Brandt and Paul Rozin, eds., *Morality and Health* (New

York: Routledge, 1997), p. 42. The International Classification of Diseases, Ninth Revision, Clinical Modification, used a nonspecific code 760.71 for FAS.

14. James Q. Wilson, *Moral Judgment: Does the Abuse Excuse Threaten Our Legal System?* (New York: Basic Books, 1997).

15. Jeanice Dagher-Margosian, "Representing the FAS Client in a Criminal Case," in Ann P. Streissguth and Jonathan Kanter, eds., *The Challenge of Fetal Alcohol Syndrome: Overcoming Secondary Disabilities* (Seattle: University of Washington Press, 1997), pp. 125–133; David Boulding, "Mistakes I Have Made with FAS Clients," http://depts.washington.edu/fadu/legalissues/lawarticles.html. For cases involving FAS and waivers of rights, see "Court Cases on the Waiver of Rights," http://depts.washington.edu/fadu/legalissues/cc.waiver.html.

16. A summary of court cases can be found online at http://depts.washington.edu/fadu/legalissues/.

17. See http://www.cdc.gov/ncbddd/fas/secondary/htm; Candis McLean, "A Home of Their Own," http://report.ca/archive/report/20010122/p3li010122f.html. See also D. K. Fast, J. Conry, and C. A. Loock, "Identifying Fetal Alcohol Syndrome among Youth in the Criminal Justice System," *Developmental and Behavioral Pediatrics* 20 (1999): 370–372, and on detention facilities, *State v. Sidwell* 1997 WL 1340003 (Wash. App. Div 1), as described in http://epts.washington.edu/fadu/legalissues/cc.general.html.

18. On the role of narrative in death penalty cases, see Austin Sarat, *When the State Kills: Capital Punishment and the American Condition* (Princeton: Princeton University Press, 2001), pp. 158–184. Denise Ferry, "Fetal Alcohol Syndrome: An Effective Capital Defense," *California Attorneys for Criminal Justice Forum* 24 (1997): 42–50.

19. Janet Rae-Dupree, "Jury Recommends Life Sentence for Killer of 2," *Los Angeles Times,* 30 August 1990, LNAU. "What's Wrong with My Child?" *20/20,* ABC News, 30 March 1990, LNAU. The show was rerun two years later. For other cases in which death-penalty convictions were reduced to life in prison, see "FAS and FAE Sufferers 'Consciously Do the Wrong Thing,'" http://www.tucsoncitizen.com/local/archive/fas/part3.html; Ginny McKibben, "Jurors Often Balk at Death Penalty," *Denver Post,* 14 March 1994, LNAU; Michael G. Mooney, "Clerk's Murder Trial Delayed until January," *Modesto Bee,* 26 June 1998, LNAU.

20. Bowers and Steiner, "Choosing Life or Death," in Acker, Bohm, and Lanier, eds., *America's Experiment with Capital Punishment,* pp. 309–349. Tom Uhlenbrock, "Missouri Executes Murderer," *St. Louis Post-Dispatch,* 31 August 1990, LNAU; AP, "Missouri Executes Man Convicted of Killing 5," *New York Times,* 1 September 1990, LNAU. Harriet Chiang et al., "Triple Killer Executed at San Quentin; U.S. Supreme Court Denied Final Appeal," *San Francisco Chronicle,* 3 May 1996, LNAU; AP, "Virginia Executes Man for Murder," *New*

York Times, 21 July 1990, LNAU; Ed Housewright, "Execution Debate Centers on Killer with Low IQ; Several States Ban Practice," *New Orleans Times-Picayune*, 16 August 1998, LNAU; Christopher Thorne, "Sullivan's Plea for Life Rejected by State Pardons Board," AP, 21 September 1999, LNAU; Amy H. Holmes, "Commentary: States Shouldn't Kill Childlike Criminals," *USA Today*, 1 October 1999, LNAU.

21. *The State of Washington v. James Leroy Brett*, Supreme Court of Washington, 126 Wash. 2nd 136; 892 p. 2nd 29; 1995, Wash. Lexis 146; "Guilty Plea Brings Life without Parole; Victim Slain during 1991 Home Invasion Robbery," *Columbian* (Vancouver, WA), 23 March 2001, LNAU. Frank Green, "Death Row Veteran's Life Spared," *Richmond Times Dispatch*, 15 November 2000, LNAU. For a case requiring expert testimony before sentencing, see *John Walter Castro, Sr. v. State of Oklahoma; Daniel Reynolds, Warden, Oklahoma State Penitentiary; and Larry Fields, Director, Oklahoma Department of Corrections*, U.S. Court of Appeals for the Tenth Circuit, 71 F. 3d 1502, 4 December 1995. For other cases of FAS and claims regarding counsel, see "Court Cases on Ineffective Assistance of Counsel," http://depts.washington.edu/fadu/legalissues/cc.ineffect.html.

22. Beverly Ford, "Saugus Woman's Killer Executed by Injection in Ariz.," *Boston Herald*, 14 January 1999, LNAU. Supreme Court of North Carolina, *State of North Carolina v. Clinton Ray Rose aka Wayne Raymond Grice*, 393 N.C. 172; S.E. 2d 211; 1994 N.C. Lexis 718, 14 April 1994, LNAU. *Cherry v. State*, 781 So. 2d 1040, 25 Fla. L. Weekly S 719 (Fla. 2000), cited in http://depts.washington.edu/fadu/legalissues/cc.wit.html, and *State v. Rose*, 339 N.C. 172, 451 S.E. 2d 211 (N.C. 1994), cited in http://depts.washington.edu/fadu/legalissues/cc.wit.html.

23. *Bobby Marion Francis v. Richard L. Dugger, Secretary, Department of Corrections*, U.S. District Court for the Southern District of Florida, 697 F. Supp 472, 7 October 1988, Case No. 88-10075-CIV, LNAU. Chris Lavin and Charlotte Sutton, "Florida Executes Killer," *St. Petersburg Times*, 26 June 1991, LNAU; Centers for Disease Control and Prevention, National Center on Birth Defects and Developmental Disabilities, National Task Force on Fetal Alcohol Syndrome and Fetal Alcohol Effect, "Minutes of Task Force meeting, September 20–21, 2002," p. 21, http://www.cdc.gov.ncbddd/fas/taskforce.htm.

24. Supreme Court of the United States, *Atkins v. Virginia*, No. 00-8425, Decided 20 June 2002.

25. Charles V. Vorhees, "Origins of Behavioral Teratology," in Edward P. Riley and Charles V. Vorhees, eds., *Handbook of Behavioral Teratology* (New York: Plenum, 1986), pp. 3–13. The FDA did not require testing for behavioral teratogenesis because of the problems in measuring such effects. See Ernest L. Abel, *Behavioral Teratogenesis and Behavioral Mutagenesis: A Primer in Abnormal*

Development (New York: Plenum Press, 1989), pp. 227–233; L. W. Buckalew, Sherman Ross, and Michael J. Lewis, "Behavioral Teratology: A Formalization," *Journal of Pediatric Psychology* 4 (1979): 323–330.

26. Peter A. Fried and Barbara Watkinson, "36- and 48-Month Neurobehavioral Follow-Up of Children Prenatally Exposed to Marijuana, Cigarettes, and Alcohol," *Developmental and Behavioral Pediatrics* 11 (1990): 49–58; Ernest L. Abel, *Fetal Alcohol Abuse Syndrome* (New York: Plenum Press, 1998), p. 137.

27. Sharon Landesman-Dwyer, Arlene S. Ragozin, and Ruth E. Little, "Behavioral Correlates of Prenatal Alcohol Exposure: A Four-Year Follow-Up Study," *Neurobehavioral Toxicology and Teratology* 3 (1981): 187–193. *Tenth Special Report to Congress: Alcohol and Health* (Rockville: U.S. Dept. of Health and Human Services, 2000), p. 301.

28. Kathleen Stratton, Cynthia How, and Frederick Battaglia, *Fetal Alcohol Syndrome: Diagnosis, Epidemiology, Prevention and Treatment* (Washington, DC: National Academy of science, 1996), pp. 63–81.

29. Ibid., p. 301. For studies of neuropathology linked to prenatal alcohol exposure and the developmental consequences, see, e.g., Beatrice Larroque and Monique Kaminski, "Prenatal Exposure to Alcohol and Development at Preschool Age: Main Results of a French Study," *Alcoholism: Clinical and Experimental Research* 22 (1998): 295–303; Tresa M. Roebuck, Sarah N. Mattson, and Edward P. Riley, "A Review of the Neuroanatomical Findings in Children with Fetal Alcohol Syndrome or Prenatal Exposure to Alcohol," *Alcoholism: Clinical and Experimental Research* 22 (1998): 339–344; Campbell M. Clark et al., "Structural and Functional Brain Integrity of Fetal Alcohol Syndrome in Nonretarded Cases," *Pediatrics* 105 (2000): 1096–1099; Elizabeth R. Sowell et al., "Regional Brain Shape Abnormalities Persist into Adolescence after Heavy Prenatal Alcohol Exposure," *Cerebral Cortex* 12 (2000): 856–865; Fred L. Bookstein et al., "Geometric Morphometrics of Corpus Callosum and Subcortical Structures in the Fetal-Alcohol-Affected Brain," *Teratology* 64 (2001): 4–32; Ilona Autti-Rämö et al., "MRI Findings in Children with School Problems Who Had Been Exposed Prenatally to Alcohol," *Developmental Medicine and Child Neurology* 44 (2002): 98–106.

30. Centers for Disease Control and Prevention, National Center on Birth Defects and Developmental Disabilities, "Living with Fetal Alcohol Syndrome (FAS) Secondary Conditions, http://www.cdc.gov/ncbddd/fas/secondary.htm. Marita Aronson and Bibbi Hagberg, "Neuropsychological Disorders in Children Exposed to Alcohol during Pregnancy: A Follow-Up Study of 24 Children Born to Alcoholic Mothers in Göteborg, Sweden," *Alcoholism: Clinical and Experimental Research* 22 (1998): 321–324.

31. On the benefits of early diagnosis, see Larry Burd et al., "Screening for Fetal Alcohol Syndrome: Is It Feasible and Necessary?" *Addiction Biology* 5 (2000): 127–139; Barbara A. Morse and Lyn Weiner, "Rehabilitation Approaches for

Fetal Alcohol Syndrome," in Hans-Ludwig Spohr and Hans-Christoph Stein-hausen, eds., *Alcohol, Pregnancy and the Developing Child* (New York: Cambridge University Press, 1996), pp. 249–268. On secondary disabilities linked to FAS, see "Secondary Conditions," Fetal Alcohol Syndrome Branch, Division of Birth Defects, Child Development and Disability and Health, Centers for Disease Control and Prevention, http://www.cdc.gov/ncbddd.fas/secondary/htm; "Living With Fetal Alcohol Syndrome," http://www.cdc.gov/ncbddd/fas/fassc .htm; "Living with Fetal Alcohol Syndrome (FAS) Protective Factors," http:// www.cdc.gov/ncbddd/fas/protective.htm. Hans-Ludwig Sphor, "Fetal Alcohol Syndrome in Adolescence: Long-Term Perspective of Children Diagnosed in Infancy," in Sphor and Steinhausen, eds., *Alcohol, Pregnancy and the Developing Child,* pp. 207–226, and Hans-Christoph Steinhausen, "Psychopathology and Cognitive Functioning in Children with Fetal Alcohol Syndrome," in ibid., pp. 227–246.

32. Ann P. Streissguth et al., *Understanding the Occurrence of Secondary Disabilities in Clients with Fetal Alcohol Syndrome (FAS) and Fetal Alcohol Effects,* Final Report to the Centers for Disease Control and Prevention (Seattle: University of Washington School of Medicine, 1996) pp. 4–7, 62–63.

33. Karen L. Lungu, *Children with Special Needs: A Resource Guide for Parents, Educators, Social Workers and Other Caregivers* (Springfield, IL: Charles C. Thomas, 1999), p. 5. Susan B. Edelstein, *Children with Prenatal Alcohol and/or Other Drug Exposure: Weighing the Risks of Adoption* (Washington, DC: Child Welfare League of America, 1995). Judith Kleinfeld and Siobhan Westcott, eds., *Fantastic Antone Succeeds! Experiences in Educating Children with Fetal Alcohol Syndrome* (Fairbanks: University of Alaska Press, 1993).

34. National Public Radio, *Morning Edition,* 21 April 1992, LNAU; Harry Smith, *CBS Evening News,* 17 April 1992, LNAU; Carla Wohl and Howard Thompson, *The Crusaders,* WNBC-New York, 2 July 1994, LNAU.

35. Dorris is quoted in AP, "Doctors Criticized on Fetal Problem," *New York Times,* 11 December 1990, LNAU.

36. Danielle Saba Donner, "The Emerging Adoption Market: Child Welfare Agencies, Middlemen and 'Consumer' Remedies," *University of Louisville Journal of Family Law* 35 (1996): 473–535.

37. Marci J. Blank, "Note: Adoption Nightmares Prompt Judicial Recognition of the Tort of Wrongful Adoption: Will New York Follow Suit?" *Cardozo Law Review* 15 (1994): 1687–1743; UPI, "Couple Who Adopted Psychotic Boy Gets $70,000," 4 January 1988, LNAU; Dan Rather, *CBS Evening News,* 11 November 1992, LNAU. AP, "Agencies Blamed in an Adoption That Went Awry," *New York Times,* 9 August 1992, LNAU. On foreign adoptions see, e.g., Connie Cass, "Family Sues over Adoption Gone Terribly Wrong," AP, 21 September 1992, LNAU.

38. Dan Rather, *CBS Evening News,* 11 November 1992, LNAU; Dianne Klein,

"Adoption Gone Awry: Psychotic Child Disrupts a Household," *Washington Post,* 5 January 1988, LNAU; Jeff Stidham, "Couple Want Their Adoption of Boy Annulled," *Tampa Tribune,* 24 November 1998, LNAU; David Postman, "Sins of Silence: One After Another, Adopted Children Were Causing Turmoil in Their New Families. The Parents Frantically Sought Answers, Only to Learn, Too Late in Some Cases, That State Social Workers Had Known What Was Wrong from the Beginning," *Seattle Times,* 14 January 1996, LNAU. See also Bruce Westfall, "Adoptive Parents Sue State," *Columbian* (Clark County, WA), 27 December 1994, LNAU; "Fetal Alcohol Syndrome on the Rise," *New Orleans Times-Picayune,* 11 February 1996, LNAU.

39. Elisabeth Rosenthal, "When a Pregnant Woman Drinks," *New York Times Magazine,* 4 February 1990, p. 61. Dru Wilson, "Danger in the Womb: Pregnant Women Taking Even Small Amounts of Alcohol Raise Chance of Profound Lifelong Damage to Children," *Albany Times Union,* 11 August 1998, LNAU. For a story quoting a medical professional, see Daniel J. Anderson, "Drinking while Pregnant Risks Damaging the Fetus: The Result Can Be Fetal Alcohol Syndrome," *Minneapolis Star Tribune,* 7 June 1994, LNAU. AP, "Campaign to Prevent Fetal Alcohol Syndrome Stepping Up," *Santa Fe New Mexican,* 7 May 2000, LNAU; Sue Major Holmes, "Fetal Alcohol Baby on Mission: Woman Speaks Out on Drinking Perils," *Denver Post,* 14 May 2000, LNAU. Joan Whitely, "Troubled Lives," *Las Vegas Review-Journal,* 3 August 1997, LNAU.

40. The ruling is *Sullivan v. Zebley,* 493 U.S. 521 (1990). See David G. Savage, "U.S. Illegally Denied Poor Children Aid: Supreme Court: The Justices Find Eligibility Guidelines for Disabled Youngsters Are Unfair: The Ruling Could Affect Tens or Hundreds of Thousands," *Los Angeles Times,* 21 February 1990, LNAU.

Acknowledgments

The best part of writing a book is thanking the people who made it possible. The worst part is the worry that I'll forget to acknowledge someone. In many ways this book has been a collaborative effort. Without the financial support of various institutions, the help I received from archivists and librarians, the friends who read and criticized the text, the opportunities to present my findings in talks and publications, the outstanding efforts of my research assistants, the cooperation of the many people I interviewed, and the support of my family, this book would not exist.

A number of institutions made it possible to write this book. I thank the American College of Obstetricians and Gynecologists for the fellowship that made it possible for me to use its archives; the National Endowment for the Humanities, which awarded me a Research Fellowship for College Teachers; the National Institutes of Health, which awarded me Research Grant 1 RO1 LMO6567-01NIH. My own institution, Rutgers University, awarded me a Grant to Get Grants, Research Council Funds, and support from the Center for Children and Childhood Studies. The author expresses appreciation to the University Seminars at Columbia University for their help in publication. Material in this work was presented to the University Seminar on Women and Society.

I am deeply grateful to the many librarians and archivists who helped me locate materials and offered me space in which to work. At the American College of Obstetricians and Gynecologists, archivist Susan Rishworth and reference librarian Pamela Van Hine made my fellowship month a productive one. At the Bureau of Alcohol, Tobacco, and Firearms I was fortunate to have the kind assistance and support of Vicki Herrmann, known to everyone as Vicki the Librarian. Ed Morman assisted my research at the New York Academy of Medicine, and at the College of Physicians of Philadelphia Charles Greifenstein and Chris Stanwood helped me locate critical materials. Suzanne White Junod and John Swann of the Food and Drug Administration were of great assistance. At Rutgers, History Librarian Julie Still helped me figure out where to look for materials and assisted me in collecting the images I needed for the book. I also want to thank Mary Anne Nesbit and Judy Odum for handling what must have seemed like far too many interlibrary loan requests. Finally, in the age of the Internet I need to thank the unseen members of the Kettil Bruun Society listserv who answered my questions and provided important insights into the recent history of alcohol research. I want to acknowledge in particular Kaye Middleton Fillmore, Lee Ann Kaskutas, Nancy Olson, Robin Room, and Ron Roizen.

I owe a great deal of thanks to the individuals who helped me conduct my research: Jeffrey Anderson, Jessica Bluebond-Langner, Erin McCleary, and Heidi Triesch. Loretta Carlisle provided critical assistance in preparing the manuscript and in helping me access materials. I am deeply grateful to the friends who hosted me when I conducted research in Washington, D.C., and New York City, and who helped me spend evenings not thinking about my work: Janet Joy and Bob Joy, Jeff Levi and Bopper Deyton, Nancy Steifel and Tom Tuthill and Joan Zoref and Roy Israel. I want to thank two other friends who helped me not to think about work but to understand the politics and meaning of work: Ellen Garvey and Gary Stoller.

Thanks to friends and colleagues, I got to try out my ideas before a number of different audiences, beginning with an intellectually outstanding conference at the College of Physicians of Philadelphia organized by Sarah Tracy and Caroline Acker, where I received wonderful comments and advice from John Burnham and Ron Roizen as well as others in attendance. Students often asked the toughest questions, and I thank Rima Apple of the University of Wisconsin, Jennifer Gunn and John Eyler of the University of Minnesota, Janet Tighe of the University of Pennsylvania, and Arleen Tuchman of Vanderbilt University for inviting me to speak at their campuses. Invitations from the Washington, D.C., History of Medicine Society and the Columbia Seminar on Women and Society allowed me to speak to professional colleagues at an important stage of my research. A faculty fellowship allowed me to participate in a year-long seminar organized by Cynthia Daniels at the Center for the Critical Analysis of Contemporary Culture at Rutgers, and gave me a chance to interact with a diverse group of scholars who share my interest in the culture and politics of reproduction.

Portions of this book began life elsewhere in vastly different form. I am grateful to the editors of the *Journal of Social History* and the *Social History of Alcohol Review* and to Howard Markel and Alexandra Minna Stern, the editors of *Formative Years: Children's Health in America 1880–2000,* for allowing me a forum to explore some of my ideas. I want to thank the editors of the *Journal of Health Politics, Policy and Law* for permission to reprint here portions of the work I first published in that journal.

I began my career as a historian of the late nineteenth and early twentieth centuries. As I sometimes told people, all my subjects were dead. Writing about the late twentieth century gave me the opportunity to meet living subjects and to conduct oral interviews. Many of those I spoke with are not directly quoted in the book, but everyone I spoke with contributed something important to my understanding of the subject. I thank Ernest Abel, Megan Adamson, Sheila Blume, Mary Dufour, Susan Farrell, Jan Howard, Kenneth Lyons Jones, Louis Leavitt, Louise Melling, Lynn Paltrow, Carrie Randall, Patricia Smith, and Kenneth Warren.

My first group of readers was a group we quickly dubbed the Janet group, since three of us share that name. Monique Bourque, Janet Theophano, Janet Tighe, and Elizabeth Toon helped me turn my first jottings into real chapters. At the meeting of another group, the Chester Avenue Seminar, Adele Lindenmeyer told me I had to gather more studies of death penalty cases, and I did. At Rutgers, Drew Humphries taught me how to use television news broadcasts and to overcome the sense I had from growing up in the 1950s that watching TV was a waste of time.

Many scholars carefully and critically read my chapters and offered superb advice. I am deeply grateful to Bert Hansen, Harriet Friedenreich, Cheryl Grames-Hoffman, Margaret Marsh, Philip Pauly, Charles Rosenberg, and Jonathan Tittler for their wise words. Arleen Tuchman not only read my chapters, she also held my hand over the telephone as I struggled to write. Laurie Bernstein forced me to rewrite and reorganize, and, as always, she made my work better and my life more fun. The two anonymous readers for Harvard University Press did their jobs well and I thank them for their criticisms and their kind words. I also want to thank Ann Downer-Hazell and Sara Davis at Harvard University Press for putting up with so many questions and a few delays.

My most profound debt is to my family. My husband, Eric Schneider, read every draft of every chapter more times than either of us would like to remember. His help was invaluable but not as important to my life as his love and support. My children, Ben and Alex, will no longer be able to answer my insinuating question, "How is the homework going?" with their own special reply, "How is the book going, Mom?" Usually this was an effective rejoinder and brought a laugh; once in a while it really got me. Of course my children are not there to remind me to work. I love not working and being with them, and it is to them and to Eric and to my late best friend Joani Unger that this book is dedicated.

Index